ARCHITECT'S PROFESSIONAL PRACTICE MANUAL

James R. Franklin, FAIA, ASLA

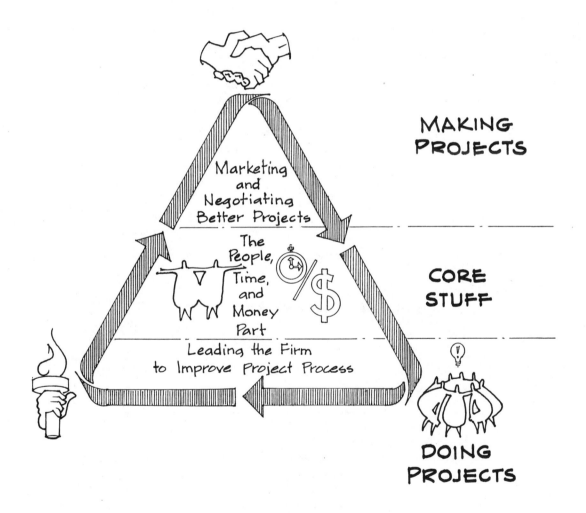

MAKING
PROJECTS

Marketing
and
Negotiating
Better Projects

The
People,
Time,
and
Money
Part

CORE
STUFF

Leading the Firm
to Improve Project Process

DOING
PROJECTS

McGraw-Hill

New York   San Francisco   Washington, D.C.   Auckland   Bogotá
Caracas   Lisbon   London   Madrid   Mexico City   Milan
Montreal   New Delhi   San Juan   Singapore
Sydney   Tokyo   Toronto

Library of Congress Cataloging-in-Publication Data

Franklin, James R.
    Architect's professional practice manual / James R. Franklin.
        p.   cm.
    Includes index.
    ISBN 0-07-135836-6
    1. Architectural practice—United States—Management. I. Title.
NA1996.F728   2000
720'.68—dc21
                                     99-054059
                                         CIP

McGraw-Hill

A Division of The McGraw·Hill Companies

   2 3 4 5 6 7 8 9 0 KGP/KGP 0 6 5 4 3 2 1 0

ISBN 0-07-135836-6

The sponsoring editor for this book was Wendy Lochner, the editing supervisor was Stephen M. Smith, and the production supervisor was Sherri Souffrance. It was set in Melior by Nicholas A. Bernini Graphics.

Printed and bound by Quebecor/Kingsport.

McGraw-Hill books are available at special quantity discounts to use as premiums and sales promotions, or for use in corporate training programs. For more information, please write to the Director of Special Sales, Professional Publishing, McGraw-Hill, Two Penn Plaza, New York, NY 10121-2298. Or contact your local bookstore.

This book is printed on acid-free paper.

CONTENTS

3

PART 2. CORE STUFF: THE TIME, MONEY, AND PEOPLE PART

ABOUT THE AUTHOR

James R. Franklin, FAIA, ASLA, has had an illustrious career as an architect, landscape architect, consultant, educator, trainer, and author. A practicing architect for 35 years, he led a firm that employed 85 people and won 18 design awards. A member of both the AIA and the ASLA, he edited the Eleventh Edition of the AIA's *Architect's Handbook of Professional Practice* and contributed major sections to the Twelfth. Named a Fellow of the AIA and the organization's first Resident Fellow, he has conducted numerous highly popular seminars for that group, the ASLA, and individual firms for many tears. In 1995, he joined the faculty of California Polytechnic School, San Luis Obispo. In 1999, he received the prestigious Edward C. Kemper Award from the AIA for exemplary service to his profession. He resides in San Luis Obispo, California.

PREFACE

This could only have been written—drawn, lettered, pasted up—for architects. The rest of you can idle through the hodge-podge format with a smirk, but architects will understand, since it's how we've always best communicated with each other—with notes and sketches of great immediacy. I submit it to you in a spirit of immediacy—this is a book not meant to be read so much as browsed, surfed for tips about what's on your mind. It talks about what I see happening in and to the profession right now. On the one hand, there is the proliferation of those paraprofessionals and quasi-disciplines out there offering to eat your lunch—that's urgent. On the other hand, our profession has oft weathered greater threats than this. I'm not worried about you. Just thought it high time we got better at getting and doing our projects on terms and in ways that permit us to turn out our best for those we serve—society. That's important.

The Preface, as I understand it, is the place I'm supposed to thank all those without whose input this would not have been possible. So I do. What's not possible is thanking you by name, since I don't even know most of you. What's put together here are gatherings from my having facilitated over 14 years of workshops and seminars in this country, Canada, New Zealand, and Australia, plus about 35 years of learnings from that ever-shifting Braille system we call practice. Thank you one and all. I'll let it go at that.

This is also the place for disclaimers is case you get into trouble doing what I say has worked for someone else. So I disclaim. Never having seen an architecture practice that wasn't unique, I have to say you're on your own using what's here—so what's new? A lot of what this addresses is that part of all our practices that most closely resembles an impromptu combination of herding housecats and freestyle wrestling—the people processes and management part—the soft skills that are so hard. Wouldn't be so hard if the most difficult one to deal with wasn't yourself. So a lot of the book is really on self-management. My hope is to give you tools for doing well by doing good, while at the same time producing better projects.

So welcome to my workbench. Jumbled here are tools I have used for some 50 years without wearing them out. *Never force a part, get a bigger hammer—Mash till it fits—Use it or lose it*—but you know all that. Old tools are meant to be tinkered with and honed. If you pick one that doesn't work for you—or if you think of another that might work better—call me. We'll talk about it. I'm a good listener, and though you'll doubtless know the remedy as soon as you say it, this (like everything I undertake) is really a work in progress—the feedback will help me a lot in making the next one better:

James R. Franklin, FAIA, ASLA
College of Architecture and Environmental Design
Building 05-212
Cal Poly State University
San Luis Obispo, CA 93407
tel: (805) 781-8420, fax: -8421
e-mail: jfrankli@calpoly.edu

INTRODUCTION
And some thoughts on the profession at Y2K

WHAT THIS IS AND WHY

This book is a gathering of experiential learnings—what the Army calls "ground truth"—except it's about the design and practice of architecture rather than warfare. What they—and I—mean by *ground truth* is the study of what was different in action on the ground from what had been anticipated and planned. The point is to consider how reality got dealt with, what worked, and what might usefully change the theory of how to go about it better next time.

I frankly borrow this term from tactics for dramatic effect. It fits because so many architects still behave as though they'd been air-dropped into an endless battle for survival. I use it to heighten the contrast between the *tactics* architects have been taught the last 50 years and where, as a profession, we need to be moving strategically. I like the term for its acceptance that there's no one grand absolute truth by which to correctly determine courses of action—that ground truth is really a jumble of small transactions that worked—stuff that was immediately operative and successful.

Strategic change in the market position of architects will come only through changes in how we as individual practitioners deal tactically with reality on the littered ground of practice day by day. The purpose of this book is to help architects transform and transcend the adversarial—Lord knows, the aggressive—factors in daily practice on an individual basis. That militant business metaphor is a guy thing we need to get over and I work very hard to keep war stories out of this. Just the reverse—here I seek to affirm the collaborative, and not just among our side in order to beat theirs.

My basic premise is that adversarial and other value-lost project activities can be significantly mitigated through unilateral transformative practices, skills, and day-to-day work behaviors involving all stakeholders. While these exemplary individual practices have been generally acknowledged, mandated, and trained-for in other fields, they have not yet been researched in detail for application on architectural projects. Here I report anecdotal findings from consulting and seminar facilitation, along with findings from such literature as exists, with proposed extrapolations useful to architects.

Everything here has worked on the ground—either for me or for those architects who reported it— and while that in no way assures it'll work for you, it does provide you a resource to browse for processes you can tinker with—can hone to fit your needs. It's a compilation of how-to information and do-it-yourself tips about what works for individuals—processes, procedures, communication methods, and behaviors that can change interactions from adversarial to collaborative, from transactional to transformative, even when the other party to the interaction is not necessarily similarly inclined to collaborative effort.

WHAT'S AT STAKE

In assessing our profession's services, what's meant by the jargon term "value added" is hard to quantify, but the reverse—the quantification of value-lost activities—is easy to estimate rather reliably. In workshops around the country I ask practitioners how many hours per week they work, their utilization ratio, and their billing rates. I then ask for an educated guess as to what percentage of their time is spent dealing with others in adversarial, blame-fixing or cover-yourself ways that add no value to the project.

Several thousand answers to this line of questioning roughly average out at about $27,000 worth of time per architect per year[*] that is reported as spent in these negative, debilitating, and frustrating activities. You can do your own calculation, but to look at the aggregate problem, and assuming roughly 100,000 architects in practice, even a 10 percent improvement would result in almost $30 million worth of additional productive (and chargeable) time available annually, professionwide.

Or look at it from the other side. Project owners across the country—both public and private sector—are increasingly electing to procure projects through design/build (D/B) or construction management (CM) delivery methods. Whether this is a passing trend or the long-term standard condition is not yet clear, though the message certainly is. Our society has rejected litigious dispute resolution and the bid-low-make-it-up-in-change-orders mentalities that ruled the construction industry in recent years. Litigated losses incurred by architects are reported by insurance companies to average some $125,000 per loss and to take from 1 to 2½ years to decide.

Clearly the need for transformation is great and the stakes are high. So high that, while this is written primarily for practitioners, my hope is that it can also be useful for students and teachers of architecture.[†] In facilitating forums and retreats about bridging the gap between practice and the academy, I frequently ask architects to list core competencies in today's market. In addition to AutoCAD 13 proficiency, their typical responses include the abilities to work in teams, deal well with people, communicate, and the like. They then invariably complain[‡] that these skills are not taught in school. The extent to which such allegations are true probably results from two things:

• Rather than knowledge-based information, these *are* skills that probably, as Schön[§] said about design, can be learned but not taught. With the fortuitous exception of the design studio, few opportunities exist in most college classes to learn by doing. Virtually none exist for teams learning by doing.

• The paradigm for architectural education in general, and design studio education in particular, remains based on a Howard Roark model of the lone individual heroically assimilating knowledge and demonstrating competencies. Early on, we've all played the protagonist in the same Gary Cooper movie.

In general, the operative basis for higher education remains, "Know the truth and the truth shall set you free." The prevailing idea seems to be that ingested knowledge will lead to greater awarenesses and understanding leading to modifications in attitudes and behaviors. Without disputing the efficacy of that sequence, and at the risk of sounding like *The Music Man* of Broadway fame, let me say that in my experience the reverse sequence can also work.

---

[*] 50 hours/week × 50 weeks/year × 0.65 U.R. × $85/hour × 0.20 of chargeable time in value-lost activity = $27,625.00. While it may lack academic rigor, the fact that the process has been replicated in some 60 workshops with several thousand architect-participants involved lends considerable credibility.
[†] Dana Cuff, writing on professions, in *Architect's Handbook of Professional Practice*, 12th Edition, David Haviland, ed. (AIA Press, 1994), p. 9.
[‡] This can be anticipated in any such meeting, e.g., most recently at Cal Poly in February 1998.
[§] Donald Schön, *The Reflective Practitioner* (Basic Books, 1983).

If one adopts and uses appropriate behaviors and attitudes as a matter of second-attention habit, the resulting positive reinforcement can lead to increased awarenesses and eventually even wisdom. Though that's admittedly an ameliorist attitude, it invites resolution of the old polemic of whether it's best to teach architecture or to teach students how to act like architects. The obvious challenge, as posed so well in *Built to Last*,[*] as well as in the Boyer Report, is to do both, so perhaps in today's world of fast-paced change even the medieval paradigm of higher education is no longer immutable.

As Joel Barker points out,[†] paradigm shift occurs when the number of intractable problems not solvable by the prevailing system reaches a critical mass. With so much information overload readily available through current technology, and such topics as "edutainment"[‡] so hotly debated, perhaps our architectural education paradigm is preparing to shift as well. If so, my hope is that this work can be useful in that process.[§]

THE MARKET SITUATION

It is widely proclaimed that the marketplace is in the midst of a paradigm shift—that the rules of the game are changing as well as the tactics and methods by which one can achieve success within the limits of those rules. Dr. Deming[¶]—acknowledged as a seminal figure of the new order of things—called for a *new religion* of continuous improvement in quality, both in tangible and ineffable terms. *Learning circles, TQM, ISO 9000, partnering,* and now *learning organizations*—all these can be seen as sequential expressions and extensions of that single theme, a global movement, the new paradigm. The need for collaborative work is inescapable in today's market.

Consider the following lists taken from the best-seller *Reengineering the Corporation*,[**] which of course has nothing to do with engineering and is instead written by management consultants for industrialists and corporate leaders. In addition to usefully summarizing the differences between the old and new paradigms of the widget makers' world, what's fascinating is that the lists could have been written by architects to describe the ways the majority of our firms (the two-thirds with fewer than a staff of five) have always practiced.

This brings back wry memories of the 1950s when all the big architecture firms departmentalized because business management experts were saying that's the way to increase productivity and profits. By the 1980s, all but a few big EA firms had quietly returned to a studio organization, having found that's still the best way to do good projects. Today it's customary for big-firm brochures to proudly boast of project teams—firms within the firm—who will personally see your project through from beginning to end.

---

[*] James C. Collins and Jerry I. Porras, *Built to Last: Successful Habits of Visionary Companies* (HarperBusiness, 1997), p. 40.

[†] Joel Arthur Barker, *Paradigms: The Business of Discovering the Future* (HarperCollins, 1992), p. 51.

[‡] Kenneth R. Weiss, "A Wary Academia on Edge of Cyberspace," *Los Angeles Times*, March 31, 1998, p. 1.

[§] A note on semantics: Given the focus here on day-to-day practices in the field of design and construction of architecture, I will primarily be speaking of practice as a verb. Obviously, many exemplary skills and practices are used with the intention of transforming groups of project stakeholders within a firm into effective teams, for providing organization development for firms—practices in that other sense of the word. For clarity, I'll try to say *firm* or *organization* when I'm referring to practice as a noun—a venue.

[¶] Mary Walton, *The Deming Management Method* (Putnam, 1986).

[**] Michael Hammer and James Champy, *Reengineering the Corporation* (HarperBusiness, 1993).

All this suggests it's finally safe to listen to business management consultants, or at least that the current movement is toward a comprehensive and intuitive approach to work, regardless of the product or service. The problem that remains with management literature is simply that it's written for corporations. Though the architectural project team is a virtual corporation, it is only assembled for the duration. Therefore, the vast bulk of the literature that deals with corporate sustainability needs to be recouched into vision-making and organizational development for short-term project teams rather than any enduring firm.

Anyway, here are the lists:

CHARACTERISTICS OF THE NEW WORKPLACE

Several jobs combined for each position.	Work performed wherever it makes sense.
Workers make own decisions.	Checks, controls, and audits minimized.
Work delinearized—is holistic.	A project manager provides single point of contact.
Multiple versions of task processes.	Hybrid centralized/decentralized operations.

CHANGES IN THE WORKPLACE

Issue	Old paradigm	New paradigm
Work units	Departments	Teams
Jobs	Simple tasks	Multitask holistic work
Roles	Controlled	Enabled
Job preparation	Training	Education
Performance evaluation	Criteria: activity	Criteria: results
Advancement criteria	Performance	Capability
Values	Protective	Productive
Managers	Supervisors	Coaches
Organizational structures	Vertical hierarchies	Flat
Executives	Scorekeepers	Leaders

While none of that seems more than business as usual to most of our profession, *Reengineering the Corporation* was a best-selling call for revolution in industry. A quick perusal of the sheer shelf-footage accorded bookstores' stocks of offerings on business management is clear evidence of both the intensity and the degree of innovation required of corporate America as it moves to embrace the new ways.

Perhaps even more telling are the incremental changes in even the titles and jacket blurbs of today's management literature. I routinely scan the catalogs of a national publisher and distributor of organization development publications for consultants and in-house trainers.[*] For the past several years, I had noted their titles were heavily weighted toward the creation and control of work teams— presumably by HRD departments of large corporations and industry—in order to increase productivity. The latest edition of the catalog shows a remarkable shift to titles such as *Leading with Soul*, and Max DePree's *Leading without Power*.

---

[*] Jossey-Bass Pfeiffer, 350 Sansome Street, 5th floor, San Francisco, CA 94104.

I take it as a sure sign that the new paradigm—that of working collaboratively—is firmly in place when the training materials and management literature typically focus on how leaders in large companies can lead by serving—can practice leadership as a support function—can effectively relinquish control and should. This positional shift mandated for leadership in the marketplace is especially relevant to architects, given that we have carefully put ourselves in a support role. In a backhanded way we may even have positioned ourselves for the new leadership by having previously refused the top-down controls the old paradigm prescribed for leaders.

It is only in the last 2 years that the AIA has finally acknowledged the fact that—out of fear and a desire for risk aversion—we spent the last 50 years yielding control in direct proportion to the amount of project accountability we evaded. Today, with CM and D/B emerging as preeminent project deliveries for sizable projects, it's useful to note that both are disciplines our profession carefully and emphatically distanced ourselves from in the past. Both now proclaim themselves professions—an increasingly vague and ubiquitous term. Suddenly it is encouraged and acclaimed when architects undertake to be CMs or provide D/B. The boundaries blur.[*]

MARKET PREDICTIONS AT Y2K

A couple of years ago I was asked to write an article called "The Future of the Architectural Profession,"[†] which immediately suggested the question, given our new-found pluralism, as to whether the noun should be singular anymore. *Professions*, plural? Consider the recent phenomenal shift in our view of ourselves. One might have suspected the broadening of membership categories by the AIA was mainly a self-serving strategy to get more dues. But when the traditionally conservative National Documents Committee unveiled the new B141, 1997 Edition, the message of a new inclusiveness among us can no longer be ignored.

That venerable workhorse document—the B141, 1987 version—was over 3 times as long as the original. It got that cumbersome from our 50-year accretion of incremental tinkerings to plug legal loopholes that opposing lawyers had punched. And, over all those years, we thought the intent of the document wasn't really changing much. Mostly, we just kept trying to revise what we wished we'd said better in the beginning, not realizing that the accumulation of defensive changes was actually self-limiting. The web always traps the spider, only sometimes the fly, and the smaller the web, the worse it became for this particular spider (us) in three ways:

- The more explicitly we said what we would not be accountable for, the more accountability we left for others such as CM and D/B to get paid for taking.

- In the process of abdicating accountability, we gave away market share, not only to the new professions, but to engineers and contractors as well.

- Finally and most important, we lost the joy to be experienced through leading by serving. We gave away leadership.

---

[*] David H. Maister, *True Professionalism: The Courage to Care about Your People, Your Clients, and Your Career* (Free Press, 1997), p. 15.
[†] *Hawaii Architect*, Fall 1997.

Rather than being just another revision, the new B141[*] reflects the ongoing process for our redefinition of practice, even the profession. It acknowledges the plethora of ways we can serve the needs of clients and users, yet still be architects. With the new document, an architect can furnish only schematic sketches on this project, and a full turnkey package preceded by facilities management and feasibility studies on the next. Whatever. I see the new B141 as saying that if it has to do with the built environment, is legal, ethical, within your areas of competence and is of value, go for it. And still be an architect. So yes, it's still one profession—now encompassing a dazzling array of project, practice, and career options. So much for the question. Now for the predictions.

Some years ago, a futurist friend shared the trade secret of all his profession's practitioners. He said they just tell you what's happening now that you haven't noticed or won't accept. Invariably that sounds so bizarre, it takes us quite awhile to acknowledge—then quit denying—the reality of it. By which time we're all prepared to be duly impressed and amazed by the futurist's "brilliant forecast" having proved true.

So here I'll play futurist—shifting to future tense—as though the following six "predictions" hadn't happened yet. But we all know better, since each is just a de facto result of the whole world being automated, which nobody can deny.

1. More and more we'll be doing **design/build**, and the options as a private-practice architect will include—though not be limited to:

   • Doing it all yourself, offering architectural, CM and design/build services, depending on client need and project size or type.

   • Partnering with a contractor, either on a full-time legal, or on a project-specific, strategic-alliance basis.

   • Marketing yourself as a design consultant to contractors as well as clients.

   • Becoming an employee or subsidiary of a general contractor.

2. The **polarity** in architecture firm size will increase. The big will get bigger, and the very small will proliferate, as both extremes use technology to reach farther vertically for market share. Even tiny firms will be capable of providing meaningful contributions to larger projects by means of their enormous electronic databases and efficiency. Very large firms will reach farther down into the market for small projects and still turn a profit, since individuals will have the capability to operate as "one-person studios" within the firm.

3. **Intranet hookups** will provide all the stakeholders in the typical project with full access to all project information. Each will be able to log input or questions instantly about design, billings, change orders, certificates of payment, RFI status and decisions. There will be only a single set of project records fully shared instead of separate and conflicting sets kept by different parties to the contracts.

---

[*]AIA Document B141–1997, *Standard Form of Agreement between Owner and Architect* (American Institute of Architects, 1997).

4. We'll be seeing more project-specific, **virtual firms**—ad hoc consortiums of individuals meeting in cyberspace from anywhere on the globe—for design crit, coordination and team meetings. A variation on this will be the global proliferation of large-firm "branch offices" consisting of minimal staff who establish a local presence and do marketing. They'll either modem the projects home, or host globe-trotting SWAT-teams that show up from the home office for the duration of on-site, project-specific services needed.

5. Instead of technological expertise (which will become increasingly unremarkable) **interpersonal skills** will be the key to professional success. We'll still be getting things done face-to-face (though more of it electronically), and the higher the tech, the softer the touch to be required. Firms of all sizes will work hard to become learning organizations that automatically and continuously learn from experiences within the larger system, adjust and self-correct—all with less cumbersome hierarchies, company policies and the like.

6. Since that larger system we work within includes clients as well as architects, builders and suppliers—and since 70 to 90 percent of each firm's projects will come from past clients or direct referrals—successful architects will treat **clients as career-long account**s instead of one-off project sources.

Each of those "predictions" reinforces the mandate for architects to practice transformative skills, to get better at the core competencies of interpersonal skills. Most stakeholders in architectural projects today can be roughly categorized into two groups, call them *transformative* and *transactional*.[*] The transformative group aspires to collaborative effort as the best hope for quality projects and the realization of the long-term interests of all. In contrast, the transactional group remains convinced that personal success can only be achieved through relentless adversarial competitiveness for immediate gain.

Three situational combinations exist: When project teams have comprised only stakeholders from the transformative group, often the efficacious overall results have been reported in justification of the quality movement. Specific day-to-day individual processes leading to these results, however, have been poorly documented. Obviously, the litigious and confrontational methodologies, tactics, and manipulations engendered by 50 years of transactional project teams have been exhaustively documented in insurance company advisories, books, contract forms, and court records.

The frustrations caused by project team mixtures—hybrids of the two categories of stakeholders—have also been widely reported anecdotally, mostly by participants of the transactional persuasion in backlash to the quality movement. Again, details of the behaviors and daily practices employed are largely matters of hearsay.

It is this last situation—the hybrid project team—that can be most usefully examined. What works when one side doesn't want it to? When the dichotomy in values is made a de facto part of the project problem to be solved? What can the individual do to change the rules of the game?

---

[*] As presented by James McKensie of the Collaborative Institute to the Cal Poly Executive Management Program, January 10, 1998.

It's important that we address the problem at the individual level for several reasons. The new paradigm—being still in its infancy—has not proved either its principles of implementation or its endgame results to be overwhelmingly efficacious in bad market swings. Moreover, quality-movement practitioners have yet to agree on effective details of implementation, even in the good times. Deming pointed out that the standard principles of accounting are the result of 200 years of refinement, that the quality movement has really been around only about 20 years. He predicted we've got a lot of trial-and-error evolution to go through before we can agree on the how-to part—an authorized set of canons—for the "new religion." In the interim, even the true believers remain under the gun—potential cannon fodder—for the cumbersome legal recourses of the previous paradigm, all of which remain in place as the last resort.

So there's confusion, even among zealot transformationists, certainly when paired in the workplace with nonbeliever transactionists. Witness in our industry the ongoing contentions over design/build versus up-front negotiated partnering versus low-bid as the "American way" versus multiprime and unbundling of project services.

Given this situation, small wonder there exists a formidable dichotomy at the level of individual project participants. On the one side are those in denial about the whole quality movement being any more than a repackaging ploy by management consultants. On the other are the confirmed zealots who're fully committed to the new goals and vision, but can't agree about which processes can best lead us from here to there. What all of us can agree on: That openly adversarial—much less litigious—practices do not add value to our projects, to our clients' or our collective well-being. We agree that collaborative practices are in every stakeholder's interest, though we are often still far from agreeing on the details of exactly what that means.

There exists a shared body of knowledge—though very little data. Many architects consistently get good projects done well in spite of the dichotomy of values among members of the project team. Obviously the profession knows more than it knows how to talk about. That this knowledge is experiential caused me to begin this with the metaphor of the Army's "ground truth"—what was different in the field from what had been planned, what actually worked on the ground and how.

For the Army, this experiential wisdom can be confirmed by data. Our first problem is that there is virtually no data available in the design and construction industry because of the assumption that each project is a one-of-a-kind, one-off assemblage of firms, people, systems, and materials. So how can statistics be meaningful, we ask? What compounds the problem is that such case study information as does exist is about projects that went wrong. My objective here is to report what went right—exemplary project practices.

My problem has been the sheer complexity of situational information needed, given the diversity of project-and-client types and procurement methods being used. Even if there were only one project type, what's needed is knowledge about an incredible range of exemplary practices. But over the years—in countless consultations, workshops and seminars—there emerged a definable list of what practitioners wanted to talk about. That list, and the data collected and investigated in trying to respond to those practitioners, evolved into the 14 chapters that follow.

PART 1.
MAKING
PROJECTS:

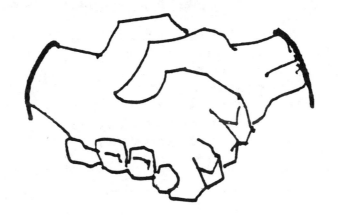

MARKETING
and
NEGOTIATING
YOUR WAY TO
BETTER PROJECTS

CHAPTER 1. MARKETING

PROCESSES FOR

Everything You Do .... **INDIRECT MARKETING**

Always with an ear out for people's wants and aspirations.

Always with an environmental scan for ways your services can help achieve their goals, meet needs, and make this a better place to live and work.

FOLLOW UP

- Phone Calls
- handwritten notes
- e-mail
- visits
- faxes
- media clippings about their business
- market tips

This has more to do with buying than selling -- buying into their network of common interests among people whose success or sense of well-being can benefit from your professional services.
Tell, don't sell.

PAST CLIENTS

Keep in touch - Most of your projects will be for them or come from their referrals......

On the other hand, keep broadening your network to target new client types, consultants, civic groups, contractors.

LEADS LIST

Try keeping a or tickler file to remind you whom to call this month

What you don't do is sell -- in indirect marketing, the goal is to build name recognition and relationship.

What you want --

a Leads List & early-warning system.

When the RFP comes out, it's generally too late to start

None of this need necessarily be sequential -- a cold call can turn into negotiation in a heart beat.

- Asking all the open-ended questions -- what-if's --
- Full disclosure and discussion of all their options ---
- Real concern for their success .... These are value-added services that can get them what they need, and you the project.
- Perhaps most important, it's this approach that helps them set realistic expectations.

Selection process? Is it a real project?

Who? Program? what How big? Funded?

when Schedule?

DIRECT MARKETING

Site constraints? where How Budget?? Delivery options?

What's the real need? why Their true aspirations?

Whenever possible, sell to their perceptions -- why it's in their interest to hire exactly the sort of person or architect they perceive you to be -- but stay honest and don't leave any misperceptions about time, fees, or budget.

Who's my competition? What's the clients' perception of me?

Keep the whole process -- Marketing, Presentation, Negotiation -- all horizontal -- neither side talking down or up to the other.

PROPOSAL and PRESENTATION

- Cover
- Executive Summary
- Project as Understood
- The Challenge & Why
- Our Approach
  Team
  Qualifications
  Experience
- Terms, Time & Money

Rather than past projects, what you're selling is the best professional approach to design and construct their unique future one -- talk process -- with lots of Enthusiasm, open disclosure and humor

NEGOTIATION

Reaching agreement on roles, responsibilities, process, schedule, money, scope -- all the terms and conditions of how you'll work together to achieve a great project.

From 1st meet til final agreement -- same skills all the way -- and at any point be ready to openly talk time & money. They won't let you not.

AN OVERVIEW OF
MARKETING !

① Get the project.
② Get the project.
③ Get the project.

The old and oft-quoted three most important rules for sucessfully practicing architecture ⤴

There's a lot more to marketing (much less practice) than that, though.

You're offering services and extended relationships that are not yet fully defined ....

To people you may not yet really know.

Marketing architecture is the art of making projects good ones while you're in the process of getting them.

It involves clients in designing the best ways to attain their aspirations for the project. You're selling roles and relationships, not buildings.

Two kinds of MARKETING

① **DIRECT:** What you do that targets a specific project.

② **INDIRECT:** Everything else. Everything.

Quotes for Indirect marketing:

Proper manners is nothing more than treating everyone in precisely the same way. (Shaw)

80% of winning is just showing up. (Woody Allen)

Of the two kinds, indirect is probably the more important in the long run. It's a knack for influencing others in ways that help them help you. It isn't a separate activity or sequence of procedures so much as it's a mind-set, and an attitude pervading all your interactions.

We've all grown up in this profession acknowledging that beyond the guy who writes the checks are the users of our projects -- many of us talk of them as the "real clients".

And who knows? In today's world almost anybody can turn up on tomorrow's building committee.

What if you started treating everyone as a client?
Marketing is less about what you do than how you go about it.

Cesar Pelli says that for him, the design process is more a spiral than a series of sequential steps.

At every turn, he's always reconsidering the same issues again -- each time with a higher level of information with which to build on previous levels of insight, understanding, and excellence.

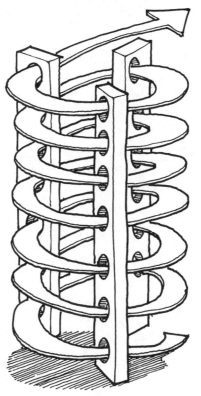

Same thing with marketing and negotiation.

It's a holistic process, not a series of steps. Keep it moving, building always to higher levels of mutual trust and shared understanding of how your interests, theirs, and those of their project can best be achieved. The lines between negotiation, direct and indirect marketing often blur or cease to exist!

How you go about this depends on situational variables -- your levels (and kinds) of experience, contacts, positions in the industry and community, knowledge and skills, personal styles.... I can only tell you some of what (to me at least) are BASIC PRINCIPLES:

Values—double-entendre: First, your set of personal core values (*principles* or *standards*), then a clear understanding of the value (second meaning, as in *value-added*) that your services bring to others. Could have put this in terms of self-worth, self-assurance or self-esteem if I hadn't feared too many *self* words smack of cockiness or arrogance. Here, I'm talking more about a deep level of professional commitment to what you do—and knowing why.

Interests—the real reasons to be doing what you do: What it is you seek in practice to bring personal fulfillment. What makes architecture—for most of us—a way of life at least as much as a way of making a living. Being secure in your sense of true self-interest frees you to intuit and confirm the real interests of others. Serving those interests is what both the practice and the marketing of architecture is all about.

Full disclosure about yourself, your practice, your own interests: Help them voice the long-term aspirations and values that lie behind stated positions about what they immediately want. I'm always fascinated to find how affirming it is for people to talk out true interests, and how woefully inadequate most are about bringing the subject up.

Open-ended questions and never saying *NO* to a client—unless their intention is illegal or unethical: Even then, try to respond with caring questions that lead to their discovering why what they propose is wrong-headed, inappropriate, or not in their long-term best interest.

Caring—the core of professionalism: Doing all you ethically and reasonably can to serve clients' true interests, even when that means they're using less, (or none) of your services. Demonstrate the agency relationship you offer—prove you'll think and act on their behalf.

MARKETING TOOLS

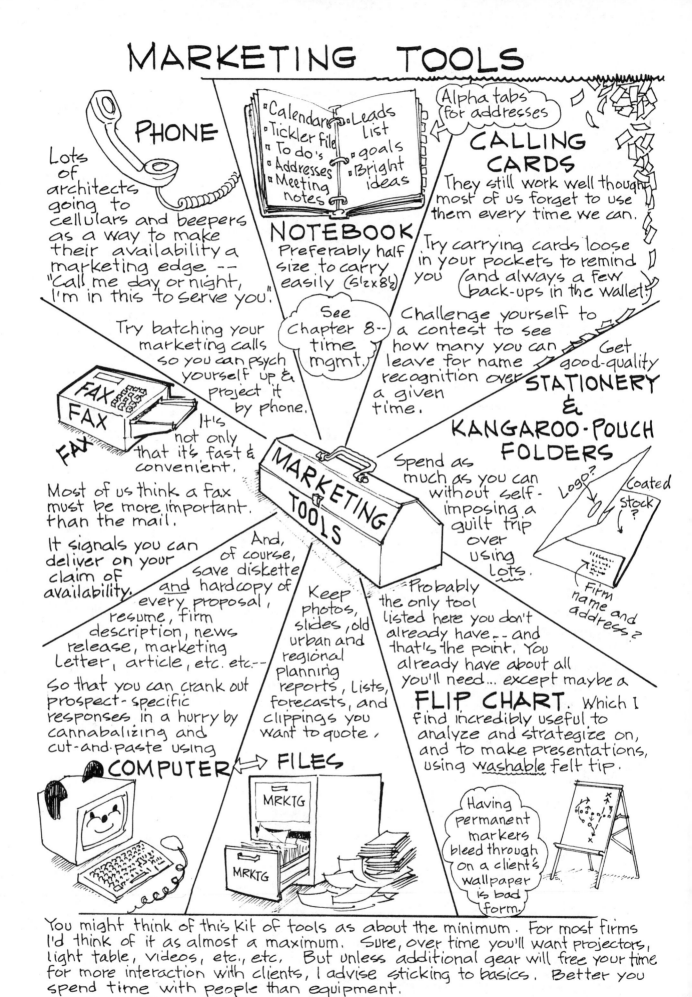

PHONE

Lots of architects going to cellulars and beepers as a way to make their availability a marketing edge -- "Call me day or night, I'm in this to serve you."

Try batching your marketing calls so you can psych yourself up & project it by phone.

NOTEBOOK

- Calendar
- Tickler file
- To do's
- Addresses
- Meeting notes
- Leads list
- goals
- Bright ideas

Preferably half size to carry easily (5½x8½)

See Chapter 8-- time mgmt.

FAX

It's not only that it's fast & convenient.

Most of us think a fax must be more important than the mail.

It signals you can deliver on your claim of availability.

CALLING CARDS

Alpha tabs for addresses

They still work well though most of us forget to use them every time we can.

Try carrying cards loose in your pockets to remind you (and always a few back-ups in the wallet!)

Challenge yourself to a contest to see how many you can leave for name recognition over a given time.

STATIONERY & KANGAROO-POUCH FOLDERS

Get good-quality

Spend as much as you can without self-imposing a guilt trip over using lots.

Logo? Coated stock? Firm name and address?

And, of course, save diskette and hardcopy of every proposal, resume, firm description, news release, marketing letter, article, etc. etc.--

So that you can crank out prospect-specific responses in a hurry by cannabalizing and cut-and-paste using

COMPUTER ⟷ FILES

Keep photos, slides, old urban and regional planning reports, lists, forecasts, and clippings you want to quote.

Probably the only tool listed here you don't already have -- and that's the point. You already have about all you'll need... except maybe a

FLIP CHART.

Which I find incredibly useful to analyze and strategize on, and to make presentations, using washable felt tip.

Having permanent markers bleed through on a client's wallpaper is bad form.

MRKTG

MRKTG

You might think of this kit of tools as about the minimum. For most firms I'd think of it as almost a maximum. Sure, over time you'll want projectors, light table, videos, etc., etc. But unless additional gear will free your time for more interaction with clients, I advise sticking to basics. Better you spend time with people than equipment.

KEEP IT SIMPLE

The larger the organization, the more people actively marketing, the more it will make sense to systematize. Some firms set and assign quotas of calls and mailings, devise marketing systems to measure and manage. They track separate activities such as:

Positioning
Public relations
Marketing research
Lead development
Proposal writing
Etc., etc.

Some measure their "hit rate"—the ratio of projects won in presentations to the number of presentations made. Or the average number of leads required to produce a project. Stuff like that. There are no industry standards, of course, and comparisons with other firms make no sense.

If you're an organized type that likes systems and sequential steps with quantifiable milestones, fine. Do as much of that as it takes, remembering that clients are brought in mostly by the the people who will provide the services, rather than by brochures, systems, marketers, even companies.

People deal with people. Prospects are a lot more interested in how well you can do their project than how efficiently you manage your firm, or how slick you make your marketing materials.

For me, even when I was bringing in the majority of work for an 85-person firm, the system had to be simple enough to have with me all the time— I used my organizer.

Perhaps what's most useful about that marketing tool kit diagram is what got left out. Needs differ according to market, clients and project types, but in my experience:

1. FOUR COLOR PROFESSIONAL BROCHURES

There are a few markets where brochures are almost demanded.

One option: a series of quick in-house flyers on specific project types -- done over time and as needed.

☐ Cost a bundle.

☐ With more than one person in on the design, it takes months of debate before sign-off on the final.

☐ If only one person does the design, nobody else is satisfied with the result.

☐ No matter who's involved, the brochure is out of date by the time it's back from the printer.

☐ Long before the minimum print run is exhausted, you're too embarrassed by the brochure to ever use it again.

2. 35mm SLIDES

And then I did this project. And then we did this one. And then I did..... And then

Think clients hold selection interviews for the chance to watch you show off your past projects? **NOT.** You're selling process, not buildings. They're shopping for their best option to get the services and relationship and team needed for this project. They've already agreed you can design, or you wouldn't be there. Now they need to know the approach you propose for getting them the best for the money available within the time frame they've got. Slides, if any, should only be cues to further the dialogue.

BELLS AND WHISTLES

- Digital cameras
- Videos
- PowerPoint
- 3D CAD walk-throughs
- Web pages, etc., etc.

You might buy plenty of other gadgets for marketing, if you're unable to resist. My advice: Don't read airlines magazines, keep it simple, save yourself a lot of money, get more projects. Not to mention avoiding those painful moments when the PowerPoint won't boot up and all your assurances about your firm's fool-proof electronic technology begin to ring a bit hollow.

So what does an old guy like me know? I know if I were out marketing, I'd give breezy assurances about all our electronic tools for *doing* projects, but I wouldn't be showing any off. I'd tell how we've improved efficiency and accuracy while assuring them we'd never let technology get in the way of our dealing personally and immediately with our clients, their design, our project details. I'd find some excuse to sketch or diagram on the spot, just to demonstrate that's how we'd be working together.

Most especially, I'd never *ever* turn the lights off to let them doze through a media show of past projects. If the RFP required one, it would be made with prints I'd draw all over with felt-tip. At most I'd use an overhead projector with the room lights on, full eye contact, and the viewgraphs or prints only there to prompt all the points to make, the questions to discuss about their project. I'd be talking process, and scribbling notes for all of us in felt-tip.

We've all been exposed to electronic marvels and film animation to the point that we're no longer impressed. Actually, I can't remember a PowerPoint presentation that *didn't* go wrong, perhaps indicating that nothing short of equipment failure ever caused one to be interesting enough to make it memorable. What's even more boring is that displaying technology these days more often invites discussions of software comparisons than architecture.

On the other hand, if you're up to the inconvenience of promising them constant access to you and to the project through modems, intranet, beeper, cell phone, whatever—by all means tout it. The new communication technology is *wonderful*. It's the edutainment and infomercial stuff that sends dangerous subliminal messages:

1. **It's canned.** Even if it's specifically prepared for them and only them, it says I've determined (and edited) what they will see. By rote and by God, you're going to hear me out. Listen up.

2. **It talks down.** Or up. Either way is a wrong-headed introduction to the personal and intensely horizontal interaction ahead of us, if we're to do a good project together. I'm there to find out what they need, not tell them I already know more than they do.

3. **It's a blatant sales pitch**, and that lumps me together with all the other vendors pushing commodities.

4. **It says I'm not busy enough** if I've got the inordinate amount of time it takes to put together electronic presentations.

5. **It warns of my overhead** (which I'll be asking them to pay) being burdened with the cost of technology and techies to do this stuff.

I know. I know. Technology is improving daily and I may regret having said this—I can't wait to apologize.

CHAPTER 2
INDIRECT MARKETING
It's not something you get to choose whether to do.
You're doing it constantly-- either poorly or well.

STATISTICS
Across the country,
architects report:

A. They're averaging
   50- to 60-hour workweeks.

B. A majority of their time
   (say 60%) is spent interacting with
   others—one-on-ones, meetings,
   phone calls, etc.

C. A majority of their projects (70–80%)
   come from repeat clients and direct
   referrals.

GO FIGURE

1. Jot down your own numbers.
2. Multiply A×B.
3. Add in a safe estimate of hours
   you spend per week with all those
   people not directly
   connected with your firm or your
   work.

Try this exercise to get a rough idea of the extent to which you're already doing indirect marketing.

But I have too much to do already just trying to meet project deadlines.

Oh well-- if it's going to keep happening to me, might as well get good at it.

Right on both counts. Instead of trying to do more, focus on getting better at-- and enjoying more -- all that you're already doing.

I'm not surprised if as much as 50% of your time is spent talking with people who will find themselves in a position to:
  ☐ Hire you
  ☐ Recommend you
  ☐ Decline to do either
for 3/4 of all your projects for quite some time to come!

So what am I looking for? It's a jumble out there.

Like good design, good marketing is more a matter of consequence than sequence.....

What's of real consequence-- Your values and theirs

From values come interests and vision.

What you're looking for are clients whose values and vision for projects have a sufficient overlap with your own to allow you to work creatively and well together.

WHAT ARE YOU MARKETING ?

...... There are lots of options ......

You can develop a specialty by service type...

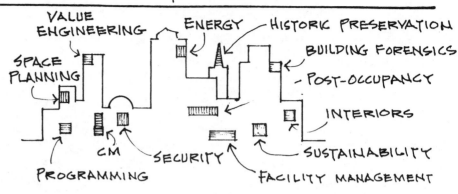

VALUE ENGINEERING — ENERGY — HISTORIC PRESERVATION — BUILDING FORENSICS — POST-OCCUPANCY — INTERIORS — SUSTAINABILITY — FACILITY MANAGEMENT — SECURITY — CM — PROGRAMMING — SPACE PLANNING

Even a subspecialty...

Bite off a chunk of architectural services you are good at and enjoy sinking your teeth into ....

B141 SERVICES

Scrutinize them -- pull them apart -- expand, perfect, and repackage them as your specialty.

You can specialize in one or a few project types

☐ Industrial
☐ Schools
☐ Entertainment
☐ Institutional
☐ Retail/hospitality
☐ Multifamily
☐ Life care
☐ Religious
☐ Medical
☐ Corrections
☐ High tech
☐ Government

etc etc etc. etc etc etc. etc etc etc.

We all tend to do this inadvertently as good projects lead naturally to similar ones. Problem, of course, is weathering the market swings. Some avoid excessive specialzation by joint ventures and alliances to break into new markets.

Or you can see the B141 services as a narrow window of opportunity -- qualify yourself to provide project services long before and after.

Planning | Market Studies | Feasibility Studies | Real Estate Development | Environmental Impact Studies | Landscape / Interiors / B141 Services / CM & D/B | Finishing out | Post-occupancy | etc. etc. etc.

The point of including these options is only that they exist. At age 65, I still carry a list of things I want to do when I grow up. It's the awareness of options--knowing *this is not the only lousy job I can get*--which bolsters the self-esteem so necessary for marketing and negotiation. Add your own options--teaching, product design, film animation--whatever. On the other hand, if something listed here really rings your bell--check it out--go for it!

WHAT ARE THEY BUYING ?

"What do clients want from their architects?" The National AIA asked that question by survey of both architects and clients in preparation for drafting the B141, 1997 Edition. Here's a summary of what got reported.

CLIENTS EXPECT AND DEMAND:

1. **Good design.** They expect this as a matter of course. Client and architect may differ over some particulars of what constitutes good design, but they are probably in broad, general agreement. Otherwise that client wouldn't have selected that architect.

2. **Good management**, which primarily means their projects completed on time and within budget.

   - When owner input was gathered for use in drafting B141–1997, one of the principal complaints expressed was that architects wouldn't "stand behind" their cost estimates.

   - Budgeting is also a value issue: Clients are concerned about getting value for their money.

   - Their projects completed on time. Time may be more important than money: On an elementary school, for example, timely completion has monetary, political, and personal ramifications for owner and users alike.

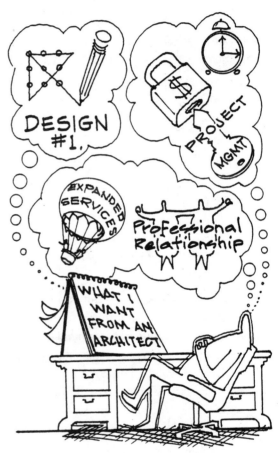

3. **Expanded services.** These include planning and predesign, construction, post-construction, and other related services—broadly speaking, services other than design that are needed to transform design concepts into brick and mortar.

4. **Professional relationship.** Along with services comes the sizzle of the professional relationship. Elements of it can be listed—availability, communication, responsiveness by the architect, and anticipation by the architect of the client's needs—but no list is complete. Clients recognize it when it is present, and can probably best be characterized as understanding by the architect of the client's needs and capabilities, and by the client that its needs will be met. One gauge of its importance is the fact that for the successful firm, repeat work is the main source of new business. It adds up to a good working relationship, with all the human and management lessons that it entails.

FROM THE AIA SURVEY OF THE MARKET:

The object of the game is to offer the services the client wants and needs—problem seeking in a truly global sense. Probably the best gauge of client wants and needs is what clients are buying. According to the firm survey:

1. **Expanded services** accounted for 40% of architects' billings in 1996, as against 20% in 1990.

   - Expanded services are growing much faster than core design services, which only grew 11% in 1990–1996.

   - Expanded services (i.e., planning and predesign, construction, post-construction, and other related services) allow firms to diversify within their specialities.

   - Contributing to architect/client understanding, expanded services allow the client to:
     a. Reduce the number of service providers it deals with.
     b. Hire a team that will coordinate all phases of the project.

   - The construction stage, not surprisingly, has seen the greatest increase in architectural services in recent years. Evidently, a lot of architects have understood clients' need to have somebody take charge of the project.
     a. 25% of firms now provide CM.
     b. 23% of firms now provide D/B.
     c. In all, 43% of firms appear to provide some form of construction services beyond conventional contract administration.

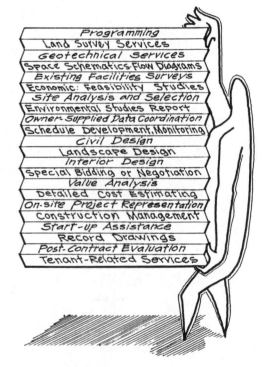

Programming
Land Survey Services
Geotechnical Services
Space Schematics-Flow Diagrams
Existing Facilities Surveys
Economic: Feasibility Studies
Site Analysis and Selection
Environmental Studies Report
Owner-Supplied Data Coordination
Schedule Development, Monitoring
Civil Design
Landscape Design
Interior Design
Special Bidding or Negotiation
Value Analysis
Detailed Cost Estimating
On-site Project Representation
Construction Management
Start-up Assistance
Record Drawings
Post-Contract Evaluation
Tenant-Related Services

EXPANDED SERVICES

Some firms are now offering "One-Stop Shopping"

2. **Pass-through billings** more than doubled in 1990–1996. This suggests that many expanded services were provided by consultants.

3. **Rehab/renovation** accounted for over 40% of firms' billings in 1996. Figures for 1981–1985 suggest 30% for those years.

You might diversify to serve a chosen client base long term

Some architects serve clients throughout the life-cycle of the buildings. In CPA jargon, they become "account executives," not just doing one-off projects, but acting as consultants on any built-environment issue. They read and listen for anything that could help their clients be more successful. They mail clippings "FYI" and become de facto partners in the clients' firms.

30 years of service opportunities in the life-cycle of your buildings....

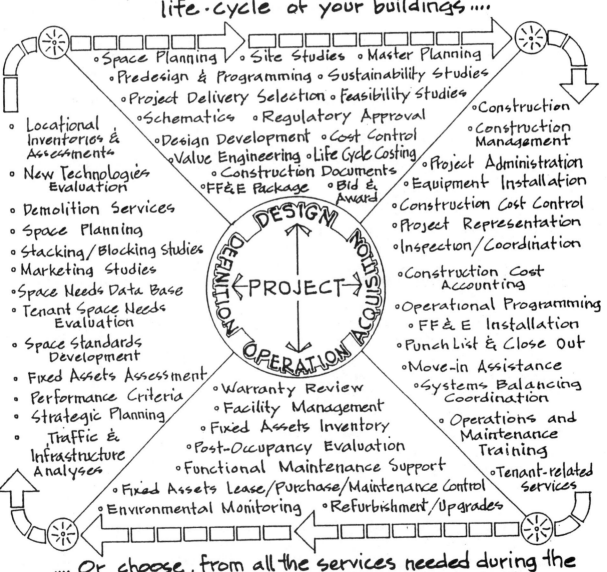

- Space Planning • Site Studies • Master Planning
- Predesign & Programming • Sustainability Studies
- Project Delivery Selection • Feasibility Studies
- Schematics • Regulatory Approval
- Design Development • Cost Control
- Value Engineering • Life Cycle Costing
- Construction Documents
- FF&E Package • Bid & Award

- Locational Inventories & Assessments
- New Technologies Evaluation
- Demolition Services
- Space Planning
- Stacking/Blocking Studies
- Marketing Studies
- Space Needs Data Base
- Tenant Space Needs Evaluation
- Space Standards Development
- Fixed Assets Assessment
- Performance Criteria
- Strategic Planning
- Traffic & Infrastructure Analyses

- Construction
- Construction Management
- Project Administration
- Equipment Installation
- Construction Cost Control
- Project Representation
- Inspection/Coordination
- Construction Cost Accounting
- Operational Programming
- FF & E Installation
- Punch List & Close Out
- Move-in Assistance
- Systems Balancing Coordination
- Operations and Maintenance Training
- Tenant-related Services

DESIGN
DEFINITION
←PROJECT→
OPERATION
ACQUISITION

- Warranty Review
- Facility Management
- Fixed Assets Inventory
- Post-Occupancy Evaluation
- Functional Maintenance Support
- Fixed Assets Lease/Purchase/Maintenance Control
- Environmental Monitoring • Refurbishment/Upgrades

.... Or choose, from all the services needed during the life-cycle to design an alternative career in the corporate or public sector.

THE B141 AS A TOOL FOR DIVERSIFICATION

Strange choice of tools, you say—hard to think of using contract forms to market projects, much less qualitatively transform your practice. Most contracts just record quantifiable expectations and obligations for short-term transactions. They define punitive consequences of breaching one's duty. And they do all that in lawyerly talk to be warily approached (and avoided where possible) by the rest of us.

In spite of this, the new B141 is a good tool for both direct marketing and for diversification through expansion of your scope of services. **The 1997 version of B141 is philosophically different**—not just better—and it sets up new ways for you to:

- Add value—and fees—by expanding your scope of services if you choose to do so.
- Educate clients to set realistic expectations and get better at all they have to do.
- Get the vital project parameters on the table up front—instead of finding them out the hard way as the project evolves.
- Place limits on how much unnecessary and unpaid-for time you'll have to spend on the project.
- Talk the client through the whole process-to-come as collaborative teamwork instead of being potentially adversarial-from-the-get-go.
- Develop relationships of mutual understanding that can help make clients yours for as long as you want them—career-long accounts for common cause, rather than sporadic and potentially arms-length encounters.

That's the good part. The hard part is that no longer is the B141 just something to be filled out for the file drawer, just in case something goes wrong later. The new document is best thought of as a working agreement to evolve along with the demands of the situation and the emerging best interests of the owner, you, and as always, the project.

For me, the bad part about the B141 is the order in which the content is presented. As always, rather than reflecting the architects' sequence of doing things, it's written in the lawyers' order for formatting and reading contracts. Doesn't correlate at all with the way we actually use the documents as working tools for projects. In fact it's bass-ackwards. For that reason, different parts of the B141 are dealt with in several places in this book, depending on whether we're talking about getting, negotiating, or doing projects.

Here, we're interested in your figuring out just what services you want to market and provide, and for that, check out Article 2.8.3 on the opposite page. It's a list (you guessed it—at the tail end of the contract) for review with clients in order to scope out exactly what services they'll need to buy in order to get their project designed and built. But you can use it here as a checklist for a little ad hoc strategic planning.

1.14

B141 Article 2.8.3 The Architect shall furnish or provide the following services only if specifically designated:

.1 Programming

.2 Land survey

.3 Geotechnical

.4 Space schematics/flow diagrams

.5 Existing facilities analysis

.6 Economic feasibility studies

.7 Site analysis and selection

.8 Environmental studies and reports

.9 Owner-supplied data coordination

.10 Schedule development and monitoring

.11 Civil design

.12 Landscape design

.13 Interior design

.14 Special bidding and negotiation

.15 Value analysis

.16 Detailed cost estimating

.17 On-site project representation

.18 Construction management

.19 Start-up assistance

.20 Record drawings

.21 Post-contract evaluation

.22 Tenant-related services*

This list provides a good place to start looking at ways you might want to diversify your services and develop an "account" relationship with clients. What might you offer throughout the project's *life-cycle* so that they look to you for help on any issues dealing with the built environment? If 70 percent of your projects come from repeat clients, how can services to them suggest a major piece of your marketing effort?

As a practitioner, it never occurred to me to even hesitate—if the project needed it and the owner wanted to pay for it, I was ready to promise the service on the spot. Talk about lifelong learning! Meeting clients' needs led to our firm's diversification into the planning, interiors, and civil engineering markets—and to my getting grandfathered registration as a landscape architect. Point is, soul-searching strategic planning isn't the only way to transform practice—just doing what the project needs next can work as well.

MAKE NO SMALL PLANS.......

By now (if you've surfed the previous pages) you know you've already got all the marketing tools you need—we all do—as well as a staggering array of possible services to offer, and lots of optional niches you might fill. Perhaps you're feeling that what you lack now is a marketing plan. If so, I say good for you and leave it like that. My idea of a good marketing program is that it's infinitely more a matter of attitude than checklists.

I'm a strong believer in the marketing planning process, however, in setting goals, making performance commitments to oneself and others—all that. It ought to happen a lot more often than it does, and the resulting self-assignments are best kept posted on the wall, in your organizer, your wallet—wherever they're useful reminders to you, day by day.

Where they're not useful is ring-bound and dust-gathering 'til they're hauled out for collective guilt trips or the settling of arguments at year-end or performance evaluation time. Who needs it? After all, they weren't really worthy goals if mere humans could have attained them—right? Let's shoot high, but not lowball ourselves subsequently.

POSSIBLE AGENDA FOR A PLANNING RETREAT

1. **Hold planning sessions away from the office and on weekends,** if at all possible, with the projects quiet, and the phone and fax unable to spread their deadly lure.

2. **Tell your story**—review the history, recall the operative myths or milestones for the firm and for those gathered. If this sounds like a time waster, think of the plan as a design problem. Every design begins with consideration of the site and the context—telling your story provides essential context for the better future you're here to plan.

3. **Brainstorm** (the how-to for that is in Chapter 10, Groupwork) to evaluate current strengths, weaknesses, opportunities, and threats (check the S.W.O.T. diagram, opposite page).

4. **Split the group** to have half brainstorm what it is like working here 5 years from now because we continued with business as usual and made no changes today. The other half brainstorms a description of the best of all possible worlds 5 years out. Both groups are writing scenarios in the present tense as though it's already happened. If I were there with you, we'd have covered a wall by now, with flipchart paper posters of issues to be dealt with.

5. **Work in subgroups,** half on the positive side with ways of enhancing and taking advantage of the strengths and opportunities—the other half devising ways to mitigate the negative weaknesses and threats.

6. **Plenary show and tell** to clarify, explain, and modify subgroupwork, then a tape-dot poll at break time. Give each participant three to five of each of two colors of Avery file-label tape-dots—one color for the most important ideas listed on the wall—the other color for the most urgent. Also during the break, number the ideas that got dots.

7. **Evaluate the prioritized ideas for quick wins.** Draw a four-square matrix with the vertical axis a minimum-to-maximum continuum labeled "bang-for-the-buck" and a continuum on the horizontal axis labeled "time required." Pick a number and ask the group to point up, down, left, right to tell you where to write the number on the matrix.

8. **Commit to making it work and self-assign tasks** using the R-charting method in Chapter 10.

.......AS OFTEN AS POSSIBLE

Actually, 9 out of 10 firms (especially small ones) don't need hard copy marketing or strategic plans though a few *feel* a need for them by reason of angst, temperament, leadership transition, or sheer firm size.

Of course, if you're in the *big* big-firm category, doubtless there's already an intensive annual process in place, with consultants like me hired on to facilitate the year-end retreat that fires us all up to meet next year's challenge goals.

So this is really for the systematic or worried practitioners, mainly in midsize firms. If you're one of those and want more on the subject, look in Chapter 11, Getting the Firm Out of the Way, under the section titled Don't Call It Quality Management. There is a more complete discussion of planning processes there, along with a bibliography. I warn you in advance, though, that I'm dead serious about those titles. They're among the best tips I can give you.

For our immediate purposes —though the diagrams pretty much tell the story— I've thrown in a possible agenda for a planning session on p. 1.16.

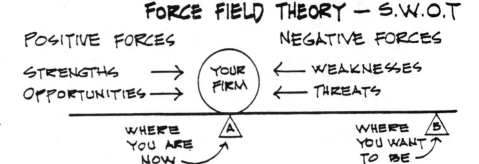

FORCE FIELD THEORY — S.W.O.T

POSITIVE FORCES   NEGATIVE FORCES

STRENGTHS   →   YOUR   ← WEAKNESSES
OPPORTUNITIES →   FIRM   ← THREATS

WHERE (A)   WHERE (B)
YOU ARE   YOU WANT
NOW   TO BE

OR PRACTICE "EMERGENT" PLANNING

① Just decide what you do or have done that you like or do well, and that others want and need....

② Versus what you don't like or do well.

③ Then figure a way to do more of what you like and are good at!

1.17

IT'S ABOUT AVAILABILITY AND....

We all get frustrated by this automated and digitized world we live in. Lobotomized electronic voices instruct us to push buttons according to a lengthy menu with every choice but that of a real person responding. Then we're put on hold with elevator music and sporadic admonitions that this may be recorded "for quality purposes." Given that some 70 percent of architects are introverts working, on average, about 60 hours per week—it's enough to give us an attitude. *Hey, I don't have time for this hassle and besides, I hate telephones, and I just dialed 33 digits and you want three more, and just wait'l I reach a real human being, and I hope to hell that's recorded, etc.!*

It's important that people calling you don't get put through some version of that—since some 70 percent of your mid-future projects might come from those trying to contact you these days. I remember David Maister* warning us some 10 years ago that success in this or any profession depends on three things:

- **AVAILABILITY**
- **AFFABILITY**
- **ABILITY**

He was talking to the AIA National Board and, looking at them intently for a long pause, he emphatically added, ***And in That Order***. What he meant was that clients wouldn't consider doing business with you if they didn't believe you a competent professional. As such, they expect you to respond with all the thoughtful, professional compassion you can muster when they reach you. But first, they also feel harried, overworked, and in immediate need of the real you—a caring consultant—every and any time they call.

This mandate gains considerable urgency if the project is under way and you're the guy who brought it into the office. A recurring complaint from clients about big firms is that the only hope of ever seeing the principal again—the one who marketed them—is at the groundbreaking and dedication ceremonies. None of us enjoys being delegated down the ladder. So the market standard for professionals now is that phone calls get same day response—within 24 hours max —and then with credible reasons for any delay.

Your choice—you can continue to regard the telephone as an invasion of privacy, an interruption of important work—or you can join your competition in accepting it along with the other fax of professional life. Lots of architects are out there marketing the assurance they'll be available 24 hours a day for the life of the project—and backing it up with beeper and cell phone numbers. It's a judgment call.

---

*David H. Maister came out of teaching at Harvard Business School where he researched our profession along with those of medicine and law. He's just written a wonderful book about his years spent since consulting with CPA and law firms. I highly recommend it—it speaks to architects: *True Professionalism* (Free Press,1997).

PLAYING THE TELEPHONE

Your objectives for marketing calls:

- To make friends—at least friendly contacts.

- To learn about potential projects.

- To learn the hierarchy of the place, then how things *really* work there and who makes it go.

- To make appointments, if there's reason.

Don't sell. From incessant dinnertime experience, none of us, clients included, is enraptured with, or easily captured by, tele-marketing. Especially when the next building project represents the biggest capital outlay in next year's or any other budget. But though you can't expect to sell by phone, it remains a very viable environment for information gathering if you take the time to build a relationship—which, oddly enough, can be done rather easily by phone.

Build relationships. Keep your organizer and pencil handy to note particulars about anything discussed, even mentioned. In subsequent calls, to be able to make follow-up inquiries about personal matters alluded to now will be incredibly flattering.

Cluster outgoing calls. Though it's poor practice to shield yourself from incoming calls, you can bunch your outgoing ones and prepare for them with agenda notes and lists of numbers. Improves both the work time and the telephoning.

Get yourself up for phoning—both psychologically and physically. Stand up, dial the number, and talk as though you were in the room with the person you're phoning—pace, gesture, nod, smile. Not sure how it works, but any good disk jockey can tell you that your bodily movements and facial expressions somehow add life and meaning to the expressions you broadcast electronically. Helps you "come across" with greater presence. Sounds crazy, but close your door (so staff won't think you've totally lost it) and give it a try. It works!

Lighten up. Use first names, open-ended questions, and lots of self-confidence to get past any screening system. But slow down enough to show genuine interest in and concern for the gatekeepers along the way. If you disclose personal data or opinions for openers, chances are that they will in return. As Maister points out, many of them are more professional than some of the people they work for. Many an executive assistant has strong influence on corporate decision making and it doesn't hurt to acknowledge that and have friends in high places.

LATERAL LEADERSHIP

A few pages back I asked what you're marketing, then clouded the issue with stuff about diversifying and specializing—in either project types or services. All good stuff, but it begs the question.

Let's start over—
What are you *really* marketing?

Answer: **Yourself**, and your ability to think, design, and act on behalf of clients who come to you for change—**a change agent for projects.**

Architects do projects, which is like saying apple trees make apples—projects are what we're here for. Problem is, lots of other people now do projects, too—claim they manage the process better, and often do. The new two-letter acronym disciplines—CM, VE, PM, D/M, and FM—all that competition for project control is our legacy from 50 years of architects' abdicating responsibility and accountability. In the face of increasing complexities in the practice and design of architecture, and in reaction to litigious threat, we ran scared. As we gave up project control, others managed to assume it—all in the name of management. Our world became digitized, its currency became information, and access to that currency is now available to anyone.

Question now is, if everybody has access to the same CAD and software systems for designing and managing construction of buildings, what real need is there for architects to lead projects? How do you differentiate yourself from the others?

First option: Go head to head. Get better at using and managing technology in order to meet expectations. Many architects—especially the younger ones—are proving themselves wonderfully proficient with the new technologies, and fully capable of holding their own against the competition. Some firms—and not just the big ones—are responding well to the market complexities by taking back their roles from the two-letter acronyms. The whole profession is reacknowledging the breadth of our accountability, the diversity of possible services, what and how much value we can responsibly offer the project.

That's *transactional* leadership, where position and power are ceded to the one best qualified to achieve the short-term goals of their constituency. Management is one essential subset of skills we need for leadership in today's market. But it's not the whole thing.

Another way: Architects have special capabilities of a different kind of leadership, which aims at transcending constituents' immediate expectations to achieve long-term shared interests, hopes, and aspirations—*transformative* leadership. We offer this through our professional agency relationship, our bedrock commitment to serving societal, client, and project interests. That's a concept very different from the marketplace quality management dictum of selling only what customers know enough to be able to specify. Given our edge of professional commitment, then, what is leadership and how can we get better at it?

Leadership is change. Management is maintenance. Management applies yesterday to today. Leadership joins today to tomorrow. Waiting for the design and construction industry to "return" to the way it should have been does neither.

Leadership is vision, is seeing the essence of a dream, a world to be created—then motivating others to help achieve the transformation. With all the stakeholders having access to the requisite technical knowledge base, the biggest design challenge today is in process, not just product. And Howard Roark is a lousy role model.

Leadership is personal, is the person of the leader as it connects with the person of the follower. Leadership is not position or title. Leadership is covenants, not contracts. Leadership is extending the collegial working relationships of the studio to encompass all the project stakeholders.

Leadership is learned. Life, not genetics, yields leaders. Hence leaders come in all shapes and sizes (Napoleon and Lincoln) and emerge at all ages (Alexander the Great and W. Edwards Deming). The good news is that the world beyond architecture is full of examples, even mentors. But mentorship requires mentees. Lao-tzu: *When the pupil is ready, the teacher will come.*

Leadership is highly marketable.
Leaders do the same things managers do, but couple those capabilities with vision and the ability to get others' help to attain it. That vision, those abilities, are the essence of marketing, of getting people to go where they wouldn't—or couldn't—have gone by themselves.

Leadership is decision. Decide if you will lead. If you will, begin with yourself. Know who you are.
Discover the sources of your enthusiasm. Acknowledge the attributes of your style. Examine the limits and potentials of the projects at hand, your life in a firm, your career in this profession. Like most things, you can undertake this as a design project—the most important one of your career!

Point of this page is that while you're naturally in a position to lead projects, you still have to decide whether you will. Leadership doesn't just happen to you, though plenty of opportunities for using it happen to you daily.

In today's world, the most effective, easily marketed, and highly sought after form of leadership gets done using *power with*, rather than *power over*.

That means there's a lot best left unsaid. Like prescriptions or top-down proclamations. It's leading by doing rather than directing.

Especially if you don't call it that.... the word makes some people leery--Just do it-- don't call it.

So whatever the jargon:

Lateral leadership
Leader as server
Change agent
Your architect

The first step in assuming leadership is to be very clear about your core values—why what you're doing in architecture is vital.

KEEP IT HORIZONTAL!

and

IMPROVING YOUR SELF-IMAGE

Of course, you're forever meeting people who ask what you do for a living. Any one of them might turn into a client—or lead you to one—and first impressions go a long way. Here's a worksheet to remind you of categories of facts about you and your practice. Try filling it out, just stating each fact, then putting a positive spin on stating why that's of benefit to your clients. Self-esteem and assurance being so essential in making that good first impression, it helps to prepare yourself. Be your own spin doctor.

FACTS/BENEFITS WORKSHEET

SIZE
Fact:
Benefits:

SERVICES
Fact:
Benefits:

EXPERIENCE/EXPERTISE
Fact:
Benefits:

SPECIALIST/GENERALIST
Fact:
Benefits:

SKILLS/CAPABILITIES
Fact:
Benefits:

LOCATION
Fact:
Benefits:

AUTOMATION
Fact:
Benefits:

PARTNERS/CONSULTANTS
Fact:
Benefits:

QUALITY MANAGEMENT
Fact:
Benefits:

WHAT BEST DESCRIBES DESIGN EXCELLENCE?

For this exercise, assume your latest project has been selected for a design award and will be published in your favorite magazine.

STEP 1. Quickly scan the three statements across each horizontal line in the matrix. There are no wrong answers, but of the three choices, put a check mark by the one you prefer be used to describe your project. Total the check marks in each vertical track at the bottom.

Track I	Track II	Track III
Context is the departure point, the inspiration for a bold, innovative statement about it. ✓	Recognizes, recalls, and builds harmoniously on local cultural and physical context. ✓	Sets strong image; distinct and new to its location; stands out.
Advances the art of architecture through a significant design statement; explores new ideas.	Altogether pleasing, a place to visit over and over; user-friendly.	Striking and handsome; meets or exceeds program requirements.
Technologically innovative; demonstrates uses of new materials and systems, or new uses for proven ones.	Great flexibility, functionally innovative; circulation easy and self-evident. ✓	Uses readily available materials and systems in proven and efficient ways.
Uses highest-quality materials commensurate with its use.	Public and community support assure economic viability; excellent life-cycle costs.	Best possible value for the construction money. ✓
Great clarity of concept; transcends style categorization. Is arresting and thoughtful. ✓	Good human scale, timeless in its design; invites participation and reflection/activity. ✓	Timely, current design, strong, compelling, marketing image.
Elegance in both materials and craftsmanship sets new standards for quality at all levels of detailing.	Appropriate durability for its intended use; excellent operating costs.	Builds easily and well. Meets schedule and budget.
Explores new ways to satisfy client and user needs.	Sustainable—environmentally responsible, accessible, safe.	Meets or exceeds all codes and regulatory requirements.
Expands our theory of design; challenges future designers.	Satisfies, but transcends client's program to also respond to community needs.	Meets stated expectations of the client in an exemplary way.
Totals		

STEP 2. Review your list of preferred clients. Which is their favorite magazine? Now retake the exercise, putting yourself in their shoes and marking their choices with an X. How much correlation between the totals in each track of the matrix? The point is to see if your marketing message needs rephrasing so as to be more compelling.

(handwritten margin notes: SUNSET / INSPIRED HOUSE / COASTAL LIVING / ? OTHER)

CRAFTING A MARKETING MESSAGE

Try this exercise:

Step 1. Name the top five.
In 1 minute, list the five best projects in which you've played a substantive role in the last few years.

Step 2. What are you selling?
Decide what you offer that is of most value. In some measure, architects provide all four things listed below on every project. If you had to pick *only one* of those as the primary, bedrock, foundation on which your practice is based, which would you pick?

A. **DELIVERY**   Timely performance. good production capability, etc.
B. **QUALITY**   However you define it —minimum change orders, sustainability, design excellence, functionality, etc.
C. **COST OR PRICE**   Initial or life-cycle cost, competitive fees, whatever.
D. **SERVICE**   Close personal attention, availability, agency relationship, etc.

This exercise was suggested by hearing Ryc Loope, FAIA, head of Durant Group, quote management guru Tom Peters. The message was that for survival in the 1990s you have to be *ultrafast, error-free, and dirt cheap.*

The first three choices I gave you just paraphrase that message into acceptable architectese and the fourth choice, *service,* invariably gets added by workshop attendees discussing Tom Peters's semantics.

In workshops across the country, virtually all architects pick either B. Quality or D. Service as their priority. What about the clients?

Step 3. Speaking for the clients.
Imagine the clients you dealt with on the projects listed in step 1. Put yourself in their place. Which one of the four choices would they honestly say is the primary reason to hire you again?

The purpose of the exercise is to help you develop a target profile of preferred clients and take a look at projects through their eyes. If there are correlations among either project or client types, it can be especially useful. If your target profile echoes your choice of the number one value you have to offer, you're either very fortunate, or else firmly in a market niche, which may or may not be fortunate.

Step 4. Put it in writing.
Still putting yourself in your target profile client's shoes, outline a letter of reference that your preferred clients would be happy to send on your behalf.

The end result should be a good start on your marketing message, subject to wordsmithing. Whole point is to write—in their words—the best and most important things your clients would think to say about you. Present your true strengths in language your target profile clients will resonate to—even find compelling. Sell what your preferred clients want to buy.

What do clients want? On this issue I agree with Weld Coxe, who on the eve of retirement, entreated every architect to overtly stress to all clients the value of the agency relationship you offer.

As the client's agent, you do your best to stand in their place to see the project through from beginning to end. Right? Then Tell 'em so!

1.24

ARCHITECT SELECTION: Why do clients pick one architect over another? Usually for **one** of the reasons listed in Column A along with a combination of some of the reasons listed in Column B.

A

√ ① GOOD PERSONAL EXPERIENCE WITH THE SAME ARCHITECT

√ ② THE ARCHITECT HAS DONE EXCELLENT PROJECTS JUST LIKE THE ONE THIS CLIENT WANTS

③ THE ARCHITECT HAS DONE PROJECTS OF A DIFFERENT BUT RELEVANT TYPE THE CLIENT LIKES

④ THE ARCHITECT IS KNOWN FOR DOING EXCELLENT PROJECTS (OF any type)

Lot of times, that A-1 reason just plain boils down to "It's who you know."

B

☐ A perception of excellent service
☐ Good general reputation
☐ A perception of a unique or impressive approach or service
☐ Technical competency
☐ Financial stability
☐ Adequate staff for the project
☐ Assurance of speed of service
☐ Good proximity to either the client or the project.
☐ Connections/experience in the project location re: anticipated political, regulatory, or funding difficulties
☐ Price or terms
☐ Good chemistry
☐ Good references
☐ Innovative or excellent design

Column A is in typical priority order. Column B is in no order at all — priorities vary with client, project type, and local conditions or business practices.

As a general rule, if you are below the midpoint in Column A for a particular project, you'll need a lot of strength in Column B.

Notice most of the criteria in column B are intangibles. They are largely a matter of perceptions that you can influence or create through marketing.

The best marketing of all is to have good past clients eager to say how great you are.

Which is why so many firms focus on — and succeed by reason of:
☒ Chemistry
☒ Service

ARCHITECTS SAY THEY NEED :

From the AIA firm survey, here's another excerpt on what architects say they need and expect from their clients.

ARCHITECTS NEED AND EXPECT:

1. **Compensation** that reflects the value of what they do. This means more than "more money." Here it may be we architects who are looking for understanding: We would like our clients (and, if possible, the public) to know enough about architects' work to understand the relationship between our efforts and the results in the built environment.

2. **Professional fulfillment.** This is a mixed bag made up of the less tangible motivators. There are probably as many kinds of it as there are architects, but the list would include:

   - Opportunity to do good design.
   - Recognition by peers and public.

3. **Better control of risk**—not less risk, but tighter linkage between liability and what the architect really does.

4. **The ability to compete** for expanded business.
   - This means particularly the ability to complete against CMs, D/Bs, and others who have carved out roles at the expense of the profession.
   - Even in boom markets there are choices to be made. As the firm survey shows, most firms specialize. So what piece of the action—or pieces, more likely —do you want? Which ones will work best for you?

5. **Enhanced communication** within the entire project team, so that problems can be identified and addressed quickly, effectively, and economically.

CHAPTER 3.

DIRECT MARKETING ......

All the stuff you do from the time you get the lead till you get the project.

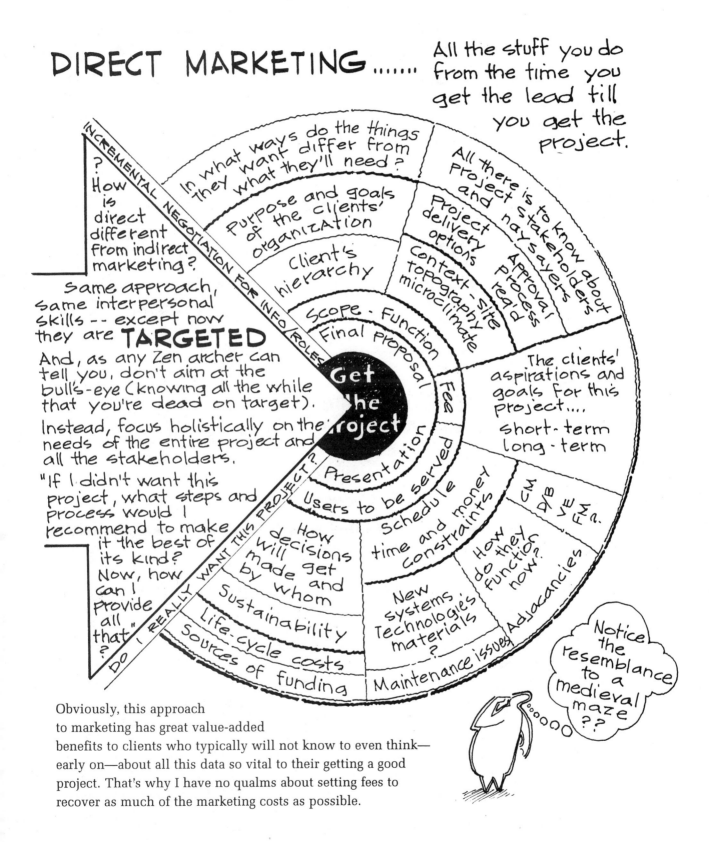

Obviously, this approach to marketing has great value-added benefits to clients who typically will not know to even think— early on—about all this data so vital to their getting a good project. That's why I have no qualms about setting fees to recover as much of the marketing costs as possible.

1.27

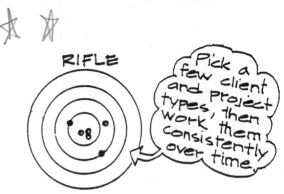

- Requires a lot of resources over time to be successful

- Lets the market (and luck) control your destiny

- Can tempt you to undertake projects outside your area of competency

- Can lower your hit rate and eventually your self-esteem and credibility

- Requires tremendous energy and time

- Is frequently the essential strategy for starting a practice

- Lets you act on the market, not just react

- Lets you build a body of work and a level of expertise in project types you choose

- Is good risk management

- When you lose, it hurts more

- Leads to specialization—and almost every project type has market slumps

- Allows better ability to size up and accept or reject clients

- May result in missed opportunities

For most firms doing good work, a major percentage of projects—at least 70 percent—come from repeat clients or direct referrals by them. So often the problem is a high degree of specialization whether you want it or not.

Regardless of your approach, be selective about the clients you take on. Takes a lot of nerve and will power, I know, but on projects gone sour, most architects report they had ignored an internal "warning bell" right from the very *beginning*.

Next time your alarm bell goes off about a prospect or a potential project, listen to it. Call time-out long enough to quietly check with other consultants who've worked with that client, or to check on credit rating, history of litigation, turnover among their staff—that sort of thing. At least wangle an invitation to spend some quiet, in-depth time with the prospect. Arthur Erickson told me he refused to work with a client until he'd spent an evening at dinner in their home to size them up—assess their wants, their needs.

A MARKETING FORM

Big-firm marketing departments seem to keep files full of marketing forms and statistics. Here's the only marketing form I ever found really useful—there was only one copy at a time and it was always in my organizer.

My banker loved to see it for one thing—gave him the illusion it told me where I'd get the middle-distance money to pay him back. And when I put it together with a bar chart of work I already had in-house, it almost did. So I used it for yearly budget planning.

Its main utility was to indicate where I'd best spend my marketing time and resources.

For example: A developer asks you and four other architects for free sketches on a million dollar building he says will be a "prestige project that will make your name." You figure you'd spend at least $10,000 to compete.

Estimated fee (This is a guess; you don't know how hungry the other four are.) $75,000

Times % go: (After all, he doesn't have the
odds this is   money;   he'll use the sketches
a real project   to raise it.)   × .50

Times % get: (You're only one of five.)   × .20
odds you'll get $ 7,500
the project

Now the $7,500 isn't a real number—as my CPA rolled his eyes and reminded me—but it would tell me I'd be far better off spending my time marketing those first two jobs on the chart below. I can do a whole lot of marketing for $10,000.

Project and status	Est. start	Est. cost	Est. fee	% go	% get	Projection
Spurlock dc. 4500 #	Feb	550,000	35,000	90	75	23,000
Blakely House	Dec	1 mil	100 K	50	50	25,000
Buster's Shipping Rehab	Apr	75000	7500	100	100	7,500
Sovran Branch Zoning Fight	Sep	1.2 M	675 K	20	30	4,000
~~Steakly House~~ ~~Divorced~~	~~June~~	~~475000~~	~~50,000~~	~~80~~	~~80~~	~~32,000~~
Rich's Sea Food Cafe On hold: 7/12	May	150,000	75000	10	30	2250

CLIENTING 101

Bracket the Time & Money and Warrant Your Work.

You can't *not* talk time and money. They won't let you. They can't. Best case: This is the most money they ever thought about spending all in one place. Worst case: They do this for a living and their job's riding on buying out this project for the best dollar. Either way, from the first meeting they're wanting and *needing* to know *HOW MUCH AND HOW LONG?*

My favorite rejoinder: *How long is a string?* Delivered with a grin, of course, and quickly followed with my spiel about how we were in this together to achieve an—as yet—undefined goal. Went something like this:

Minute I know the time and money answers we'll both *know, but this was no place you can kick the tires, read the sticker, and start the haggle.*

I'm in this for quality and to provide whatever services you and the project need. Total fees—me, surveyors, engineers, the whole thing—will range around 10 percent of construction cost. If it were a commercial office building project, total construction cost and fees would be in the range of only some 7 percent of life-cycle cost you'll be paying. Decisions we could be making in the next few weeks might easily save you way more than my fee over the life of the building—in such things as energy conservation, labor savings, maintenance required, and value added at resale. But if you have to have low dollar, I'll be happy to give you names and phone numbers of three architects who work that way.

I meant it and they knew it. Took some nerve on my part to pull this off—always thought I badly needed every project—but to me this was Clienting 101. If they couldn't accept this, we weren't going to last long together anyway, and I wanted to know as soon as possible. In actual practice it always worked—no one ever walked off at that point—though some did later when I actually quoted the fee. But at this stage I was testing intentions. Then I gave them a sop by **bracketing**—first tenet of Clienting 101.

When it comes to bracketing, there's an oft-quoted truism (because it's true). You set the low-end estimate *above* the maximum you think it could ever possibly end up costing in time and money. *They only remember the low figure.*

Best bracketing tactics I've heard of come from those small-project practitioners (lots of them) who carry an entire project file—from a previous and similar job—to the initial client meeting. Or have the client in to the office to review one.

Sketches, memos, check sets and final drawings, correspondence, faxes, job record—everything's arrayed and reviewed chronologically to educate the clients. They're always amazed by how much was required to get that project designed and built. They get full disclosure of what it had cost—in the undeniable form of project records. They help set a factor to be applied to their own project based on comparative complexity, size, quality level, and escalation in market costs. They work on programming the space they'll need, then multiply by the estimated cost per square foot.

The client goes away knowing more than they ever dreamed about all that's going to be required to get their project done. Which compensates a bit for knowing less than they had come to find out about how much it's really going to cost.

The second tenet of Clienting 101 is that you always **warrant your work**. I never took a project without giving an *unconditional guarantee* that there would be errors in my working drawings and there would be change orders during construction. After we shared a good laugh we talked about reality, how much contingency they needed, and how we could deal with it together when the tough times came.

Too many times it subsequently turned out to be vitally important—even crucially urgent—to be able to remind them of this conversation.

CHANGE ORDERS HAPPEN

1.31

CLIENT SELECTION

If you look back to the beginning pages of this part of the book, marketing gets broken into *indirect*, *follow-up*, and *direct* marketing. My hazy differentiation moves from the general to the particular, somewhat like this:

- **Indirect**: Everything you do with no specific objectives about getting projects. You're establishing presence, name recognition, and reputation.

- **Follow-up**: Things you do that specifically target people but not projects as yet. Lots of relationship building, disclosing, networking.

- **Direct**: Activities to reach specific people with a targeted project in mind. Actively going for it.

This page and the next can be useful in bridging all three of those activity categories. The headings for what's listed here frame the sort of information you can look for in indirect marketing, to clue you in to the people you want to follow up on. By this stage you've begun to home in on the specific concerns listed here. Your answers to the questions presented here might strongly modify your approach and behaviors when you're pursuing a specific project. They're definitely on your mind and often your agenda by negotiation time.

The list isn't intended as a yes/no way of deciding whether to work for a client—most of us seemingly being congenitally incapable of saying no to a project.

Think about the factors listed here to help frame your inquiries during marketing, and stiffen your spine during negotiation.*

FACTORS TO CONSIDER

1. **Client history.** What baggage do they bring to the project from their previous experiences in design and construction? Ask them or those who worked with them for the story and consider it in terms of your own capabilities, needs, and current situation.

   Whether the previous architect was so fine as to leave a hard act to follow —or so bad you're about to inherit a cynical and paranoid client—either extreme can cause you problems in controlling and meeting their expectations.

2. **Management structure.** The real one— not the Org. Chart in the annual report—how things get done and who has to bless them first. When there's a tough project problem, will you have access to the person who will fix it? Who will be evaluating your performance? How?

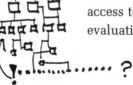

3. **Client attitude.** When the tough decisions have to be made, how will the client weigh your professional expertise?

   - Rely on it?

   - Fight it?

   - Ignore it and turn to others?

---

*This list is from Ava J. Abramowitz, former VP for Victor O. Schinnerer Company and teacher at Harvard GSD. Ava is a favorite at AIA conventions and a consultant to the profession nationwide.

4. **Time.** Does the project demand a schedule you can't commit to meeting? Will it require too much of your workforce for too long a time?

5. **Money.** Does the client have the funding for

- Your services?
- The project?
- A healthy contingency?

6. **Reputation.** When things go bad, how does the client resolve disputes?

- Confrontation or pollyanna style?
- Attack or negotiate?
- Problem solve or panic?

7. **Community ties.** Does the client's standing and network of contacts help or generate problems in the

- Local community?
- Financial community?
- Regulatory and political arenas?

8. **Chemistry.** The best projects derive from mutual trust and respect for the strengths, leadership, and expertise that both client and architect bring to the project.

Warm personal bonding is a bonus, though not necessary. Some of the best clients are tough, brusque, demanding— and fair. On the other hand, you want to check yourself for signs of incipient fear or loathing. Are you *really* willing to talk to and deal with this client—every time they feel like it—for the entire life of the project?

9. **The project's fit.** This one got added to Ava's list at the Signature Firm Roundtable in 1989. Star designers tend to consider projects according to their degree of fit into the architect's body of work in the long view.

- Will you be proud to have done this project?
- Is it a project type the firm can do well? Efficiently? Profitably?
- Will the project offer learning opportunities?
- Will the project improve or damage the firm's position in desirable markets?

Or at least ought to be, if you harbor any illusion of being in control of your professional destiny.

Even if you don't, this is a useful guide for issues to discuss with potential clients

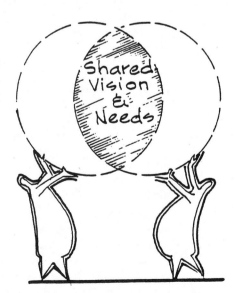

UP-FRONT WORK — Talking it out.

B141 Article 1.1 Initial Information does nothing more than call for you and the client to jointly list the assortment of roles, facts, and assumptions needed to start work together. It's a place to jot all that stuff you're used to finding out from each other—or disclosing in bits and pieces—as the project progresses over time. This gets it up front in one checklist, so that the two of you can agree on when and how the information can be developed and documented, if it's not initially available or needs verification

Whether or not the B141 will actually be used for the project, this list still furnishes a good tool* for starting the joint education of you and the client about how the project can be set up to best succeed. And during marketing is the time to do that.

B141 Article 1.1 Initial Information

1.1.2 PROJECT PARAMETERS

.1 The project objective or use
(owner's goals)

.2 Physical parameters
(size, location, dimensions, geotech, etc.)

.3 Owner's program
(identify documentation or process for getting it)

.4 Legal parameters
(surveys, legal descriptions, regulatory restraints, etc.)

.5 Financial parameters
(owner's overall budget and the budget for the cost of the work)

.6 Time parameters
(milestones, durations, fast-track scheduling, etc.)

.7 Proposed procurement or delivery method
(D/B, CM, design/build/leaseback, negotiated vs. bid, bridging)

1.1.3 PROJECT TEAM

.1 Owner's designated rep

.2 Others required to review architect's submittals

.3 Owner's other consultants and contractors

.4 Architect's designated rep

.5 Architect's consultants

What can you add to this list? One architect starts every project with a vast list of data she develops with the client and lists in four columns-- FACTS, ASSUMPTIONS, WHO and WHEN. The who column lists the person responsible for verifying that assumption or changing it to a fact -- and by when. Until proven otherwise, they agree the assumptions will operate as though facts -- will be the basis for project decisions.

etc., etc. This list gets longer all the time!

On sizable projects, here's a good place to deal openly with a problem before it becomes one: CONTINUITY. The client wants you personally, full-time, the life of the project. Can you jointly design an acceptable alternative? A protocol and process for when project reps get replaced?

---

*You can also make good use of Articles 2.1 to 2.9, the *scope of services*, at this stage. (See pp. 1.67 to 1.69.) Comes as a neat and separate package for review with potential clients, which allows talking through all that's required of each of you without worrying about them chancing upon all those pesky terms and conditions. Trying to formulate scope while they're hung up in the fine print about consequential damages could really put a damper on that positive marketing tone you want to maintain in your discussions for now.

PREPROPOSAL MEETINGS
HELPING THE CLIENT ACHIEVE REALISTIC EXPECTATIONS

Make notes. Better yet, sketch & diagram what's being said.

You might agree on an agenda and how much time you'll spend on this today.

What do you hope to accomplish in the meeting? What are the client's intended outcomes? Sharing expectations can be a good way to start the meeting.

Before the meeting, review your true interests in the project and those you assume that the client has. (Chapter 5 covers this in detail.)

Ask open-ended questions -- show genuine interest and concern for the client and their activities -- how they function.

The message: Respect for them and what they do. You want to know what makes them tick so you can help not only meet their needs, but their aspirations.

KEY to all this:
1. STRAIGHT TALK
2. ACTIVE LISTENING
3. THE COURAGE TO SAY WHAT IS, AND YOUR JUDGMENT OF WHAT IT WILL TAKE TO MEET THEIR REAL NEEDS AND EXPECTATIONS

By now they should realize you'll act as their agent-- think and work in their best interest. Confront the tough issues jointly in a problem-solving mode: 
- Schedule
- Funding options
- Project delivery options
- Quality control
- Change orders
- Claims and risk allocation
- Scope of services
- Payment
- Budget
- Approvals

Don't hesitate to dream a bit out loud about your aspirations for the project, but listen hard for theirs.

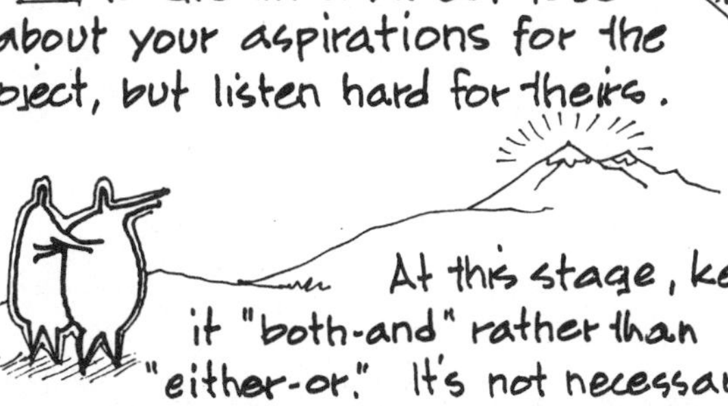

At this stage, keep it "both-and" rather than "either-or." It's not necessary you share the same vision, but you want to be sure of enough overlap to be able to work well together.

Be very open about what you don't know -- how you'll go about getting answers for them, and when.

It's a good idea to leave some things unresolved so as to justify the next meeting to provide information to help them. Set the date!

WINNING THE RFP GAME

Most architects seem congenitally incapable of turning down *any* project that walks in the door. One good thing about the request-for-proposal (RFP) process is that it's so much trouble to answer one! It virtually forces you to consider whether and how much it's actually desirable to get the project. So when you open the mail and it's an RFP, the first question is whether you want to play the game at all. Do you want to answer what—as is often the case in today's consumerist market—is no more than a bid solicitation for architectural services as a commodity?

Consumerism is based in part on the assumption that regulatory law keeps competing commodities within a tight range of performance standards. If we're all the same, it's only prudent to buy whichever's cheapest. For architects, winning in such a game is sometimes second prize, so how do you decide whether to compete? And if you choose to play, how do you go about winning?

Here are some tips, tricks, and traps to keep in mind.

1st Question: Do I want this Project ?

How to decide?

THE PROJECT
- Size
- Type
- Schedule
- Budget
- Client

YOUR
- Workload
- Capability
- Aspirations
- Experience
- Staff
- Availability

A. What's the project size and type and how do either of those fit with your needs and goals?

B. What sort of schedule does the RFP imply and how does that fit with your workload?

C. Is this client someone you know—have been building a relationship with—have marketed or worked for?

Even if the project and client are both news to you, there are clues available from the very nature of the RFP:

- A performance-based and open-ended RFP indicates the owners don't yet know their highest and best use. That can be fun. It allows for creative planning and visionary thinking. It also allows most anybody to compete and you may find yourself up against some atypical teams with blue-sky promises that are hard for owners to resist.

- A highly prescriptive RFP complete with schedule, budget, contract form, building description, and program indicates it may have been authored by an engineer or architect—even someone outside the client's organization writing in their own favor. You need to know.

Two kinds of RFPs

OPEN ENDED

Blue sky time. They're shopping for innovation, expertise,

Detailed and Prescriptive

They know exactly what they want.

Beyond immediate general questions of this sort that are instinctive for all of us, you might want to put yourself in the client's place and try to analyze—or guess—the reasons prompting their use of the RFP process at all. Prequalifying architects; designing, writing, and mailing the RFPs; dealing with all the subsequent queries, responses, and proposals; final evaluations, notifications, and follow-ups—that's a labor-intensive job of considerable duration. As a client, why put yourself through all that?

The point is, their motivation and needs for handling selection through an RFP process can tell you lots about how they would be to work for and with, whether or not you want to undertake it, and if so what might be your best approaches. The following table lists reasons they might have issued the RFP, along with tips on how you might best approach getting the project.

Their situation (more than one may apply)	Advice
They live in a fishbowl of scrutiny by public, shareholders, members, or architect customers and want to demonstrate they've used "due process."	Get ready for lots of careful documentation and tedious review up through their hierarchy—sell on the basis of impeccable service and due diligence.
They want to carefully prequalify potential architects in order to get top quality in design and service for the money.	Where are their priorities among design, service, economy, and delivery—and how well do those match your strengths?
They consider architectural services a commodity and want the low bid.	Your choice—either sell what they want, help them discover what they need, or turn it down. The uphill alternative is to get to know the client well enough to reeducate them.
They're naïve first-time clients and found out RFPs are the way the big guys do it—their government, or school district, or whatever.	In addition to ability, sell trust and agency relationship—that you'll shepherd them safely through this alien territory.
They're sophisticated project reps and use the RFP to qualify firms in an equitable, efficient, businesslike way.	Try to get past business to relationship. The due process of business is only the price of admission.
They've already decided whom they're going to use, but feel required to demonstrate they're being fair.	Research them, their business, and their project til you can demonstrate you know more about their true interests than they do—certainly more than any competition.
They've been approached by so many architects about the project, they need a process to cull the list down.	Follow all their rules so as not to be disqualified, but somehow differentiate yourself.
They have a unique project with special requirements or processes and need an RFP to find architects who can meet them.	Stress that they're right—their project is unique—then push team building and your interdisciplinary strategic alliance capability.
They don't really know yet what the project should comprise and the RFP is a way to get free opinions.	Sell planning and flexibility in approach—stress openness rather than any preconceived solutions.
They have an incredibly complicated set of users and the RFP process is a way to get all stakeholders on record in advance as having committed to project goals and expectations.	In addition to competence, sell people skills.

OK, so that table was a trick, but it's no joke. Looking over that column of advice, is there anything on the list that doesn't apply at some level to virtually every project, every client? Brings you back to the original question, doesn't it—do you want the project? At least enough to take the next step?

Last chance—do you really want the project? And, if you elect *not* to go after it, should you answer the RFP? Yes.
Of course; the only question being how.
Under what circumstances would you:

- Have somebody call and regret?
- Send a form letter saying thanks but no thanks?
- Call and talk with them, then write that you're too busy?
- Research the client and the project, then write a personal letter about:
  - The important aspects of their project.
  - How you would have approached it.
  - Think it can best be approached.
  - Your deep regrets, wishing them best of luck.
  - How much you look forward to working with them in the future.

If you decide not to play this game, yet they really are clients you'd like to work with, try to refuse in such a way that they'll later be sick that they didn't get your services instead of what they deserved and got. Refuse this one in a way to put you high on their list for the next one. It's an investment. Some 70 percent of future projects will come from people who know you. Besides, you may be hungrier by then.

Say No in a way

That makes you a hard act to Follow!

If you're seriously interested in the project....

Research the client among people you know who have worked with and for them in the past (especially consulting engineers and construction people). Try everything you can to arrange to meet with the clients. Your overall purpose at this point is twofold:

Research the project	Research the client
What's the schedule? How rigid is it and why?	Why the RFP process? What's been their experience in design and construction?
Project type and size—what fit is there with what you've done or want to do?	Motives and intent—what does the client do that this project should make easier or better?
Project site, topography, subsurface, history, context, access, traffic circulation?	Client expectations, needs, the context within which they function?
Microclimate—ecology?	What are the client aspirations—their highest hopes for what they do? Can this project help?
Funding process and schedule?	What's their financial ability and how realistic is their expectation of cost plus contingency?
Regulatory constraints?	What's their structure and hierarchy—who has the final say and will you have access to them?
Program status and how was it authored and agreed to? Did all stakeholders have a say?	Dispute resolution history—have they typically negotiated, mediated, or litigated?
Are there advocates for opposition to the project? Is it controversial?	Who'll make project decisions, how, and how fast? How's the initial chemistry with them?
Special considerations—sustainability? Preservation?	Number, identity, and roles of all stakeholders? Will they respect your opinions? Get second ones? Fight among themselves? With you?
What's your track record with this project type or the approaches, technologies, or processes you think it demands—how qualified are you?	Do you know somebody—either among the project stakeholders or their friends—who can help you get the project?

Architect selection committees first cull and _then_ pick, so assuming you _do_ want or need to compete, it's essential you know and follow their rules. And the first rule is that following their rules doesn't win you any points—it only keeps you in the game until the real judging starts. To help you survive the qualifying round, here's a checklist of content for answering virtually any RFP:

- **Your understanding of the project** (and _their_ true interests _that will be met_).

- **Your approach and work plan** for doing the project (_how that's unique, at least exemplary_).

- **The team members** you propose to carry the project out (_along with the expertise they offer, their 24-hour availability, and that they'll stay on for the project duration_).

- **That team's experience** on a few similar projects (_or projects of different types requiring your proposed approaches or expertise_).

- **References** they can call (_and that you_ have talked _to about being called_).

- **Proposed schedule and fees** (_at best, how you'll work with them to determine that and when_).

- **That you intend to be their agent**—to put yourself in their place and act on their behalf through the life of the project. (_This one is so second nature to architects, they often forget to say it._)

- **What makes you different** from the competition (_and why that's in their interest as your client_).

Remember... First they cull

Then they pick.

SELECTION COMMITTEE

Not a bad outline for content, but don't forget the importance of format. Be sure your proposal is in _exactly_ the sequence they ask for and in strict compliance with their RFP—any deviation is grounds for trashing it. Then plant some zingers in it—if only in syntax or vocabulary—to make it memorable. Make them want to at least talk with you personally.

The trick is to follow their rules <u>exactly</u> in order to keep from being disqualified ....

Yet somehow differentiate yourself from all the competition.

The real question is how to *differentiate yourself*—but especially your understanding of their project—within the narrow limits the system allows. You have to somehow show that what you offer is more than a consumable. That you're more than a vendor. That the project's unique and so your approach to it is appropriately nonstandard. Here are some tips:

1. **Lots of research.** When you can demonstrate understanding of their needs, site, microclimate, business situation, and organizational context that is greater than they expect (or know themselves) you're way ahead.

2. **Call your references.** This bears repeating because the potential client *will* call, and you want to be sure what they'll get told will be in glowing terms. Besides, references may have moved, and giving a nonlocatable one is a no-no.

3. **What you offer is not a consumable.** Keep that in mind so it will somehow project through your writing. Unlike automobiles, this year's clothing, even the building that gets built—good design and a life-cycle service relationship is value added that won't wear out.

The Big Trick .....

Be somebody they know knows them.

Disclose far more than you ever thought wise -- It builds trust.

Besides .... they'll find it all out in the first months of the project anyway and you'd rather it have your spin on it than theirs.

4. **Piecemeal the fee.** Whenever it can be justified, quote only the fee for the first step, telling them how the rest of the fee will be established and when in the course of the project it will be possible to do that equitably. But put enough spin on it to make them realize they don't know how to price what they need either—why an easily quoted market rate percentage won't meet their true interests.

5. **Do *not* cannibalize** (in any recognizable way) previous proposals. If spotted, it's an immediate circular file justification.

6. **Check attribution.** Be sure the projects you claim will not be claimed by competitors —more research needed. If the client is considering anybody outside your present organization with whom you have worked on a project for which you want to claim attribution—former employers, employees, joint venture partners, even consultants— verify with those people the proper attribution. Photos of the same project showing up in submittals from different companies are *automatically* grounds for trashing both proposals. Improper project attribution is the preeminent allegation brought before the AIA Ethics Council year after year.

When possible, quote only the fee for the 1st phase. ¢

And how, together, you'll arrive at a fair fee for the rest later

You'd be amazed how easy it is to spot-- just changing names won't hide it.

Hey guys! No point in all of us getting thrown out of the running for new work by all showing the same photos and claiming the same projects we did together. Let's have lunch and sort out how we'll handle attribution!

Unfortunately,
The answers are
all time intensive....

1. **Know somebody.** There's an old truism in the profession—by the time the RFP comes out it's probably too late for you to get the project. Winners get there way early to build relationships and form strategic alliances intended to not only cut costs but increase profits for both parties. Takes marketing time and research to learn enough about their true interests to be able to help them venture into project acquisition, but doing so can result in your actually writing the RFP for them when they're required by regulations or policy to go through the process. It often results in their somehow finding a way to eliminate the RFP process entirely. But don't despair if it's too late this time—losing one in spite of great people process now can put you in line for the next.

2. **Use due diligence** to find out their true needs—and to be sure that some other architect hasn't already gotten a lock on the job. If they have, that's not necessarily cause to abandon the quest. Just be sure that they—and /or the owner—have done their due diligence and actually posed the right problem for the proposed project to solve. The most compelling response to an RFP can be to convince them they've asked the wrong question and that you know the right one.

3. **Prescriptive RFPs asking for bids** call for special attention. The more prescriptive it is, the greater the chance that an architect or engineer wrote it—either as staff or as consultant. If consultants, they may have positioned themselves for the project. If staff, it tells you immediately that—with full knowledge of the difference between vendor and agent—they've chosen to ignore that, and it's not likely you'll change their minds. In most cases, holding a job there requires such an attitude, which tells you a lot about the organization.

   If they've hired design professionals to take bids they're probably street-smart, bottom-line companies that are frequent clients for professional services—rather than naïve first timers who, without professional input, just naturally assume they should bid it as the Great American Bottom-Dollar Way.

4. **Performance-based RFPs** deserve special attention and frequently a team response. On the one hand they're enticing because they allow you more freedom to invent not only your approach, but the scope of the project as well. On the other hand, that same invitation is practically extended to the world at large and you may find yourself competing with a weird assortment of spin-doctor paraprofessionals/turned/ consultants—some of whom are terribly quick-witted and convincing.

5. **Write the way you talk** when you're with bright friends who enjoy exciting and meaningful discussion. Proposal writing falls somewhere between technical writing and an ad campaign. Don't use jargon on the one hand, or stilted legal-sounding language either. Draft anything that really says what you want to actually do, then edit out one-third. And while you're editing, work for 21-word sentences and 3-syllable words, max. Then get a nonarchitect friend, family member, or significant other to read it and tell you where they stumble or get bored.

6. **Legal stuff.** With *all* RFPs, remember that a proposal by you, accepted without change by them, becomes a binding legal contract. Read their RFP carefully from a legal point of view, looking for exceptions to it—if any—that you need to make in your proposal. Their reference to using their own in-house form of agreement, for instance, might suggest your proposing the industry standard form B141 "modified if and as necessary." Or at least that reaching a mutually agreeable form of contract for services is an item in your work plan. Say what you mean, mean what you say.

Neither that last tip—nor any of this—is aimed at scaring you away from undertaking any project you're interested in and for which you can put together the right team to handle it well and profitably. What this does counsel is to manage your risks (and your clients) up front, provide them the services they need, and price your services equitably to allow you to do great projects!

MARKETING PRESENTATIONS

Marketing presentations vary, of course, from sales pitches for selection committees to pushing for approval from zoning boards and design review boards, to coffee-table diagramming over a set of sketches or prints. They also vary with the individual style of the presenter—so much so, in fact, that I hesitate to say much more on the subject. You have or will develop what works for you and that's as it should be—in marketing, you're selling yourself and your process fully as much as your ideas about the project. If you're a thoughtful introvert who listens carefully before responding—fine—sell that. I happen to prefer behaving like a raging extrovert with a touch of showbiz that differentiates me from the competition. And on the chance that some of what I do will be useful, here's a brief list of principles, tools, and tricks that have worked best for me over the years.

PRINCIPLES:

- **Set it all up.** I at least go look at the room in advance to pick my best position and the wall I'll use to mount posters or to draw on. If possible I want to be involving them from midpoint of the long wall of the room. My worst option is at the end of the conference table with them hiding behind each other, silently keeping score sheets in lil-bitty ballpoint.

- **Talk with them, not at them.** If I can't get them talking horizontally with me or among themselves for at least 30 percent of the time together, I figure I've lost it.

- **Make it immediate.** It's their project not mine, and it's happening right now. On-the-spot feedback on a flipchart or a stretch of poster paper rivets their attention.

- **Keep it graphic.** I can triple the effectiveness of a blue-line print carefully rendered in color if I boldly note their comments and emphasize mine on it in felt-tip. They're wincing and grinning about what they're saying being important enough that I'll graffiti it onto a finished presentation drawing.

- **Ghostwrite it** in advance. I can draw and letter faint cues to myself in 0.5-mm graphite that none of them can see from 6 feet away. They're impressed that I can felt-tip with fair accuracy, barely glancing at what I'm drawing, and talking directly to them all the while.

- **Tag team it**—with choreography. Unless you're going to be their sole contact throughout the project, take along whoever they'll be dealing with on a daily basis. Works best when that person and you can enthusiastically interrupt each other—step on each other's lines, play a little one-upmanship, demonstrate you work as a team with mutual respect and a bit of humor.

FOR FUN & PROFIT!

- **Keep it moving**—sketches and diagrams convey whole concepts. Key words and one-liner metaphors annotating the drawings give us all a handle—a set of shorthand code words for subsequent reference to those whole thoughts. To-do lists involve them in setting next steps and leave us all with future activities—unfinished business. *How can we not hire this guy? We're not through yet!*

TOOLS:

- Felt-tips: Washable—I don't need to buy anybody new wallpaper. Sanford's *Mr. Sketch* markers for large groupwork are good, though Crayola *Classic* or *Bold* markers project an ingenuous grade-school directness and mutual openness to small groups.

- Flip-chart easels need to be the heavy-duty facilitator's type with stiff backs to pound at with markers. Display tripods are too flimsy. Your best thoughts will get shot down often enough as it is. You don't want them crashing to the floor in advance.

Keep the lights on, full eye-contact, and nobody dozing.

You techies: check out the page on "Bells and whistles" in Chapter 1. That's my story and I'm sticking to it!

- Or you can use poster paper—comes in 3- and 4-foot rolls. The disadvantage of the flip chart is it's awkward to carry far. The poster paper requires a flat wall to work on and needs time to put up and take down. Your choice.

- For small groups there's a 20- by 25-inch masonite clipboard available, but that means you've got to hold it up for them to see while you write. Takes practice.

- Your choice on any or all the above, but of course you need masking tape with any of them.

- My only paperless option is an overhead projector with hand-drawn and lettered viewgraphs. Works best when I customize the viewgraphs with permanent *vis-á-vis* markers in bold colors, then scribble and write on them during the presentation with *vis-á-vis* washable markers in contrasting colors.

- 3M makes a good 8½- by 11-inch transparency film that photocopies from your paper sketches. If it's required that you show previous work, you can freehand trace photos as felt-tip sketches to mark up on-screen, and wow a committee who's dozed through your competition's 35-mm slide shows.

SELL TO THEIR PERCEPTION OF YOU

Everything till now has pushed your building a mutually trusting relationship and helping both the client and you set realistic project expectations. All that still applies to selling-- to closing the deal.

Except now, if you're competing with others for the job, things are suddenly relative. The client is trying to compare you and your firm with others. Depending on circumstances, a client may perceive you as <u>large</u> or <u>small</u>, <u>local</u> or <u>out-of-town</u>, <u>expert</u> or <u>novice</u> for the project type. Through the use of associations, joint ventures, consultants, and enough gas to drive one hour, even sole practitioners can find themselves being put in any of those six categories.

TWO CHOICES:

① You can correct their misperception--set the record straight. (And there could be times it would be dangerous not to do so.)

② You can-- within the bounds of honesty-- let them perceive you any way they want. Then put a spin on your sales message to convince them why it's in their best interest to hire exactly the sort of architect or firm they perceive you to be.

Which do you think more likely to get you the job?

Here are some examples of spins you might use

LOCAL

- We are here for the long haul. We have a personal stake in the community as well as a professional one. We intend to live with the results just as you do.

- We are here every time we are needed— we are only (—) minutes from you, (—) minutes from the site. We'll know when to be on the job, without you or the contractor having to call us.

- Fees spent locally get respent 7 times locally. Keep the money in our own town.

- Even if we end up with an out-of-town contractor, most of the actual work will be done by local people. If they screw you, they will have to work with us for years to come. We keep score . . . and they know it.

OUT OF TOWN

- We are purely professional—no local bias or pressures to use anything or anybody on your project other than what's best for it. If it meets your needs and wishes we will fight to get it for you. You wouldn't be talking to us if we weren't specially qualified.

- In an information society there's no such thing as "remote." Here is how we plan to manage project communication and coordination. . . .

- The fee for architecture services is about $\frac{1}{10}$ of 1% of the life-cycle cost of the project. Pick the best.

- We offer fresh eyes, new ideas, objective evaluation of the performance of the contractor and all the subs. And we have a basis for comparing their work to the best work in other localities.

RATHER THAN FROM HOW YOU SEE YOURSELF

Perceptions operate like facts.
When possible, it's best you operate on
the basis of theirs.

SMALL FIRM

- Today's fast-breaking technology demands a generalist overview and one-point responsibility—that's me.

- We are not encumbered by in-house engineers who try to be expert for every project type. We assemble the best team we can from consultants who are truly expert for your unique project. Most of the nationally recognized designers agree with us—they don't have engineers in-house.

- Your project is a big one to us. It means a lot and will merit our day-to-day attention at the top. It won't get relegated to lower echelons. In our firm the same architect (me) personally controls design, specs, etc.

- Just as in your business, in architecture it all comes down to people. You want to deal with the people who make the professional judgments—not with computer or technicians.

- Your job means so much to us, you can be assured we won't be shifting personnel.

- We are a close-knit office—overview and coordination of all aspects of a project are automatic—everybody in the office overhears everything—there is no compartmentalization. It's all one-on-one.

- Contractors—just like you—want to deal with, and tend to pay more attention to, the head of a firm.

- There's a limit to the number of people who can effectively work on a project. Regardless of firm size, it always comes down to the project team. We are

---

LARGE FIRM

- "Master builder" is an impossibility in today's industry. A team of specialists is required.

- We've got in-house capability and therefore have tested relationships and teamwork among well-qualified specialists—we stress coordination—we don't expect you to fund our experts' organizational learning curve. You'll get a dedicated team to see your project through.

- There is a reason we are the size we are—we have to pay attention to service and responsiveness. You'll get a project manager assigned 100% to your project with oversight by a partner.

- Technology is moving so fast, it takes a firm our size to afford CADD upgrades, quality control systems, continuing education, etc., etc. (if true).

- We have staff depth and plenty of second opinions to assure the quality of professional judgments.

- We can ride out "stop-and-go" on a project when necessary.

- We aren't dependent on outside consultants, so coordination is built in—it's automatic.

- Construction administration (or specs, design, project management, etc.) is a discipline all its own—it deserves an expert such as ours.

1.49

How do they perceive you?

VERY LITTLE EXPERIENCE

- Caudill: "An architect who claims to have done 10 schools may really have only done 1 school 10 times." We have no preconceptions. We'll be working to answer your needs as you define them.

- We'll be looking for breakthroughs. Your project and your site offer unique opportunities. You deserve more than a cookbook solution.

- Let's talk about what's unique to your project and how we would approach the design.

- No assembly line with us. We work hard at staying generalists. Similar but different project types keep us from getting stale. Here are examples of different projects we've done that had similar concerns—and how doing them gives us the diverse experience to qualify us to do well with your project.

- We do lots of different project types to keep ourselves enthusiastic and growing professionally. Nothing is by rote or done without our full, professional attention. We *have* to pay attention.

A LOT OF EXPERIENCE

- Everybody likes a winner—which is why we keep being selected for projects like yours. You've got a lot at stake here. We've got a demonstrated track record.

- We have no learning curve on this and won't ask you to pay our tuition. Instead of our time being spent learning the project type, we can focus on what's unique about your specific needs.

- Let me show you all the projects like yours we've done. You'll want to talk to our other clients for this type of project. Here is a list of references.

- Because your project type is one we like and work with a lot, we naturally research it and continually stay abreast of latest advances in design and technology relevant to it. We've already got a head start on anybody else you'll talk to.

- Although we are proud of our design, it's still only 15 to 20% of the service we provide. You want experts on the technical aspects—people who've been there and have seen all the variations. We've got a lot at stake in our reputation for doing this type of project.

There are, of course,

MISPERCEPTIONS YOU CAN'T LET STAND

Like how long it will take and what they can expect to pay.

How long is a string?

Hi! I'm Jill Architect.

Hi, I'm Joe Owner. How much do you charge?

At some point -- sooner than you'd like -- they'll ask, or worse, tell you. That's **when marketing becomes negotiation.**

☐ You can throw out a percentage of construction cost   ← except you'll be guessing, not yet really knowing the scope.

☐ You can estimate a range of prices or percentages   ← except they'll only remember the low one -- be sure you're covered.

☐ You can show them through the entire file of a similar project and, based on that history, estimate a range   ← Better -- you're educating them to all that's involved -- they may want a guaranteed max.

☐ You can quote a lump sum for what you agree is the first step. Tell them your hourly rates, propose to work on a pay-as-you-go basis   ← Works well for some clients and project types. They'll still want a GMP, at least a firm estimate of the total.

For most architects, most projects, **PRICING** is only reliably done when you know enough to cartoon (at 8½ x 11) each sheet of required drawings, estimate the time required for them, the specs, and all the rest of your services, based on job records for similar projects. (The AIA Architect's Handbook of Professional Practice, 12th Edition, 1994, has good stuff on how to figure the money part.)

☐ You can quote an hourly rate (It'll be a lot lower than their lawyer's or accountant's) and propose a hybrid fee. Paid by the hour, you'll work with them to define exactly what they need and want -- that's fair since neither of you can predict how long it'll take. Once the project is defined, you'll quote a lump sum. (Some go lump sum only for CD's then back to hourly for CA, since the duration of that is unknown, too.)

← More & more architects are reporting good and equitable results using this approach -- They start work with a Letter agreement, develop a scope memorandum, then lock into a standard contract later.

CHAPTER 4
NEGOTIATION

NEGOTIATION

Wish we had something else to call it. Lots of us grew up professionally believing negotiation is always about money—somehow unprofessional—a contest between two adversaries with one winner, one loser.

When that's the case, even if you win, the project usually loses. If it is to be a successful project, you and the client will need to confront lots of problems together. If, instead, you'll be confronting each other, keeping score, getting even—or with one of you unilaterally making all decisions—project quality will surely suffer.

How to avoid this? Take whatever time you can get to endlessly explore with the client all the *interests* of all the stakeholders, all the options available, all the project's demands.

Ideally, setting the fee comes last, though money is an issue for discussion all the way through. Rather than trying to evade it (they won't let you), keep giving honest estimates in ranges—brackets of cost—that they have to anticipate and within which you can live.

Meanwhile, talk them through all the alternatives from which to choose in order to get you both through the complex process of design and construction. Explain what you think the project needs and why—how you plan to approach getting it done well. Work for consensus on responsibilities and roles and aspirations. Consider what-ifs: What's the worst that could happen and who would be damaged? Who could best see that it doesn't? What will we do now to see it doesn't happen? Who will do what if it does anyway? But end every discussion headed the other way. What's the best that can happen, and how can we collaborate to make that a reality and how?

NEGOTIATION

WE ARE ALL NEGOTIATORS

Negotiating is the normal way we communicate back and forth with spouse, partner, staff to:

- GET THE RIGHT THINGS DONE
- THE BEST WAY POSSIBLE
- WITHOUT DAMAGING THE RELATIONSHIP

What's different about negotiating a project with a client?

① The stakes are often higher. (And that's good!)

② You don't have a strong relationship yet.

③ The process is usually more structured.

So what you need is a structured process for negotiating that can help build a relationship.

Coming out of research in the
Harvard Negotiation Project
and first published in 1981,
Getting to Yes is still -- for
me -- the basic primer on
how to negotiate. For several reasons:

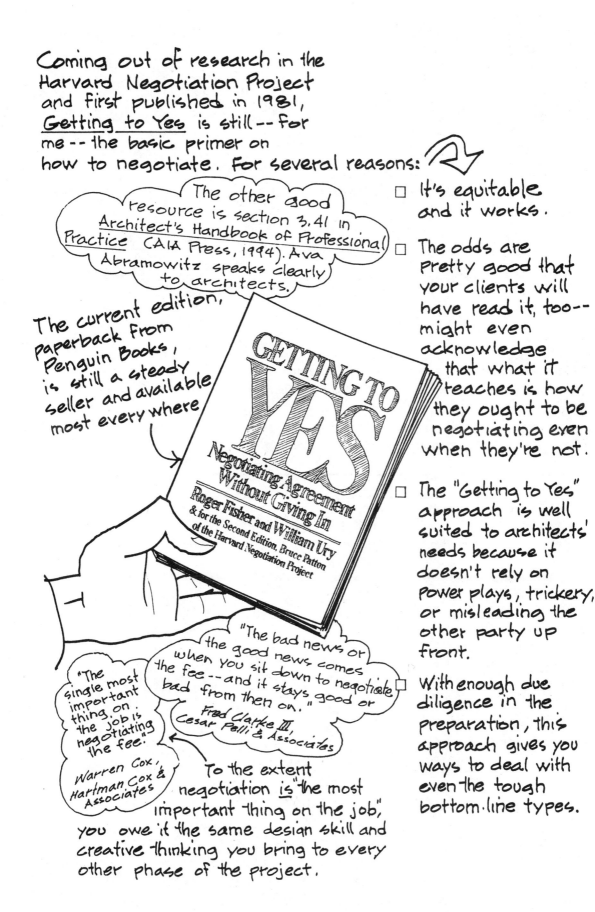

The other good
resource is section 3.41 in
Architect's Handbook of Professional
Practice (AIA Press, 1994). Ava
Abramowitz speaks clearly
to architects.

The current edition,
paperback from
Penguin Books,
is still a steady
seller and available
most everywhere

GETTING TO
YES
Negotiating Agreement
Without Giving In
Roger Fisher and William Ury
& for the Second Edition, Bruce Patton
of the Harvard Negotiation Project

"The
single most
important
thing on
the job is
negotiating
the fee."

Warren Cox,
Hartman Cox &
Associates

"The bad news or
the good news comes
when you sit down to negotiate
the fee -- and it stays good or
bad from then on."

Fred Clarke III,
Cesar Pelli & Associates

To the extent
negotiation is "the most
important thing on the job",
you owe it the same design skill and
creative thinking you bring to every
other phase of the project.

☐ It's equitable
and it works.

☐ The odds are
pretty good that
your clients will
have read it, too--
might even
acknowledge
that what it
teaches is how
they ought to be
negotiating even
when they're not.

☐ The "Getting to Yes"
approach is well
suited to architects'
needs because it
doesn't rely on
power plays, trickery,
or misleading the
other party up
front.

☐ With enough due
diligence in the
preparation, this
approach gives you
ways to deal with
even the tough
bottom-line types.

We all grew up thinking there were only two approaches to negotiations—had to be either hard or soft, depending on your position. **Avoid positional bargaining**—somebody always loses. Do that enough, the project will lose, too. Instead, **negotiate on the basis of the merits**. It's in the best interests of you, the client, *and* the project to discover and openly disclose everyone's interests, to yield to reason, though never to pressure.

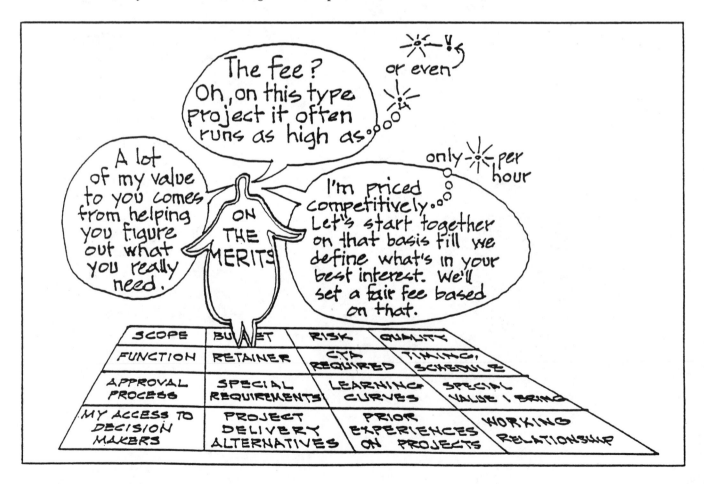

PROBLEM		SOLUTION
Positional bargaining: Neither hard nor soft negotiation is in your best interest -- you lose even when you win.		Change the game -- negotiate on the basis of the merits.
SOFT	HARD	PRINCIPLED
Relationship and esteem are as important as the deal.	Participants are adversaries; winning is what's important.	Participants are problem-solvers.
The goal is to reach agreement, avoiding a contest of wills.	The goal is winning a contest of wills.	The goal is to reach a wise outcome efficiently and amicably.
Trust others.	Distrust others.	Trust is not an issue -- proceed on reason and merits.
Concede and give in to cultivate the relationship.	Demand concessions as the price of the relationship.	Separate the people and the problem.
Readily change positions -- make offers.	Hold your position-- make threats -- dig in.	Focus on interests, not positions.
Yield to pressure-- accept one-sided losses as the price of agreement.	Apply pressure -- demand one-sided gains as the price of agreement.	Invent options for mutual gain. Agreeing to not reach agreement may be one of them.
Search for the one solution they'll accept -- insist on agreement now.	Insist on the single solution you'll accept now-- your position.	Develop multiple options to investigate, consider, choose from. Decide later.
Be soft on both the people and the problem.	Be hard on both the people and the problem.	Be soft on the people-- hard on the problem.

Adapted from Roger Fisher, William Ury, and Bruce Patton, *Getting to Yes*, 2nd Edition (Penguin, 1991), p. 13.

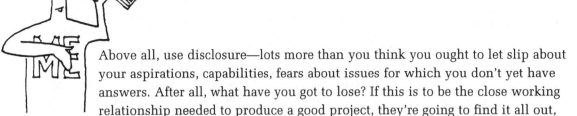

Above all, use disclosure—lots more than you think you ought to let slip about your aspirations, capabilities, fears about issues for which you don't yet have answers. After all, what have you got to lose? If this is to be the close working relationship needed to produce a good project, they're going to find it all out, anyway. There will be ample opportunity to learn all about you, your practice—how you work and think and feel—your capabilities and shortcomings

Personal disclosure up front encourages them to share what they really want and need—it moves the discussion upstream of positions to bottom-line interests. If you trust them enough to openly discuss everything, they generally reciprocate, not only with disclosure, but with trust. Trust begets trust. Disclosure implies trustworthiness.

INTERESTS vs POSITIONS

Interests are the stuff of long-range, transformative, core value. Positions are more immediate I-want-it-now transactional objectives.

Here's an analogy with which most of us are familiar. We've all known (hopefully only vicariously) the experience of a teenage driver having had the first fender-bender with the family car. The typical position ("It wadn't my fault") masks real interests, some long range, some more immediate. It's not uncommon for parents, with old tapes of their own adolescence kicking into replay, to react with position statements ranging from hard to soft.

The successful parent moves beyond positional bargaining. It's OK to express sympathy and acknowledgment of best intentions (no one sets out to have an accident). It is also OK to require retribution or set punishments. But both are *position* statements and probably not the best place to start the discussion. Instead of either, what works better is finding the interests behind each party's position—those of the kid and each of the parents. Real solutions to the problem come from jointly recognizing, then working to meet, shared interests:

- Safety—personal and public
- Equitable cost allocation of repair based on ability to pay
- Preventing reoccurrences
- Learning personal responsibility/ accountability
- Uninterrupted necessary transportation
- Etc., etc., etc. . . .

In this scenario, everybody's immediate shared interest, of course, is the kid's continued access to wheels. Who wants to be up all hours every weekend chauffeuring a contrite (much less a sullen) teenager? Shared interests. Basis for negotiation.

Getting the right fee—managing the project—even getting the project at all—involves the same process. It's based on a conviction we're all doing the best we know to get the best project possible. It depends on awareness of and ability to acknowledge interests, your own as well as those of the client. It requires the skills to move both yourself and the client upstream from stated positions. Start by acknowledging the needs, aspirations, and value systems that lie behind stated positions. Then keep looking for— designing—ways to meet both parties' interests.

We're all quick to state our expectations and positions. Often takes a lot of work to move discussions upstream to what matters most.

Often, just knowing the difference between positions and interests is not easy. Our language—and uses of it—can get in the way of understanding. Yet at any time, a proposal by you, if accepted by me, can be construed to comprise our legal agreement—particularly if we shake hands on it. Which is why it's wise to say things two or three different ways and hear them said back to you before offering that handshake. So, keep talking, asking open-ended questions, listening for nuances of meaning, looking at options!

Gold Medalist Joe Esherick once said, "We talk our clients to death. It's the secret of our success." I'm convinced that the ability to do this, coupled with a lively and sincere interest in the client's interests (and well-being) is a characteristic of virtually all great architects. It's incredibly important to start with—always return to—the underlying plain-speak interests and intentions of all parties. Risk management—terms and conditions—is only part of what you're negotiating.

Frank Stasiowski says there's more money to be made or lost during negotiation than in any other phase of the contract. I still quote Frank on that, but add the corollary that there's also more to be gained or lost in client development—clienting—by negotiation than by any other means.

It's like Pelli's partner, Fred Clark, said. "Negotiation is the most important phase of the project. By the end of negotiating, it's either going to be a good project or a bad one, and there's not much you can do to change that either way from then on." The process of reaching agreement—negotiating—is arguably a lot more important than the form of written contract that comes out of it—whether a letter agreement or a complex document.

SUCCESS COMES

Not by winning out over the other side....

BUT RATHER,

by winning the other side over.

Negotiating is the one time you *know* they're paying attention and that your verbal communication is being intently received. But even when you get the semantics straight and recognize positions as such, getting past them can be tough. They often are hard and fast rules by which you have to operate. Some are givens.

In fact, you can look at the whole body of civil law as a vast accumulation of position statement rules. Collectively—as a society—we agree on, and intend them to furnish, a reliable system by which to predict the consequences (and costs) of our actions. Or inactions.

The owner-architect agreement is a form of private law—another position statement. Whether it reflects true interests or not, the courts will almost always attempt to enforce it as law. So it's up to you to see that your contracts state positions that are based on the underlying interests of the parties to them. The tricky part—given the complexity and uniqueness of most projects—is being sure you haven't left something crucial out.

There are tools you can use to help assure that the process comprehensively covers all it should. My favorite these days is the B141, 1997 Edition, but there are other standard resources for architects:

- The scope of services list in the AIA B163.
- The commentaries on the B141 and A201.
- *Architect's Handbook of Professional Practice*, 12th Edition, AIA Press, 1994.
- *The Contract Guide* from DPIC.
- *Guidelines* publications from Victor O. Schinnerer Company.

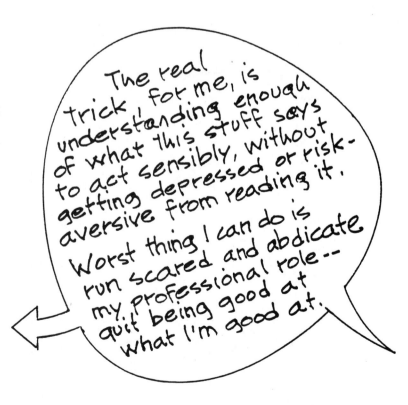

ABOUT THE STANDARD OF CARE

In the negotiation of your contract you can control the scope of your services,

a lot about the extent of professional liability exposure you'll incur, as well as the fee appropriate to those services and to your risk.

You can decide to undertake the entire project by yourself.

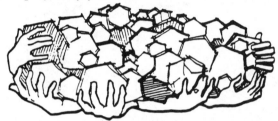

You can team with joint venture partners and consultants to provide comprehensive competency—and set a fee consistent with that approach.

 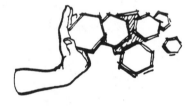

You can elect to limit your scope of services based on your personal competency and business objectives. You can decide to reject the project in whole or in part, giving up the fee but avoiding the risk. You can decide to take on the project pro bono as a donation. But once it's locked into a

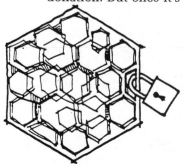

contract, the project takes over and the standard of reasonable care is determined by project requirements regardless of fee, competency, intention, or available time.

NEITHER STANDARD CONTRACTS NOR THE LAW REQUIRES PERFECTION FROM YOU.

OUR COURTS DEFINE A STANDARD OF REASONABLE CARE AS NO MORE THAN:

WHAT ANOTHER REASONABLY PRUDENT DESIGN PROFESSIONAL

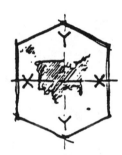

IN THE SAME MARKET AREA,

IN THE SAME TIME FRAME,

AND

GIVEN THE SAME OR SIMILAR CIRCUMSTANCES

WOULD HAVE DONE.

A good way to think about the standard of professional care is through an analogy with driving a car. The state licenses you as a driver if you qualify by passing their exam. Being a licensed driver carries the general obligation to comply with traffic laws and, in addition, to drive at all times with reasonable, prudent care. Thank goodness! Our health, safety, and welfare depend on every other driver living up to that same obligation.

It's left up to you, the driver, to choose—within a range of acceptable alternatives—any vehicle that meets regulations, your route, your time of travel, and the speed you drive.

It isn't always prudent to go the posted speed limit. When they're bumper to bumper at 85 mph on the freeway, it's unsafe to go 55. In a blinding rain you're a fool to risk hydroplaning at the posted 65 mph when everyone else has slowed to 35 mph through 3 inches of standing water. In dense fog, you can risk getting rear-ended or else maintain speed while not seeing two car lengths ahead. It's all a judgment call and often not an easy one.

One thing for sure: If you run a stop sign you've been negligent. Even if it's 3 A.M. and no one's around, you've still been a negligent driver. But then, you've also incurred no liability.

In fact, if you run the stop sign to avoid being rear-ended by a runaway bus careening down the hill behind you, you will have been a prudent driver.

But if you run that stop sign and wham! Out of nowhere there's a car and a pileup— ah. Now you have been negligent *and* there is damage *and* there is liability.

A ponderous legal apparatus is set in motion to reconstruct the scene of, and all actions and inactions leading to, the accident in order to assign blame and damages. Experts arrive, skid marks are measured, photos and depositions taken, witnesses called, and testimony given. All this to answer one question: What would a reasonable and prudent driver have done, at that time, given those specific circumstances?

Same thing in architecture. The state licenses you and gives you a limited monopoly in the marketplace because you have special expertise. In return you're obligated to be reasonable and prudent.

What constitutes reasonable driving varies depending on the situation

Architecture's like that. Or think of Nordstrom's single-sentence employees' manual--"You are hired to use your best judgment at all times." For us, you can also add the obligation to practice within one's own competencies.

PRINCIPLES FOR WRITING CONTRACTS

Here are four basic principles lawyers use in writing and reviewing contracts. You and your client can use them in discussions of scope of services, writing letters of agreement, reviewing contract language, and negotiating. Nothing hard about it, except remembering to do it at a time when all we can think of is how great this project's going to be and some neat design ideas to try.

EXPOSURE: What's the downside? What could go wrong, and if it were to, what would be the consequences? Who might be damaged? To what extent?

CAPABILITY: Out of all the stakeholders in the project who is most capable of handling the exposure -- preventing the downside from happening? Do we need to add someone else to the team to handle this?

RESPONSIBILITY: How can we write an agreement that equitably assigns responsibilities among those involved according to their capabilities?

Are the roles and responsibilities fairly and properly allocated and clearly described?

POWER: How can we have the agreement provide the authority and power needed to see that the responsibility is carried out? Is that power (information, control, money, etc.) available when and as needed?

This and the spread on the Standard of Care are included here just to remind you of things to be thinking about as you review the B141 on the following pages

CHAPTER 5: PREPARING FOR NEGOTIATION

**WHAT ARE YOU GOING TO NEGOTIATE?
USING THE B141 FOR
NEGOTIATION PREPARATION**

In the previous chapter you've dealt with the how-to part—ways to think about, approach, and carry out a negotiation—and some general principles, like starting with an understanding of the parties' interests.

But in preparing yourself to negotiate well, you also need the particulars—the specifics of the *how much* and *what* parts to be negotiated. You need a working understanding of the contract and it's language so you can discuss it knowledgeably, then thoughtfully modify it to fit the needs of both parties. Such a level of comfort with the details of the contract naturally gets built over time, of course, from studying it as each project's needs demand. But it also helps to study the contract form without the pressure of a specific application in mind. It's a good way to reconsider the principles of how you want to work.

The form to use for this, of course, is the *AIA B141-1997, Standard Form of Agreement between Owner and Architect.* Written for architects, the B141 (in each of its iterations) has long been acknowledged as the Bible of the profession, the foundation of practice. Ten years in the making, this version was drafted by, and states consensus among, representatives from across the design and construction industry about what's equitable. The meanings of all the terms used correlate with those of the same terms used in all other AIA project forms. Courts accept the B141; there's good legal precedent for using it.

Putting all that together makes this form the ultimate piece of written communication between owner and architect that you can count on everybody having read.

So use the B141, but not in the order it's written because that doesn't fit with how projects really happen. The six pages of notes which follow read the B141 from *back to front*. Working this way through the document more nearly reflects the natural sequence of discussing and negotiating projects.

It also seems to me to provide the best interface between yesterday's legal system we're stuck with, and tomorrow's business management trends we're moving into—or need to be.

Your client's response to the contracting approach outlined here can be instructive. They might be receptive to a transformative vision of working together, or may just as likely be still in denial. "Things will never be better than dog-eat-dog out there, so let's nail down obligations in lawyer talk and square off for business." Old paradigm stuff.

One major reason for writing this then, is to help you envision how to use the B141 to change the rules of the game, transform the typical project processes from the old paradigm to the new, provide a tool to improve clients, projects, and profits. It's high time we make the effort.

With that in mind, I encourage you to:

- Read what's here in conjunction with the actual document (the numbering of the articles is the same) to see if you agree with my understanding of what's meant.
- Consider whether and how the requirements of the articles might vary from how you already practice. If they do, how might you modify your practices to do better projects?
- Would you rather modify the contract language to reflect your current ways of getting projects done well?
- Much of any contract language is necessarily couched in the negative, setting out expectations and the consequences of their not being met. Read this with the challenge of adding *positive* procedures that can better serve the project and the best interests of both yourself and your clients. How might that be reflected by or called out in the contract?
- In the ideal, of course, the B141 is meant as a living document to be crafted initially in anticipation of project-specific conditions, then modified subsequently as project conditions actually evolve. Read this with the challenge of designing ways to facilitate doing so, of reminding you to update as needed, of triggering its happening. Your challenge is to use your contracts proactively to serve your clients' and your own interests better, to get better projects for more equitable fees.

That out of the way, let's get to the specifics. On the following pages, statements in italics are this layman's paraphrased excerpts from the B141 document for your consideration. The questions and comments that accompany them in parentheses are offered as practice (or negotiation) aids rather than any comprehensive commentary on the document.

STANDARD FORM OF ARCHITECT'S SERVICES
ARTICLES 2.1 to 2.9

2.1 PROJECT ADMINISTRATION SERVICES

2.1.1 Architect shall manage, administer, consult, research, attend project meetings, issue progress reports, etc. (Do you already do all this on every project? Do you want to on this one? Will they be needed? What neat processes and shortcuts at record keeping are you proudest of that can help this project? What's the minimum we can get away with—and you be paid for?)

2.1.2 Architect to initially prepare, then periodically update project schedule with milestone dates for owner decisions as well as beginning *and* completion *of construction.* (The owner always needs this. How can you—and the owner—get more reliable answers? CM? GC up front? Other consultants?)

2.1.3 Architect to consider cost/value of alternative materials, building systems, and equipment. (You always do this. What's needed to move you closer to real value engineering? Or move the owner further away from hiring an outsider to second-guess you late in the progress in a effort to cheapen rather than improve?)

2.1.4 Architect to make a *presentation to explain the design to owner reps.* (Only one? I always thought any chance to explain my design to interested parties was a free chance to market to people who could recommend—or hire—me later.)

2.1.6 Architect to assist Owner with Owner's responsibility for filing for regulatory approval. (Do you consider all that you do mere assistance? Do you want to be more specific? Should you be given the possible risks and if so, how should you be paid for accepting the risk—in some locales—of regulatory approval turning into a project all its own?)

2.1.7 EVALUATION OF BUDGET AND COST OF THE WORK

2.1.7.1 From project requirements identification until end of construction documents, Architect shall prepare, update, refine, and advise of changes in a preliminary estimate of the Cost of the Work.) (In what ways—in-house or outsourcing—can you get better at this or facilitate the owner's getting reliable second opinions? It's on issues of time and money we most often fail. How to manage that risk? Here's where my disclaimers come into play. The only things I warrant on *every* project are that the drawings *won't* be perfect and that there *will* be change orders. But in the next breath I'm assuring the owner I'll put myself in their place and act always in what I believe to be their best interest.)

2.1.7.3 To meet budget, the Architect shall be permitted to determine materials, equipment, component systems, and types of construction, and to make adjustments in scope of the project. (If you were the owner, would you give away this much power? What are some alternatives that would still enable you to perform well? I like to talk here about there only being four major categories of variables on every project (*scope, quality, price, and time*) and we get to pick any two to control—the market sets the other two.)

2.1.7.5 In the event of a cost overrun (either at bidding or negotiation), the Architect shall modify the documents as necessary at no additional cost to the Owner, but this shall be the limit of the Architect's responsibility. (Here's where you might reiterate my disclaimer, but that done, how can you use this provision to encourage the owner to a more proactive—and accountable—role in the activities listed in the two preceding articles? This limit of liability can provide a big incentive for more constant and active involvement. With involvement comes ownership of both successes and problems, so here's a good place to warn the owner of all the decisions they'll have to make—but that they'll have your presentation of options and professional recommendations at every decision point—that you put their interests first.)

2.3 EVALUATION AND PLANNING SERVICES

2.3.1 Architect to provide an evaluation of Owner's schedule, program, and budget requirements, each in terms of the others, as well as any need for other information or consulting services. (Have you *ever* designed a project without doing some programming? In virtually all of them, hasn't the design process surfaced some need for reprogramming? Hasn't that always added value to the project? How can you make the owner aware of and comfortable with the need, value, and cost of your predesign services? How can you expand your standard scope of services—and fee earned?

2.3.3 Architect shall review Owner's proposed method of contracting for construction and notify Owner of anticipated impacts the method may have on Owner's program, financial, schedule, and scope requirements. (Owner's plans for procurement may range all the way from policy, to pat answers and assumptions, to hearsay, to naïve questions. How will you deal with each or include a process for reaching the best project-specific answer?)

2.6 CONTRACT ADMINISTRATION SERVICES

2.6.1.5 Architect shall review properly prepared, timely requests for information from Contractor which shall be in a form prepared or approved by the Architect and containing detailed written specifics needed. (Sounds like another form to be added to the project manual. What project sizes, types, and methods of procurement require or warrant this for your practice?)

2.6.1.7 Architect shall interpret and decide matters concerning performance between Owner and Contractor upon written request of either. Listen up, owner. Your agent's about to turn arbiter.)

2.6.1.8 Architect's interpretations and initial decisions shall be consistent with intent of and reasonably inferable from Contract Documents. Architect shall endeavor to secure faithful performance by both Owner and Contractor, and shall be impartial. Decisions related to esthetic effect to be final. (Both these articles call for a potential change for the worst in your relationship with the owner. How can both you and the owner achieve an adequate comfort level with that in advance of it happening? Should you consider alternatives?)

2.6.2 EVALUATIONS OF THE WORK

2.6.2.1 The Architect shall visit the site at intervals appropriate to the stage of the Contractor's operations. . . (2) to endeavor to guard the Owner against defects and deficiencies in the Work, and. . . (*Endeavor*—too strong? Is this—or the disclaimer that follows in the document—strong enough? Here I make full disclosure of my lack of construction experience beyond having been a teenage carpenters' helper.)

2.6.2.4   Owner shall endeavor to communicate with Contractor and with Architect's consultants only through the Architect. (Brings up the whole complexity of today's information-transfer technology—is the project better served by simultaneous electronic information distribution? So long as you're in the loop, how much control do you really need—or want—as to who gets told what, when, and by whom? After all, with e-mail, fax, and a beeper, how much can go wrong without you being alerted? But this suggests careful indoctrination about the risks of the owner's de facto assumption of your or the contractor's roles and therefore legal responsibility.)

2.7   FACILITY OPERATION SERVICES

Upon request of Owner the Architect shall provide a post-occupancy inspection. (Do you want this a condition of the contract? How can you get the owner wanting the service and the cost of it as part of the initial contract? What will be included in the service and who will perform it? What participation from which stakeholders will make it truly valuable to the owner? To you? Do you want it at the owner's request or at a scheduled time after final completion?)

2.8   SCHEDULE OF SERVICES

2.8.1   Unless paid, Architect's services under the fee are limited to an agreed-to number of:
.1   Reviews of the same shop drawings and submittals.
.2   Visits to the site during construction.
.3   Inspections of portions of the Work for substantial completion.
.4   Inspections of any portions of the Work to determine final completion.

(To many, these two articles seem problematic, given the tenet of our profession that we do whatever the project requires, and since none of the above can be reliably anticipated before the project is under construction, much less before it's designed. A review of the new sister documents A101 and A201 will ease your agnst, along with discussions with clients about how you will certainly perform needed services while providing them the means to back charge the contractor for your fee to do so.)

2.8.2   Architect gets paid for:
.1   Review of GC submittal out of sequence from the agreed-to submittal schedule.
.2   Responses to GC's RFIs when information requested is available elsewhere. (Note above.)
.3   Change Orders and Change Directives requiring evaluations of proposals, including the preparation or revision of Instruments of Service.
.4   Providing consultation concerning replacement of Work due to fire or other causes.
.5   Evaluation of an excessive number of claims submitted by the Owner's consultants or by Contractor or others in connection with the Work. (What's excessive?)
.6   Evaluation of substitutions proposed by Owner's consultants or contractors and the making of subsequent revisions to the documents.
.7   Preparing alternate bid requests proposed by the Owner.
.8   Contract Administration services provided 60 days after date of substantial completion.

ARTICLES 1.2 to 1.5

1.2   RESPONSIBILITIES OF THE PARTIES

1.2.2.2   Owner to periodically update the budget for the project and not significantly change it without agreement of the Architect to a corresponding change in Project scope and quality. (This one begins to get at the problem of owners hiding financial capacity from you on advice of friends that "architects always spend more than you tell them—expect to need 20 percent more than whatever you tell them is your limit, so be careful what you tell them.")

1.2.3.1   The Architect's services shall be performed as expeditiously as consistent with professional skill and care and the orderly progress of the project. Architect to submit for approval a schedule to be adjusted as necessary, and to include allowances for Owner's review, for performance by Owner's other consultants, and for regulatory review and approval. Neither Owner nor Architect to exceed the schedule without reasonable cause. (Quid pro quo. But then we've always been under the gun on this one and now it works two ways.)

1.3   TERMS AND CONDITIONS
1.3.1   COST OF THE WORK

1.3.1.2   Cost of the Work to include cost to the Owner of all that Architect designs, including any cost of construction, overhead, and profit paid by the Owner for separate CM or Contractor services, plus reasonable contingencies for all this. (What contingency factors do you use? Should you use? One for design, another for construction?

1.3.2   INSTRUMENTS OF SERVICE

(This article deserves special and ongoing scrutiny, since electronic technology and the games that can be played with it keep changing far faster than practice—much less the AIA Documents Committee or the law—can keep up with.)

1.3.2.2   Architect grants Owner a nonexclusive license to reproduce Instruments of Service solely for purposes of constructing, using, and maintaining the Project, provided the Owner complies with all obligations under this Agreement (including prompt payment). Termination of this agreement prior to completion cancels license. *If Architect is adjudged in default of this Agreement, license permits Owner to use the Instruments of Service to get Project modified as needed and completed by other professionals.* (This is a trade-off for owner's right to terminate for convenience: 1.3.8.5.)

1.3.2.3   Owner is permitted to allow Contractor, subs, and suppliers to use portions of Architect's Instruments of Service. Owner not permitted to use Instruments of Service for future additions or alterations to this or other projects without written consent of Architect and Architect's consultants. Any unauthorized use at Owner's risk. (What provisions about shop drawings does this prompt? Maybe a special conditions clause to the effect that shop drawings must be based on field measurements rather than only your diskettes?)

1.3.2.4   Owner and Architect to have separate written agreement setting forth format of Instruments of Service and electronic data, including any special limitations or licenses. (Another contract?)

1.3.3 CHANGE IN SERVICES (and therefore fee)

1.3.3.2 Circumstances under which Architect's fee and schedule to be changed include:

.1 Revisions due to changes in Owner's instructions or approvals.

.2 Revisions due to codes, laws, regulations, or official interpretations being changed.

.3 Decisions of Owner not rendered in timely manner.

.4 Significant change in Project, i.e., size, quality, complexity, schedule, budget, or procurement method.

.5 Failure of performance by Owner, Owner's other consultants, or contractors.

.6 Preparation and attendance at public hearing, a dispute, proceeding, or a legal proceeding in which the Architect is not a party.

.7 Change in Project parameters or participants as set forth in Article 1.1.

(Some of these are easy to prove, others a matter of degree and a judgment call—i.e., timely, significant—any way you might agree in advance how to define or quantify them?)

1.3.4 MEDIATION

1.3.4.1 Mediation to be first recourse for settling all claims and disputes before resorting to arbitration or litigation. Cost of mediation to be shared equally. (Given the average cost and duration of either arbitration or litigation, this change is in everybody's interest. Questions: Do you want to go with the procedures that follow or, instead, agree on other mediator(s) in advance? Does the project warrant a more automatic trigger that either party can use to start the process instantly? Somebody on call?)

1.3.6 CLAIMS FOR CONSEQUENTIAL DAMAGES *mutually waived by Owner and Architect.* (Consequential damages usually arise from missed deadlines or late completion. For some clients, missing a selling season, a bond issue deadline, or a government funding cycle can be matters of survival. Amounts of damages claimed can be staggering, so it's also a matter of your survival. Might liquidated damages be an option? Outsourcing or joint venturing?)

1.3.8 **TERMINATION OR SUSPENSION**

(*1.3.8.5 This Agreement can be terminated by the Owner for convenience and without cause.* (This one relates to—triggers—Article 1.3.2.2—license to reproduce Instruments of Service canceled.)

1.3.8.7 Termination Expenses are in addition to fees; are to cover Architect's expenses plus Architect's anticipated profit for services not yet performed. (Is this last part a bargaining chip for you?)

1.5 **COMPENSATION**

1.5.1 How it's to be computed.

1.5.2 How changes in fee due to changes in services will be computed.

1.5.3 Markup Architect is to receive in event of changes in service by Architect's consultants.

1.5.4 Markup Architect is to receive on reimbursables.

1.5.6 Architect's rates and markups to be adjusted to reflect normal salary changes.

1.5.7 What initial payment is due upon execution of this Agreement. (For you, is this a retainer, a mobilization fee, an administration setup cost?)

1.5.8 When payments are due and what interest will be applied to late ones. (How many ways can you use this?)

Traditional wisdom has it that you never start work without a signed AIA contract form. The argument is that this makes sure everything's covered, keeps both you and the client safest, and enables you to settle future misunderstandings on the basis of accepted industry standards.

Based on the traditional wisdom, most architects treat the contract as something we hope we'll never have to resort to using, once it's signed. A safety net. Past-tense documentation of how the AIA said we'd work together. Just paperwork we have to get out of the way of our doing whatever the project needs done. With that attitude, many of us got in the habit some years back, of just filling in the blanks on a B141 and sending it to the owner with the breezy assurance it's the standard form we all use.

What we found out was that up-front, hardnose, hard copy isn't the answer. Architects increasingly report that to require that standard contract forms be signed up front produces a standard response—the owner's involvement of lawyers. Which leads to the lawyer's standard response—earning their fees by demanding contract modifications they believe to be in the owner's favor. Or the reverse happens. The owner insists on using *their* standard forms, sending you to seek legal help. Either way does nothing to add value to the project and misses a great chance for good clienting on both your parts.

Maybe that's what we ought to name negotiation—*clienting*. Might help us change the traditional process of episodic displays of costly defensive tactics. Turn it into an ongoing process of jointly designing creative strategies by consensus, of learning ways of working that anticipate future misunderstandings by devising processes for clearing up present ones as we go along.

This approach argues that arms-length working relationships—much less adversarial ones—more often result in standard buildings than quality architecture. It insists that quality design deals with matters of consequence rather than contractual sequence and deliverables.

Its practitioners—an increasing number of enlightened owners and architects—therefore start work on the basis of a simple letter agreement. When they're repeat clients or longtime friends, often even a handshake.

Or, if you practice in a highly litigious market, try working with your lawyer to paraphrase applicable provisions of the B141 into your own form of preliminary letter agreement suitable for front-end services. If you do that, the real trick is to use the AIA B141 as a guideline for covering all that's needed. You work to reduce what you need of it to a letter form that doesn't sound as though a lawyer wrote it.

The objective: To reserve use of the standard form of agreement itself until you have built a high level of trust between you and the client. You know you've won when later, given the standard form of agreement, they simply ask,

Though I'm no attorney, here are some things that your lawyer will want you to consider in writing a simple letter agreement:

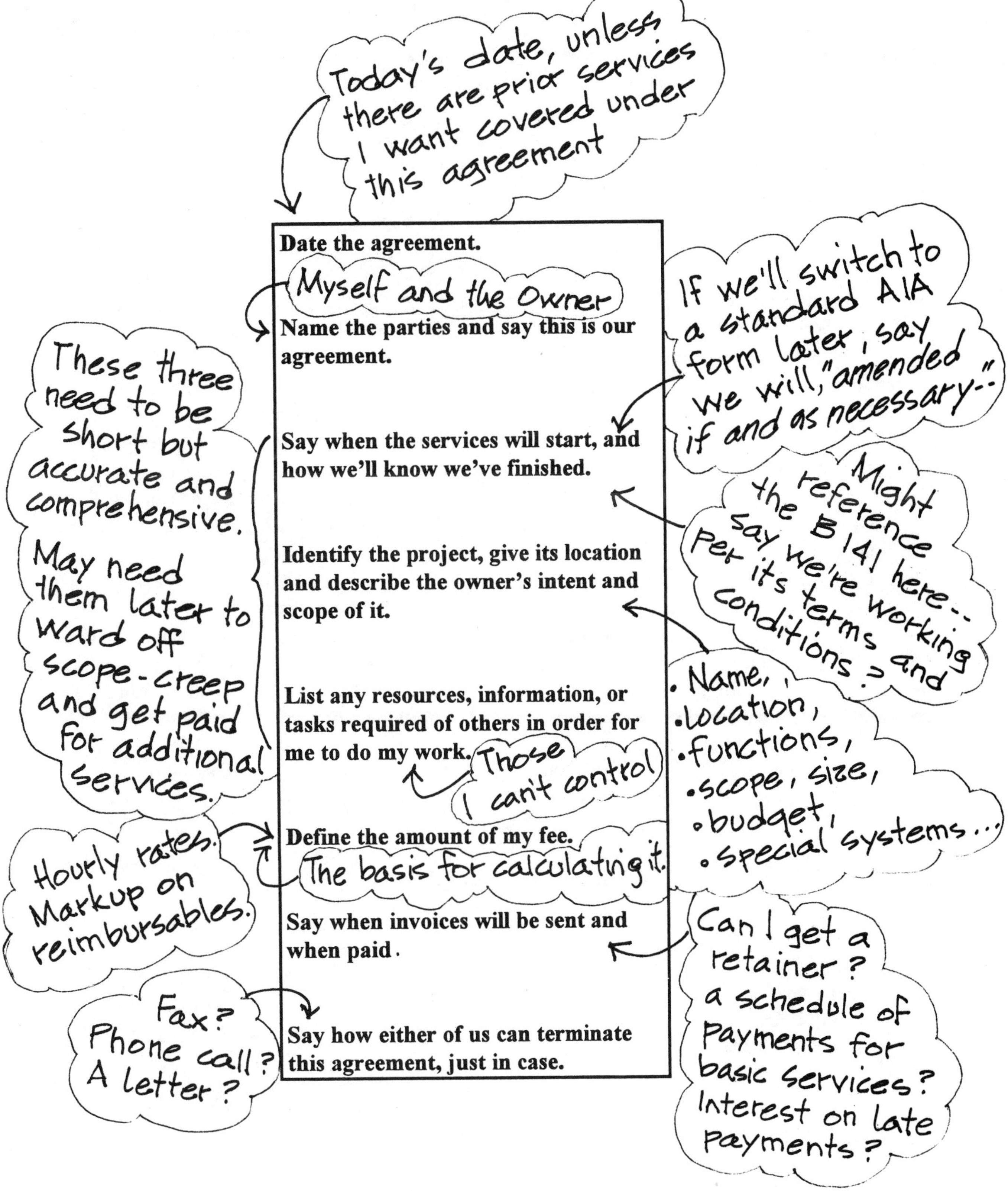

Today's date, unless there are prior services I want covered under this agreement

---

Date the agreement.

Myself and the Owner

Name the parties and say this is our agreement.

If we'll switch to a standard AIA form later, say we will, "amended if and as necessary."

Say when the services will start, and how we'll know we've finished.

Might reference the B141 here-- say we're working per its terms and conditions?

Identify the project, give its location and describe the owner's intent and scope of it.

• Name,
• location,
• functions,
• scope, size,
• budget,
• special systems...

These three need to be short but accurate and comprehensive.

May need them later to ward off scope-creep and get paid for additional services.

List any resources, information, or tasks required of others in order for me to do my work. Those I can't control

Define the amount of my fee. The basis for calculating it.

Hourly rates. Markup on reimbursables.

Say when invoices will be sent and when paid.

Can I get a retainer? a schedule of payments for basic services? Interest on late payments?

Fax? Phone call? A letter?

Say how either of us can terminate this agreement, just in case.

The letter of agreement is only the precis that gets you working—typically at an hourly rate. The actual full text of what's to be done and who's to do it then evolves in what I call the scope memo approach.

Statistically, most clients will be left brain types, or will have come up through the ranks in such a business culture. Either way, they tend to *hate surprises* having to do with numbers, dates, and especially money.

The best practitioners of the scope memo approach work with the client to develop over time an agreed-to list of everything needed (and by when) to get the project designed and built. They even furnish a cash flow projection to help the client anticipate how much money will be needed and when.

The important tip—keep it positive and keep it in plain-speak. Write it the way you talk, and instead of listing what you *won't* do, anticipate everything that needs doing and who'll provide it—all of it —the requirements that designing and building the project will make on the client, you, contractors, other consultants, anybody. This is a good place to explore project delivery options, and help the client make informed decisions.

The scope memo approach is one way to help clients develop a better understanding of all that you do—what each of you must anticipate and when. It's a good way to gently train them in the art of clienting. It's an ongoing process of incremental negotiations. It's also a way to push yourself into being better organized to do a quality project.

In the ideal scenario, before the actual "negotiation"—setting the fee—ever starts, you will have already negotiated most of the groundwork—scope of services, allocation of roles and responsibilities, schedule. You will have been paid fairly for providing valuable service and they will have become accustomed to your standard rates.

Fee negotiation can become much simpler now. A quick review to confirm the workplan already evolved, an honest allocation of hours required to implement it, and the arithmetic of determining the fee.

One favorite variation is the piecework system. Break the project into sequential pieces and negotiate lump sums for each step, before work on each proceeds. It's cash-and-carry, and either side can call things off at any point.

Another variation—the hybrid fee. Sign on for the whole project with an agreement to work by the hour to define it (schematics or design development), to set a lump sum at that point for production, and to return to an hourly rate for construction administation.

The equity in this one can be pretty compelling—you quote prices for those services for which you can be expected to know or control the duration. You're paid by the hour for the rest.

THE SCOPE MEMO APPROACH

which is essentially partnering, depends on open, on-going communication with the client-- listening to the customer.

is based on thorough working knowledge of the standards of the design/construction industry.

Project goals and aspirations--full understanding of restraints, resources, capabilities, and interests to be met-- realistic project expectations form through discussions, questions and feed back.

But the formal contract itself doesn't surface until the project is well underway and the requisite working relationship of mutual trust and respect prevails.

Initial services -- to define the project through program and conceptual design--are paid for by the hour on the basis of a letter agreement or even a handshake.

B141
B155
B727
B163

SET FEE

$$\oslash \$\$\$ REQ'D$$

WHAT WHERE WHEN

WHO WHY HOW

Fee negotiation is on the basis of the plain-speak scope memo-- if possible, the contract is provided after the fact as "industry consensus language for what we agreed to."

Frequent billings keep each party's risk in manageable chunks.

From the beginning, a plain-speak memo of scope of all services and of the work is developed.

As work continues, the scope memo is elaborated and often amended.

Along with the scope memo, project schedule and budget are developed*-- at least in brackets to anticipate. When possible a cash flow is projected -- everything the client must anticipate spending, and when.

All goals and decisions get recycled to validate the consensus. They form the scorecard for future work. They safeguard against scope creep, tangents, and rework.

Worst case scenarios are invented & talked through. "What will need to be done if that happens? Who is most capable of seeing that it doesn't happen?"

Input--and buy in--are gotten from engineer consultants & builders.

*Statistically, most clients will be left brain types, or will have come up through the ranks in a business culture that is. Either way, they tend to hate surprises having to do with numbers, dates, and especially money. Using the scope memo approach is one way to help develop a fair understanding of what to anticipate and when. It's also a way to push yourself into being better organized to do a quality project. In this ideal scenario (we should all be so lucky) you will have already negotiated most of the ground-work—scope of services, allocation of roles and responsibilities—before the "actual negotiation"—setting the fee—ever starts. And you will have been paid fairly for providing valuable service.

NEGOTIATION DESIGN CHECKLIST

Though these steps are not numbered, I'd start and end with this sequence, and in between, work in any order that seems useful. As with any design problem, work holistically—partial solutions to any part can suggest directions to take for others, even a solution for the whole. For important projects, I wouldn't leave any of these steps out. You might use this page as a checklist at the end to make sure you're ready to approach negotiation with ease and confidence.

What do you know about the project? About the person with whom you'll negotiate? The organization they represent? User groups or targeted customers? Try filling out B141-97 Articles 1.1.2 and 1.1.3. Review Article 2.8.3. What else do you need to know, and where and how can you find it out? Start open-ended lists of questions, scope, constraints. What's needed in resources, information consultants, timing, process, communication, etc., for you and the client to jointly carry out the project successfully? *Start every negotiation with questions. What will you ask?*

Brainstorm your best alternative(s) to a negotiated agreement (BATNA). If second prize were getting this project, how many productive things can you think of to do instead? Start an open-ended list or cluster diagram. No need to choose yet, but it's important to have options that are specific and feasible—things you could really do with energy and enthusiasm.

Interests versus positions. List three or more position statements—for yourself, for the person with whom you'll negotiate, for anyone they have to answer to, and for the project users. Then move upstream from each of those positions to the interests behind them using the *five whys* exercise with brainstorming and role-playing among your team. If you don't as yet know the other stakeholders' positions or interests, make assumptions, invent reasonable alternatives, put yourself in their place. The point: *Separate the people from the problem.* Never *negotiate in anger. If you're frustrated or mad at the other negotiator, start and stay with this step for as long as it takes to be able to put yourself in their place, to be able to have done yourself whatever it is they did—or didn't do—that made you mad. Doesn't mean you ever have to agree with them or what they did or do. But to negotiate well you need to find detachment, and it's not something you can fake. Be mad at the system, not at the people. They'll read it.*

Invent options for mutual gain by playing what-if, looking for innovative breakthroughs, thinking outside the box. What project processes are directly opposite to what's the expected for this situation? What advantages could possibly exist to better meet stakeholders' interests that probably won't be fully met doing this the usual way? How might this project be broken into (or combined with) several others? How many ways can the project be delivered?

What are the issues to be negotiated at this session? You want a fair and binding agreement, but for how much of the project at this time? It can vary from next-step incremental, to life-of the-project comprehensive. What best serves your interests and theirs? How many options can you offer and still live with?

Research fair standards and precedents. In today's information age you can find out almost anything—and so can they. You're looking for *quid pro quo* trading possibilities among scope, time, money, accountability, risk, etc., as well as independent standards and objective criteria to support any of the wildly different positions and options you may decide to offer.

Finalize your BATNA. Make it singular and singularly attractive—what you actually and specifically *will do immediately* if this deal doesn't go through. Image experientially how good (effective, productive, fun, educational, etc.) it will be getting that done—or having gotten it done—if you don't get this project. Your power's in your BATNA.

HOW AN "IDEAL" NEGOTIATION MIGHT WORK.

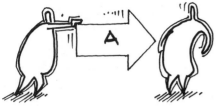

They ask for your proposal, which you give them.

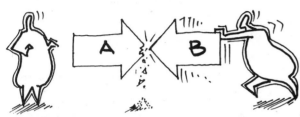

They make a counter offer, stating their position, which you listen to very carefully so as to learn the underlying interests behind that position.

You sidestep their proposal by neither resisting it nor agreeing.

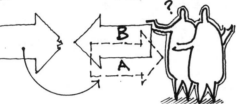

At the same time, you acknowledge their needs and interests, your respect for them personally.

You ask clarifying, problem-solving questions that are open-ended and relate to equitable principles.

You "play back the tape" of what's been said -- what issues are resolved, what's still in question....

You agree with as much of their position as possible (even the smallest parts) and expand the area of agreement, focusing on all that's positive.

Together, you then work on options available to find the break-through strategy.. a mutually beneficial solution based on the merits, rather than the relative power or strength of will of either of you.

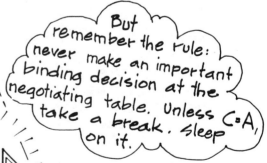

Except, you rephrase the question to include all the interests as well as the positions of both parties. The message: "The people are not the issue -- we share a problem to solve."

But remember the rule: never make an important binding decision at the negotiating table. Unless C≥A, take a break. Sleep on it.

To Make it work this well takes skill and preparation

CONTRACTING TIP-- THE HYBRID FEE

If they demand a lump sum, try to restrict it to cover only those services for which you can reasonably control scope & duration. Do the rest on an hourly basis.

THE RATIONALE:

PREDESIGN
Propose an initial letter agreement referencing the B141 as the final contract form to be used, "amended if and as necessary."

SCHEMATICS
Done on an hourly basis, the design concept sets the scope and therefore the fee for services needed.

DESIGN DEVELOPMENT
With the project defined, lump sum fees for the rest of design and for construction documents can be negotiated and the contract finalized.

CONSTRUCTION DOCUMENTS

BIDDING AND NEGOTIATION
During the CONSTRUCTION ADMINISTRATION market forces set what services are needed and for how long. Use hourly rates.

HOURLY

LUMP SUM

HOURLY

Star designers report they are doing predesign as a separate and essential phase of service. It's their key to achieving quality design. Try for an hourly basis -- at least hourly with a maximum-not-to-exceed.

Both scope and duration of schematics are controlled by others--the client, design review boards, regulatory officials, etc. Not only that, the client gets more value per hour spent here and during construction administration than they get in the other phases of service.

Some smart developers set a fixed date for completion of schematics and gladly pay for as many design hours as the architect can cram in to the charette.

As a matter of equity, the scope of the project -- or the services -- isn't really known til the end of schematics. It's only then that you should be responsible for the scope and duration of DD & CD services.

Both you and your client lose control of scope and duration of services in B/N & CA phases. Market forces, weather, supplier deliveries, and the luck of the draw on who are low bidders on all the specialty contracts-- many factors combine to set construction administration requirements.

If all this seems impractical, too complicated, or plain not useful, given your project types and practice-- fine -- at least when a project comes in "over the transom" take it on an hourly basis til the scope is set.

1.78

A MORE TYPICAL SCENARIO

At the other extreme, take a situation that we've all been caught in. Client says "We've decided to go ahead with the project and the budget's set at five million. Like to have you do it, but you'll have to get right on the fee. We're getting prices from two other architects. You interested? Quote me your best price by Monday."

Need to talk about this one in detail so for purposes of illustration, let's assume the following:

1. This is a project you've been promoting. You know enough to price what you assume will be the services required.

2. This is a past client, so you're already equipped with all the information we covered under Marketing Research.

Where those two assumptions are not the case, you've got a lot of work ahead between now and Monday. No reason not to go for the job, just a lot more contingency to factor in and the odds against success are much higher.

What to do? Keep them talking. Help them realize that for a typical building, the total cost of design *and construction* can be as little as 8 percent of the real operational life cycle cost. That taking bids is high risk for small stakes on both sides and can easily get them five quotes, each for different services. That for you to bid on what they actually need, you have to understand more about the project and what they really want. Try anything to get a meeting.

Assuming you can do that, treat that meeting itself as a design problem. And the first step in any design effort: *Image* an ideal scenario:

Image the Ideal:

- You and the client jointly explore the real interests each of you need to have met by doing this project together.

- They request a proposal and you make an offer (state your position) to which they respond with a counteroffer (a lot different than you asked) from their position.

- You neither agree to nor resist their proposal—and this is the key step. Rather, you ask clarifying, open-ended questions about intentions, scope, schedule, responsibilities, and authority. In the process of all this, you continue to acknowledge why, given their position, you'd have offered the same as they had.

- You go on to examine together how your accepting their offer would not be in your interests, theirs, or those you share. They discover why their position on fee poses problems for both of you, but mainly for the project.

- You work together to consider all the options on scope, schedule, responsibility allocations, *and* fees that could optimize the chances of all the interests of both parties being met.

You come to amicable agreement. Both of you have learned a lot; the project and the relationship have benefited in the process.

For anything like that ideal scenario to actually happen will take skill, knowledge, and not a little choreography on your part. Rather than squaring off at them, you've somehow got to get yourself on their side of the table. With them, rather than against. Carrying out such a successful negotiation takes thoughtful preparation. But throughout your preparation—and the actual negotiation—hold on to that positive image. While it won't guarantee success, it definitely improves the odds. Enthusiasm and self-esteem go a long way.

PREPARING FOR NEGOTIATION

1. Design Your BATNA

The term BATNA—your *best alternative to a negotiated agreement*—comes from the original source for this section, *Getting to YES* by Roger Fisher, William Ury, and Bruce Patton, 2nd Ed. (Penguin Books, 1991). First published in 1981, it still sells several hundred thousand copies each year. I've known clients to require that their consultants read it. If your clients—particularly public sector ones—don't have a copy, you may want to gift them with one. Might do a lot to level the playing field and turn your next negotiation into joint problem solving rather than adversarial one-upmanship.

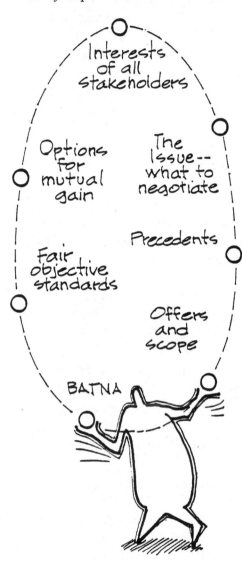

The authors point out that *the better your BATNA, the greater your power* at the negotiating table. Only quarrel I can pick with the whole book is that it lists developing a BATNA as the fifth out of six steps in preparing to negotiate. I put it first and always; maybe I'm just a wimp and need more power sooner. I'd rather think it more a matter of my intuitive, right brain preference for starting the six steps all at once and juggling them till something tells me I'm ready. For me, the BATNA is the first ball in the air, and kept in play till the final handshake at the negotiating table.

Relative strength in a negotiation doesn't come from money or clout. It depends instead on the attractiveness to each party of their options should no agreement be reached. Since I'm in business to build trust and serve my clients well, I spend considerable time inventing several BATNAs for the other side. Tremendously effective when my BATNA is so strong I can sincerely explore with them their best alternative to hiring me.

2. BRAINSTORM INTERESTS.

Especially yours. Remember that "we need this job" is not an interest. It's a position that can easily prove the old truism, *If you want something bad enough, you can probably get it bad enough.* Instead of settling for that, move upstream from that statement via the five whys method. Then do it as though you were the client. Discovering the interests of the client—putting yourself in their roles to feel what they might be feeling—is an actor's skill and can become fascinating. Not only that, there are multiple roles to assume.

To discover the interests behind positions (your own as well as theirs), start with the stated or assumed position. Keep asking why one naturally acts, feels or thinks that way.

① - - →

POSITION

② WHY?

OK, but why That?

③ yes, but why Those?

④ ⑤
- Interest
- Interest
- Interest
- Interest
- Interest

Use the 5 Whys Rule

There is the person with whom you'll actually negotiate. Their interests are virtually always different from (or in addition to) those of the marriage, company, or organization for which they are negotiating. Then there are the users of the project—the ultimate clients—whose interests need to be met if the other clients are to be successful, or at least, not sued. You need to know the interests of every client.

At this stage, it works best to involve others, but do so in your own preferred style for receiving feedback. If you are a devout introvert, you may prefer to get everything on paper and circulate that among potential team members for comments and an eventual meeting. Extroverts typically call a quick huddle and talk till they assume they have gotten all possible viewpoints.

Even as a sole practitioner, you still can call on friendly builders, consultants, significant others, or (so long as you talk interests, not fees), your own competition.

Let's assume the project in this example seems well worth the time spent to go through an actual brainstorming session. Whatever your methodology, the goal is to end up with written notes, some reminder on paper to help in your preparation for the interview.

One good format is a three-column list under the headings MINE—THEIRS—HIS/HERS. *Mine* and *His/Hers*, of course, head the lists of interests of the two negotiators. *Theirs* is for assumed interests of client organizations and users of the project. I've used that format—and shared it as an opening tactic in negotiation—to present an image of being well-organized, caring, and systematic. Don't know whether it did that. Mostly it was useful in getting them to talk interests before positions.

3.
DESIGN OPTIONS FOR MUTUAL GAIN

The steps for preparing your negotiating are all numbered here as though each must be completed before the next is begun. Not so. As with architecture, design of negotiation is a matter of consequence, not sequence. Stay loose and bounce amongst it, keeping a written or graphic record of your thoughts on each step in some form. Lots of notes to yourself.

Obviously, one set of options available in this example are those involving alternative project methods and the potential team members and activities required.

- How might the services be unbundled into multiple prime contracts with the owner?
- How many of the services listed in B163 might be needed and how might you provide them all?

- Interested in design/build? If so, what role could it (and you) play in producing a successful project?
- Are there alternative technologies for construction, electronic communication, or in-house production of documents that might provide a better project faster, cheaper? Fax? E-mail? Intranet? What could work?
- How might the services and relationships required by this project be seen as a subset or a new beginning? Is there a bigger, different project, building program, even career that this project suggests for you or for the client?

Quite apart from all the project-related options, there is another set for you to consider. Fees. There's not just one, and they vary with all the other options of what services you might provide, risks you might accept or decline.

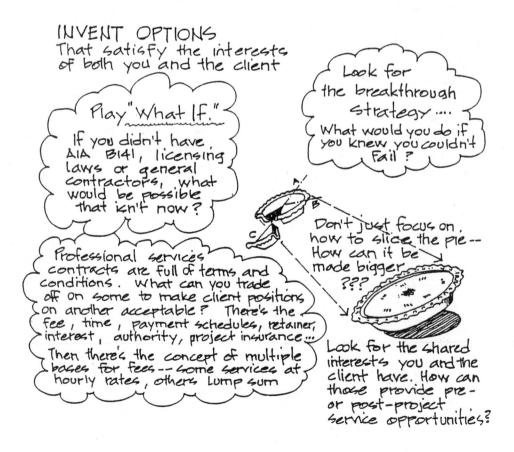

INVENT OPTIONS
That satisfy the interests of both you and the client

Play "What If."
If you didn't have AIA B141, licensing laws or general contractors, what would be possible that isn't now?

Professional services contracts are full of terms and conditions. What can you trade off on some to make client positions on another acceptable? There's the fee, time, payment schedules, retainer, interest, authority, project insurance...
Then there's the concept of multiple bases for fees -- some services at hourly rates, others Lump sum

Look for the breakthrough strategy.....
What would you do if you knew you couldn't fail?

Don't just focus on how to slice the pie -- How can it be made bigger ???

Look for the shared interests you and the client have. How can those provide pre- or post-project service opportunities?

4. RESEARCH FAIR STANDARDS

The first research, of course, comes in reviewing your own project files and pricing the project. Traditional wisdom, of course, is having whoever will actually be doing the project produce quick 8½ by 11 "cartoons" of every drawing required in the construction documents phase. They estimate the hours for each drawing and add in an allowance for checking and spec writing to come up with a total number of hours for production. From that you can easily derive an average number of hours per sheet required (adding in estimated duration of the other phases of the project) and compare that to similar previous projects. You can divide job record hours per sheet first into fees earned, and again into costs incurred—which won't be the same. But you know all this; starts around page 267 in your AIA *Handbook*, and it's the deductive part.

The inductive part—the art of pricing a project—requires subjective judgment. First about the typology of whoever (yourself included) did the deductive part. Some of us want to be heroes, start with a safe budget, and crow later about efficiency and productivity. At the other extreme, many of us have a reach that exceeds our grasp. We're prone to think each next project will go more smoothly than the last, considering all we learned from *that* experience. Either way, it's one subjective judgment to be factored in.

Another is a factor based on how much of a lock you feel you have on this project. No such thing as obscene profit to be made in architecture. You'll earn any fee you can get and add value far beyond that. Go for it, puppy, as they say in Texas.

IN-HOUSE:

Search job-files for time and money spent on similar projects. Lessons learned. Cartoon an 8½ x 11 of every sheet of working drawings.

Get ideas and best estimates from the people who will actually do the project.

SURF THE MARKET:

Call consultants and builders who've done similar projects and will want in on this one.

Check publications and out-of-state municipal clients. You can talk with other architects about project processes, deliveries, technologies -- though <u>not</u> about fees.

A lot of what you're looking for has nothing directly to do with money....

Third factor comes from comparative pricing. They'll be finding out what they'd have to pay elsewhere and, even if the competition's prices won't affect your quote, you'll need numbers to confirm or rebut them. Fee data is available to you with no violation of antitrust law, so long as you don't discuss them with other architects. Which, even if it were legal, would be a lousy way to price your fee. All this subjective stuff is in addition to—not in lieu of—the deductive work of knowing your utilization ratios, overhead, all that profit planning information discussed in the AIA *Handbook* starting on page 267. It's firm-specific.

On the other hand, architects often think that because each project design is unique, there are no useful comparative criteria or second opinions available beyond their own experience. Not so. Public projects come in all sizes and types and access to public information is the law, if you do some creative telephoning. Statistical data are published on private sector projects. There are municipal, state, and federal fee schedules available to you. Beyond those resources, there are your friendly builders and consultants. Many keep a keen eye on who paid how much for what, when, and where. On the chance they'll get future work out of this, they tend to be very interested in your being simultaneously highly paid and highly competitive.

But the researching of fair standards can be a lot more than comparative shopping about fees. Terms, conditions, complexities, and project durations—data such as these affect pricing but also enhance your ongoing lists of interests amid options to negotiate. You can assume that most good left-brained clients will have already looked at precedents. They tend to respect those you

can quote that counter theirs or offer hope as gridlock breakers. Your goal is to stay flexible, yet principled, and keep them talking till you both discover the best solution. Often this involves agreeing to seek yet more precedents and criteria.

Data reassures clients, especially those accountable to others for their expenditures. Documentation of precedents—even just your notes—can be valuable for their files. It can later prove they based their decision on the best available information and precedent after consideration of reasonable options. By benchmarking what others have done on successful (and disastrous) projects, you can better equip yourself and your client to negotiate.

All this by way of saying you don't go into a negotiation with only the one *it's-my-way-or-the-highway* ultimatum. Even where you have the power to do so, it can win the battle and start the war. Even if you "win" the negotiation, you've set the rules for a relationship—a long-term private war—that can last for years. Who needs it?

5: ESTABLISH A RANGE OF OFFERS

○ What you really want
○ What would be OK
○ The bare minimum

But avoid setting a slam-the-door deal breaker amount. Instead, design a series of deal changes-- ways to reallocate tasks, responsibilities and risks. Stay flexible.

MAKE A LIST

No matter how much you've researched the client and the project, no matter how gifted your assumptions, you can't not have questions that need asking as a lead-in to negotiation. First one is *What are your intentions for this project?* What do you need them to confirm before you can openly negotiate? Make a list to share with them for openers. Then share it. I hate it when people come to me with their closely guarded written notes. Worse than that is when they tell me my intentions instead of asking. Like some damn car salesperson starting out with "Now, what you need is...."

6. REHEARSE

Try out your opening pitch and your options for mutual gain-- <u>ALOUD</u> -- and preferably with your partner or staff til it rings true.

If all else fails, say it into the rearview mirror on your drive over.

Try it several ways. You don't want a set, memorized speech-- just a solid level of comfort in dealing with issues readily and thoughtfully.

DON'T "WING IT"-- PREPARE!

REVISIT AND PERFECT YOUR

Best Alternative To a Negotiated Agreement

The BATNA is your source of power in the negotiation. It's essential you be very specific in its design and that you be able to experience the power of it internally. Image it—like a private TV commercial—in ways that motivate you and make it a really viable alternative to this negotiated agreement—if possible, just marginally less attractive than getting this project.

When I'm at my best, while I'm walking into their office for the negotiation, my imaginary BATNA commercial is playing in my head with all the details about how great it's all going to work out.

There's always a BATNA. Take an extreme scenario. Let's say I'm down to a two-person firm, caught in a terrible market turn, and desperate for money. As a BATNA, "go after other projects" is hardly convincing—gives me no power in this negotiation. Instead I need to design an entire scenario, and for me it works best to make a to-do list of it that I definitely commit to carrying out.

- *Start calling my list of past clients tomorrow and finish doing it this week.*
- *Lay David off next payday.*
- *Take Sue up on her mention of subleasing and sharing office expenses—and if that falls through, break my lease and set up a home office first of the month.*
- *Spend 50 percent of my time marketing homebuilders—I'll get a list from their association on Monday.*
- *At minimum make three calls or visits per week to collect those outstanding fees.*
- *Finish the Hudlow and Taylor jobs myself—say 2 months for that.*
- *Call the big offices, first to find David a job and second, to offer myself as an outsource to them on fieldwork, specs, project management—whatever. I'll do that by Friday before I talk to David.*
- *Over the weekend start definite plans for that move to the coast we've always talked about. Buy out-of-town papers, check classifieds, look up AIA component execs I can call Monday. If nothing breaks for me in 2 months, we're outa here!*

1.86

WHILE NEGOTIATING

You're ready to embark on negotiation. You've got all your baggage and hopefully have lightened the load by discarding all that's not applicable for this trip. You're ready to meet for joint luggage inspection and comparison of claim checks. You're prepared to assume a big load at a fair price if you can agree to leave behind all that's not useful, and fairly allocate who handles what. Point of that convoluted metaphor is that, for projects, most unnecessary baggage is a set of wrong assumptions among stakeholders about each other. The basic principle of the *Getting to YES* approach is to separate the people from the problem. Which is why the emphasis is on identifying the interests of the parties during preparation for negotiation. And since it's impossible to really know theirs with any certainty, the first order of business in a negotiation is to openly discuss interests.

After enough introductory small talk to get the discussion going on a personal basis, ask their intentions for the project, or review to confirm those you've previously been led to believe. From their end-game goals naturally come the discussions of how best to get them from here to there—scope of services, terms, and conditions. If you've really done your homework, it's somewhere along in here—with assumptions validated or modified—that you can bring up their BATNA. Negotiation can be an opportunity to exemplify the agency relationship you offer in incredibly powerful ways by openly discussing their best alternatives.

My favorite example—an architect who never takes a project at the first interview, even the smallest of residential remodeling jobs. With scope, terms, schedule, and price all on the table and understood, she assures the clients how very much she wants the project and looks forward to working with them, provided one other step is taken.

She says she won't feel right about taking the project without their having interviewed other architects—that in addition to professional competence, personal chemistry is essential to doing good architecture. She asks that they talk with at least three other architects and select the one they feel will do the best job and with whom they can work well. She then looks up names and phone numbers and sends them off with a list of several competitors she honestly feels would serve them well. She reports she's never lost a client this way and that they always return with a lot more trust than when they left.

While I'm not suggesting you necessarily go to that extreme, the story does exemplify true professionalism—sincerely seeking and actively protecting the clients' welfare—and demonstrating that commitment at the negotiating table.

Showing you'll put their interests ahead of your own can change an arms-length negotiation into a joint problem-solving session. It not only separates the people from the problem, it goes a long way toward eliminating resistance to the negotiation. It's based on objective criteria, with interests and options openly shared. Obviously this isn't always possible, but when it is, it:

- Lets you be soft on the people and hard on the problem by first disclosing your interests, then helping them share theirs.

- Positions you in negotiation as a generalist architect with a satchel full of quid pro quo options to be explored together.

- Equips you to frame each issue as a joint search for objective criteria; to reason—and be open to reason—for the good of the project.

- Gives you the strength to never yield to pressure, only to principle.

- Permits project life after negotiation as a productive, mutually respectful partnership.

The best chance of all that happening comes from two things. The first is your having done your research. Knowing interests, options, objective criteria, and being able to apply all this to the project at hand gives you tremendous credentials. It's the insight and knowledge that earns you respect. The second and even more essential factor is how you demonstrate your commitment to use that knowledge and your professional capabilities wisely in the best interest of the clients as their agent. That earns you the trust without which your services could be relegated to commodity status and you to that of vendor. Mutual trust and respect builds professional relationships that are prerequisite to building quality architecture.

In today's "bid-nez" world, it's still possible to go up against negotiators who can't or won't play any game but that of the hard bottom line. When this happens I might well share my prize BATNA with them with a can-you-top-this smile. It's also in this type of situation that I remember Fisher and Ury's recommendation that you never reach final agreement at the negotiation table. That you always end by saying how excited you are about the project; that while you believe everything has been satisfactorily resolved, it's in the interest of both of you to think about it overnight and confirm final agreement with each other tomorrow by phone. In extended negotiation of complicated issues, and when you didn't get acceptance of much that you initially wanted, that's good advice. Sleep on it.

Treat People as People Not part of the problem.

1.88

BUT EVEN WITH FULL PREPARATION
WATCH OUT FOR THESE TACTICS...

- That's in the state contract and can't be changed.

- It's company policy.

- It's out of my hands.

- We never pay more than. . .

- We don't do business that way.

- I could never justify...

- Architects are always late and over budget.

- You had too many change orders on that last project.

- I've got 5 good architects just waiting...

- Take it or leave it.

- Don't you want our business?

- What'd you do—pull that fee out of your—

- You architects are all alike— build monuments to yourself and don't know the real world.

- Great! We've got a deal, then —except there's this one more thing—

- Hey, I'd go along, but our comptroller—

- Just go along on this and we've got this great job coming up that—

- Trust me—sign here— we can always amend later...

STONEWALL

ATTACKS

DIRTY TRICKS

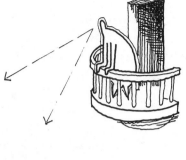

WHEN YOU SPOT ONE
Give no immediate reaction. Instead, "Go to the Balcony" for a moment and recognize their tactic for what it is. Don't get sucked into their game. They're good at it or they wouldn't play it. If you can let them know you recognize it without playing it, their game is neutralized.

DON'T:
- Counterattack
- Give in
- Give up

INSTEAD:
Listen carefully for any counter-offer hidden in their tactic.

Before leaving this chapter on negotiation, just a small-project reminder: No matter how tiny the project, and even if it's a handshake deal—never leave out getting specific agreement on three biggies:

Time, with some clients, can be as loosely dealt with as "I'll start right away," and those are the ones to worry about. A client, for whom a semester start date or Christmas retail season is a survival issue, will be sure to have hammered on it before giving you the project. It's the laid-back ones who'll say nothing at the outset, give you a grace period *they* think is plenty, then decide that if you haven't finished by now, you must not really be looking out for their interests or caring about their project. What you don't need are clients with hurt feelings. Leads to claims. Or witholding your money to retaliate. Paybacks are hell, especially when they don't even want to hear about your not really being late, that it takes this much time. Better to make sure they understand up front.

Money. Same principle here. It's the trusting ones, nodding happy acceptance at your hourly rate quote, who can get nasty surprises when it begins to add up later. Then you get nasty surprises. Remember in Chapter 3—"Clienting 101" (page 1.30)? At least *bracket the time and money, warrant your work*, and if they don't bring it up, include all this gratuitously in negotiation. If you've covered it all in marketing, reiterate it now.

Collections. Sometimes, even on big projects, this is the one they'll be glad to leave out of the negotiation—or just not think to bring up, given our world of electronic–revolving credit–pay later–no charge til next year hype. That's why the next part of the book starts with collections, which, for your projects, starts no later than at negotiations.

THREE THINGS YOU DON'T LEAVE OUT IN NEGOTIATION

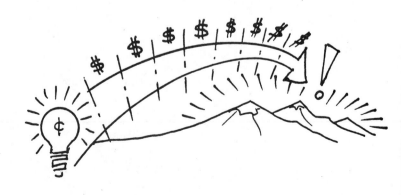

PART 2.

CORE STUFF
THE TIME,
MONEY,
AND
PEOPLE
PART

CHAPTER 6. COLLECTIONS

Collections start well before the work does. Setting up how you'll collect your fee should start well before the project begins. No negotiation is complete, of course, until there's a clear understanding of not only *how much* is to be paid, but *when*. Collections are obviously a proper element of every negotiation, letter of agreement, and contract form.

But I advise not waiting for those formal steps—I'd begin setting up collections early—often way back in marketing. The options available as to how it will actually work can furnish quid pro quo issues to be informally identified and agreed to, as elements affecting final pricing and negotiation. However you go about collections, starting with the right mind-set and strategies up front can pay off for you (literally). Some questions to consider:

- Wouldn't it be easiest to cut routine checks for basic services according to a schedule of payments in the contract? (Evens out the cash flow.)

- On a very small project, would they like a 10 percent discount for full payment up front? (You'll save far more than 10 percent by not having to worry about billing.)
- For private clients: How often are they comfortable with writing checks? Cash and carry? Every 2 weeks? Monthly? (And how often do you want to fool with the paperwork?)
- For corporate clients: How about cutting a check every 2 weeks along with their payroll and getting invoiced only every other month for additional services and reimbursables?
- Would they perceive an advantage—at no loss of control or fee for you—in unbundling the project and paying engineering consultants directly? (Would it matter? And think of the overhead saved.)
- Do they have a policy on prompt payments to secure discounts? On interest payments when delinquent? (Where's the leverage?)

These are the sorts of questions that, separately or in combination, can lead to designing a strategy for making more money and getting it in a timely fashion. Some of them you'll probably want to explore openly with the client, others you may want to quietly research and plan a strategy around.

You'll need to strike your own balance between calmly announcing *This is the way I work* and asking *How can we make this work best?*

With a schedule of payments made part of the contract, work on the project can continue smoothly even when there are reimbursables that need explanation or justification...

Great! And oh yeah—about the money part?

There are some heavy front-end costs--especially with CAD. But setting the project up carefully and right the first time saves both money and time in the long run.

Besides, the retainer helps safeguard the project from stoppages in the work in case of late payments.

Be sure to credit the retainer to their last payment on the project-- not the first.

RETAINERS

You can get a retainer, but not without asking. It's something most clients halfway expect but of course will never offer. After all, they're used to paying attorneys retainers and never getting medical treatment without prepaying or showing evidence of insurance that pays. In many areas of the country you can just calmly state that it's your policy to get a retainer that is applied to the *final* billing. In other locations you've got a lot of justifying to do. One sole practitioner told us that clients in his market adamantly refused to pay architects retainers, so he no longer asks for one. Instead he charges a standard "administrative setup fee" and gets no complaints— same money. (By the way, this tip suggests a way around one's natural reluctance to ask for a retainer from a past client.)

With new unknown clients, this is not just a matter of jump-starting and protecting your cash flow. Retainers and sizable payments made early are your best indication of the client's commitment to you and to the project, of their ability to pay, and of their ethics about doing so. Getting a retainer and sending a sizable bill early is not only good business, it's good professional practice.

People ask me how much retainer to ask. Depends on how long—or if—you're willing to work financed by your own money. It's their project, so the design and production of it should be funded by their money, not yours. How long will it take for them to pay their bills? A month? Two months? What will doing their project cost you per month? Or it may depend on what's customary in your market—10 percent? 20 percent? Or on the size of the project—for tiny ones, 50 percent? Obviously you don't want even a hint of antitrust law violation, so I wouldn't talk to other architects about this, but I know of nothing preventing you asking your lawyer or CPA for advice on local practices.

In one variation of this I've heard, the architect negotiates the fee, then gets the client's up-front list of how they'll know at the end of the project that the architect has provided great service. They negotiate how much such service would be worth and agree to that amount as a retainer—an advance bonus. The offer is that the client—at their unilateral discretion—can deduct any or all of that retainer from the final billing. I'm told he's never lost his bonus.

UP FRONT

Get to know their person who'll be handling your getting paid.

If you have an office manager and they have an accounts payable person, buy them both a lunch to review and agree on invoicing procedures.

There's considerable benefit in preproject planning about collections. The familiar adage "Bill early and often" is sound advice for several reasons:

- It keeps the invoices small and more manageable for the client.
- It tests the intentions and capabilities of the client early, before you've invested too much work.
- It requires you to organize the administrative part of your project up front.

It also implies you'll research and rehearse your justifications for realistically loading the front-end fee—and there are very real and good reasons for doing so. If you have CAD, it's relatively easy to figure. Many fully automated firms have analyzed costs to justify a heavy front-end expense, with value added later through shorter turnaround times for production, and especially for changes. Some firms report they automatically charge—as a retainer—their average cost for setting up a project on the books and in the CAD system, and that they are prepared to explain that in detail to clients.

Another highly useful front-end tactic with organizational clients, whether corporate or public, is to arrange a preproject meeting with the person who actually processes the client's accounts payable. Your stated purpose is to get their agreement on a billing format and learn how they want invoices to be handled. It helps to go over your normal invoice form with the person who'll be receiving and processing that same form every month for the life of the project.

Ask questions like:

- How might the invoice format be changed to make their job easier?
- How much detail is needed and useful; what part is clutter to be eliminated?
- Would they prefer some other format?
- How does their payables process work?
- How many people will have to sign off on payments to you?
- On which day of the month does the processing of payables start in their organization and how long does it take? (You want your invoice to arrive the afternoon before the day they start processing bills, so it's at the top of their stack, rather than buried.)
- Do they understand exactly what will be charged for and how often?
- Does he or she need anything from you before the first invoice in order to get prior authorization mechanisms in place?

The overt goal of all this is to make handling and paying your invoices a routine matter for them—last thing you want to do is surprise them. Just as important—maybe more so—you're there to build personal relationships and pick up interesting information about avocations, background, family, and their workplace as seen through their eyes. Nothing like a short, warmly personal phone chat about their personal lives at some future date, before asking them the favor of tracking down an unsigned check lost at some desk.

INVOICING

One major reason for clients to be slow—or unwilling—to pay, is when there's something about the invoice they can't understand or find too complicated. The other two possibilities: that there's something going wrong with either the project or the perceived level of services. The key to invoicing is to detect and eliminate any of those three problems, which is why invoicing is properly a responsibility for the project manager or whoever's running the project on a daily basis. Some tips:

- Phone them while you're making up the invoice and review what it will cover.
- Take pains to be explicit but succinct in detailing the written invoice. Pelli's managing partner told us back in 1989[*] that he considered filling out an invoice an art form in its own right.
- By all means, invoice them for every service you provide, even the ones on which you note "no payment required." It's good for them to realize whatever bargains they're getting and that you've been willing to go the extra mile. If or when the scope -creep gets out of hand you'll want credibility for requesting renegotiation and the complete record of what you've done pro bono can provide that.
- Then there's the tip from a small-project practitioner who puts at the bottom of every bill:

  This invoice has been carefully calculated in accordance with our agreement, but I am in this profession to serve my clients. If you are dissatisfied with my services in any way, simply mark out the amount shown on the invoice, note whatever you feel is right, and send it back with your check in that amount. I will immediately adjust my records and fee accordingly.

  She reports it's cut her collection time considerably and that she's yet to have anyone question the amount.

---

*At the AIA Signature Firms research roundtable, 1989, as reported by me in *In Search of Design Excellence* (AIA Press, 1990).

2.5

GUARANTEED SATISFACTION WITH THE SERVICE ?!?

At first it sounds outrageous, extreme, maybe unprofessional to offer to let the client adjust the amount they'll pay, based on how well they're satisfied. Like doctors and lawyers we only provide services and certainly can't guarantee results. Notice, however, that she asks clients to pay based on their satisfaction with her services—not project results. In fact, David Maister—in his excellent book *True Professionalism*—puts it even more strongly. Here's his case for your offering a *full unconditional guarantee*—but again—only on client satisfaction with the service.[*]

The marketplace is cluttered with design professionals' claims of excellence and assertions of quality, few of which are credible to clients for the simple reason that that's all they are—claims and assertions. The architect that has the courage to offer an unconditional guarantee will break through this clutter, saying to the market, *Don't take my word for it. Decide for yourself.*

Consider the alternative. Without a guarantee, what is the architect saying? *I'm committed to your complete satisfaction, but if I fail to serve you well, I expect to be paid anyway!* Leaving all considerations of ethics aside, this is just bad business—and it isn't how things really work. The reality is that if the client becomes dissatisfied, you're probably going to have to adjust the fee, like it or not.

[*]David H. Maister, *True Professionalism* (Free Press, 1997), p. 196.

YOUR MINDSET:

For some architects, collecting the fee is a social and interactive game to be played well for high stakes; for others, it's one of the niggling chores of practice. One may think it a dead serious, assertive activity required and governed by the principle of equity. Another may use the same moral imperative but with reverse psychology, telling clients to think it over and pay whatever they feel is right.

Hardball ↔ Mr. Nice Guy

It's your choice, and the method you choose for collection—from Hardball to Mr. Nice Guy—doesn't have to be the same for every project. There are judgment calls to be made based on what you know or can intuit about each specific client.

It's worked best for me—even with elusive and delinquent developers—to approach the collection process with a certain sense of detachment. I never let them sense I'd even entertain a notion of their not paying—of course I'll be paid!

But consider the worst—they won't pay.

- If I've been doing my job of billing with maximum frequency, the amount at stake should be small enough that I'll live through it even if they've hurt themselves badly—it's a small world and I know a lot of people.

- It can be valuable to learn their modus operandi now before we go further and deeper.

- If they're not happy with my performance or the project, I certainly need to know about *that* and fix it now rather than later. Not paying may be the only operative signal they've come up with to give me a heads up.

So there's value to be derived from the collection process, no matter what happens and ideally it's just another part of the project involving hard copy instruments of service. The paperwork deserves the same care as documents and specs and the same situational, reasoned judgment. The personal interaction part of collection is best accomplished using the same skills, sensitivity, and understanding I used when providing the services for which I am now collecting the fee.

While I may refer to my needs and uses for the money (if I need to pressure for payment) I avoid making strident or shrill demands. What I might think of as justifiable displays of moral outrage could invite reactions such as: "If this guy is so financially shaky, should I be trusting him with my project, the biggest investment I've ever made?" Or, "Wait a *minute*. If I'm getting pushed this hard, maybe there's something unfair or deceptive about this bill—better dig into this. Get outta my face!" In other words, I'm careful not to imply signals I don't want to send. Even the use of humor can send the wrong signal—they take money seriously, they expect you to. If you joke around about your own money, maybe you think all that money you're playing a part in *their* having to spend is also a laughing matter? Be pleasantly professional, but no jokester.

SCRIPTED COLLECTIONS

Got this one from Frank Stasiowski, and it worked well for us. It's based on the obvious fact that collections is a primary responsibility of the project manager—whoever deals with the client on a day-to-day basis. They should calendar themselves—or have somebody at the front desk reminding them from a tickler file—to call the client each week.

In our firm we all got together and decided how long we would be willing to work without pay—at that time, in our case, 2 months. We then jointly outlined eight weekly scripts for telephone calls, typed up the outline, and gave one to each project manager. The scripts —and the actors to deliver the lines—were calculated to build pressure but not animosity, the reason being you never want to damage the client/project manager relationship. Here's an example on which you can base your own script:

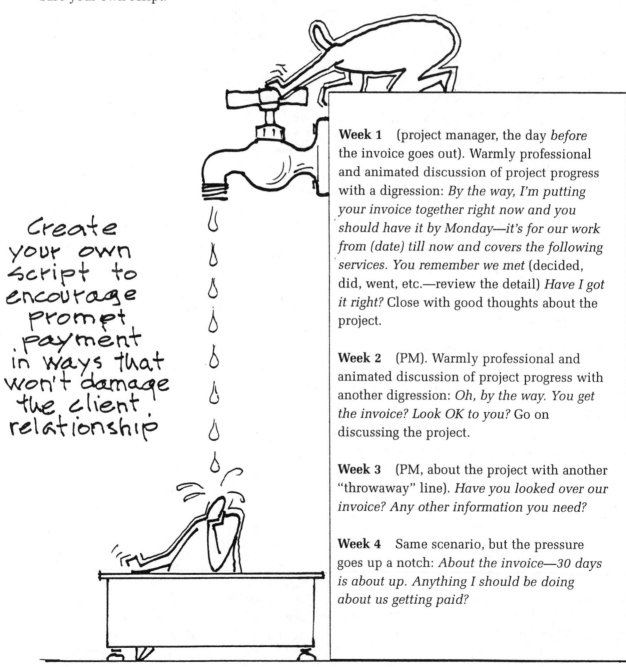

Create your own script to encourage prompt payment in ways that won't damage the client relationship

Week 1 (project manager, the day *before* the invoice goes out). Warmly professional and animated discussion of project progress with a digression: *By the way, I'm putting your invoice together right now and you should have it by Monday—it's for our work from (date) till now and covers the following services. You remember we met* (decided, did, went, etc.—review the detail) *Have I got it right?* Close with good thoughts about the project.

Week 2 (PM). Warmly professional and animated discussion of project progress with another digression: *Oh, by the way. You get the invoice? Look OK to you?* Go on discussing the project.

Week 3 (PM, about the project with another "throwaway" line). *Have you looked over our invoice? Any other information you need?*

Week 4 Same scenario, but the pressure goes up a notch: *About the invoice—30 days is about up. Anything I should be doing about us getting paid?*

Week 5   At this point someone else—who the client doesn't know—calls. The gist of the message: *I'm working on accounts receivable and I'm calling to see whether you got the invoice? Oh well, I didn't know, so I've already sent you another. Sorry about that. Well let me ask if there is any problem with it? Oh good. Can you tell me when we can expect payment? Thank you very much.*

Week 6   A principal of the firm calls: *They tell me you're overdue on paying us and that tells me there must be something wrong with either the project or with our services. I'm calling to find out which it is so that I can fix it. What can I do????* The principal is waiting with pen and paper to take down everything the client says as a memo for file, dated and signed. If something actually *is* wrong the principal gets involved and reports back to the client. If assured *it's only a cash-flow problem* or some such, the principal is prepared (in case things turn ugly later) to give a legal deposition about being assured there was nothing wrong with the service.

Week 7   The same or another "someone else" (this can be your spouse, if you're a sole practitioner) calls: *I'm still working on these accounts receivable. Should I tell the firm to stop work on your project or what? Can I come over and walk the invoice through your system? Should they call a lawyer? What do you want me to do?*

Week 8   is up to you. Above all, you never want to anger the client enough to send them to *their* lawyer.

The course in Construction 101 for law students must be exceedingly brief. So far as I can tell, it might be abbreviated as follows: *If your client is angry at his architect for any reason, immediately file suit against that architect for negligence. There are always grounds for filing a claim, whether any allegations can be proved or not. Mere compliance with due process is typically punitive enough to force said architect to accede to even specious demands.* Hate to say it, but in my experience that's almost true.

I was blessed to have a wonderful lawyer on retainer. In situations like this I was free to write my client a long letter saying *exactly* how I felt—no holds barred—so long as I mailed it to my lawyer instead of the client. The lawyer knew to calmly take *all* the anger out of it, insert about three five-syllable legal terms, and send it to the client on *his* letterhead. Worked wonders.

Obviously, waiting til payment is long overdue, then taking drastic action, is not the most effective procedure

TACTICS FOR SLOW-PAY/NO-PAY CLIENTS

These swing wildly from Mr. Nice Guy to Hardball—they're all tips from architects about what they've found works for them. Consider your own style, and the specific situation at hand. In the words of Clint Eastwood—"A man's gotta do what a man's gotta do. . . ."

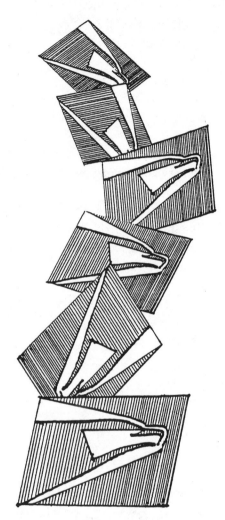

Send two invoices in the same envelope, one for the basic fee and the other for any hourly charges they don't expect and for reimbursables. Being paid the fee can smooth your cash flow while you explain or argue about reimbursables. When I've done this with clients who've previously been slow to pay, their accounts payable people hate the extra paperwork of two invoices and promise to do better in the future if I'll keep it to one bill.

Fax and mail at the same time. For some reason, people consider a fax more important than a letter.

SECOND BILLING boldly noted in major felt-tip on both the envelope and the invoice gets results—particularly when you also fax it. Think about it—the person tending the fax usually isn't the one signing the checks, so you may be fomenting some internal pressures with this tactic. *What's going on here? We're not paying our bills? Should I be worried about job security?*

Registered mail, return receipt requested works well to counter it-must-have-got-lost-in-the-mail tactics. Nothing like a guy in a government uniform asking for your signature to get your attention.

Hand carry it. Obviously, the best way to collect is to confront the person who owes you. Might go something like this: You talk with them about the project and

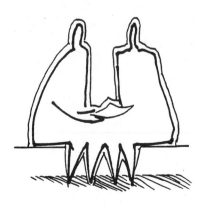

- All about progress and the good aspects of how it's turning out.
- What you're worrying about and working to keep from going wrong.
- Warning of decisions coming up they need to be thinking about.
- Unmet needs you think they might not have considered and could use your help on, etc., etc.
- Ask how they feel everything's going, listen carefully, and prove it by giving feedback.
- Then: *One other thing, I haven't gotten paid for that last invoice and we need to stay up-to-date on that part of the project, too. Can you cut me a check?*

You're using me as your bank. Several practitioners have reported they negotiate that, for late payments, there will be interest charged at a slightly lower rate than that available from the bank. This gives them an option if the client is slow to pay: *Been thinking about it and I have an idea that might help us both. You're using me as a bank and that's OK, except now I need to go to my bank, and they want collateral. If you'll just sign this promissory note. . . .* Point is, if the client were to sign, they'd give up the right to claim negligence later for all services prior to signing. It's reported that most respond with *Here, let me write you a check.* If they *do* sign, it may be a danger signal about their financial condition.

Why are you mad at me? Typical response to this one: *What? Me mad at you? What're you talking about?* Answer: *Well, you're not paying me so I figured I must have done something wrong. Can't we talk about it?* Neat thing about this one is that it deals with the possibility that slow payment means the client really *is* dissatisfied with the service.

I'll just wait. This one's really for use with the no-pay category client. The architects, after getting the endless runaround, simply show up, announcing they have to have a check today and that they'll sit in the client's waiting room. Several have reported that at quitting time, there's feigned discovery: *What! You're still here!* Followed be a frantic rush to cut a check and get it signed.

Whatever you think right. This is a last resort for some, an up-front offer from others. It's the reverse moral high-ground approach, demonstrating your trust they'll do the right thing. Best accompanied with full documentation: *This is what I have in the job. Pay me whatever you think it's really worth.*

The 1099. One final ploy for the no-pay types: Call or write to advise them you're claiming what they owe as a bad debt and submitting a 1099 to the IRS. You're doing them the favor of advising them to claim it as income on their tax statement. You'll be amazed at how many would rather pay the full fee than the taxes on it.

No liens. In my experience, filing a lien sends them straight to their lawyer and Construction Law 101 is immediately put into full effect. Thus endeth the parable. But on the other hand, there's always Clint Eastwood. Your choice.

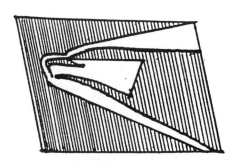

ABOUT THE MONEY....CHAPTER 7

Not going to spend much paper here on the left brain side of this issue—what little I know along those lines I managed to get included in the AIA *Handbook*.*

By the way, one of the (hopefully few) prescriptive admonitions I want to include in this is that every firm ought to have the four-volume version of the *Handbook*—and market research has shown that most do. Problem was, the same research showed virtually no one had read it, so more important, let me urge that every practitioner (from intern on up) have a copy of the *Student Edition* at their workstations.

- It's a single, paperback volume—you can deal with that.
- It's a calm and reasoned exposition on most everything you need in order to practice.
- It's a consensus document, so you're protected from the skewed bias of any particular author.
- It's still remarkably relevant to today's practice, yet it's about to be replaced by a CD-ROM version, so buy your hard copy now—it's still the most comprehensive toolkit you'll find—and besides, your system could crash.

Truth is, I think so highly of the *Handbook* that the only reason for me to be writing this is to mess with your head. Hold on—I'm still on your side. What I mean is, the *mind-set* required for successful practice has changed in the last 5 years. It's how you think about what you do, your regard for—and *collaborative relationship with*—the others you're dealing with in the doing of it that has changed. But you knew that. So what follows are a few quick head trips on the money part, because it's how you approach bean counting that sometimes matters more than the numbers. What's needed is more beans and fewer numbers.

Few years back, I was asked to facilitate part of the national Young Architects Forum on personal financial strategies. Since money management has never been my strong suit I asked friends for tips, and the best input came from AIA's Chris Clark passing on his grandfather's advice from years back.

Armed mainly with this and other folksy truisms from my own upbringing, I ventured off for a day with such experts as Peter Piven, FAIA, who wrote the book on the subject (2.53 and 2.54 in the *Handbook*). In addition to Peter we had three professional financial advisors give us a long afternoon of numbers, statistics, advice, and warning. Scary.

Pay yourself first. Don't worry about what to do with the money—hide it under your mattress if you like—'fore you know it, it'll get to be such a big lump you won't sleep sound till you've figured out someplace good to invest it. Main thing—take 10 percent off the top of anything you make and pay yourself first. You want to tithe after that, that's another issue.

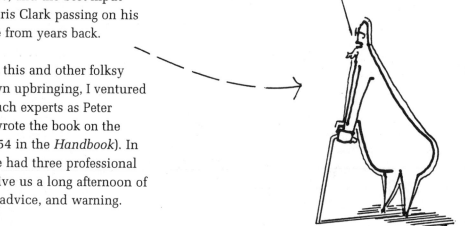

---

*David Haviland, *Architect's Handbook of Professional Practice*, 12th Edition (AIA Press, 1994).

FINANCIAL EXPERTS WARN

- You'll live longer than you think.
- So will everybody else, and medical costs for over-65ers are rising faster than inflation.
- Social Security is best thought of as only a possible bonus if you're lucky.
- Recent tax changes have cut most pension plans 10 to 30 percent.

THEY ADVISE YOU INVEST

Art, metals, gems, options, commodities, explorations, futures

No more than 5-10%

TAXES / IRA

SPECULATIVE   Hi Risk

Growth stocks or mutual funds, equity partnerships, your house

100 less your age as a %

GROWTH   EXPERT   Medium Risk

(Maybe)

60-80%

CONSERVATIVE   Lo Risk

(Maybe)

T-bills, municipal bonds, conservative mutual funds, or equities — anything where the government assures payment

And remember: A 30-year mortgage means you are paying 300% of the real cost of your house.

Pay extra and call it savings

Monthly Investments Needed Now to Fill Your Retirement Income Gap

If you expect your retirement income gap to be approximately this amount per year:

Years until retirement	$5,000	$10,000	$20,000	$30,000	$40,000	$50,000	$60,000
	You would have to invest these monthly amounts starting today:						
40	$20	$40	$81	$121	$161	$202	$242
35	$29	$59	$118	$176	$235	$294	$353
30	$43	$87	$174	$261	$347	$434	$521
25	$65	$131	$262	$392	$523	$654	$785
20	$102	$203	$407	$610	$813	$1017	$1220
15	$167	$334	$668	$1003	$1337	$1671	$2005
10	$306	$612	$1224	$1836	$2448	$3060	$3672
5	$740	$1480	$2960	$4439	$5919	$7399	$8879

Note: Assumes (1) a 7% fixed return, compounded monthly and no fluctuation of principal, (2) withdrawals for 20 years, and (3) no adjustment for income taxes or inflation during retirement. Your investment returns will vary.
Source: NPL.

But if you cut through the experts' doom, gloom, and latest professional jargon—hey!—it's Chris's grandfather from out in Utah! Making notes of what they said, at end of day, I left with two clear categories of options:

1. I can assume that I really am going to live forever and never want to retire. That it'll always be a lot easier to make money than to save it, that eventually I'm bound to inherit or marry wealth, that surely Congress is going to provide for me, etc., etc.—or…

2. I can decide some of those assumptions may prove groundless and realize that I might as well tend to this myself—nobody's gonna do it for me.

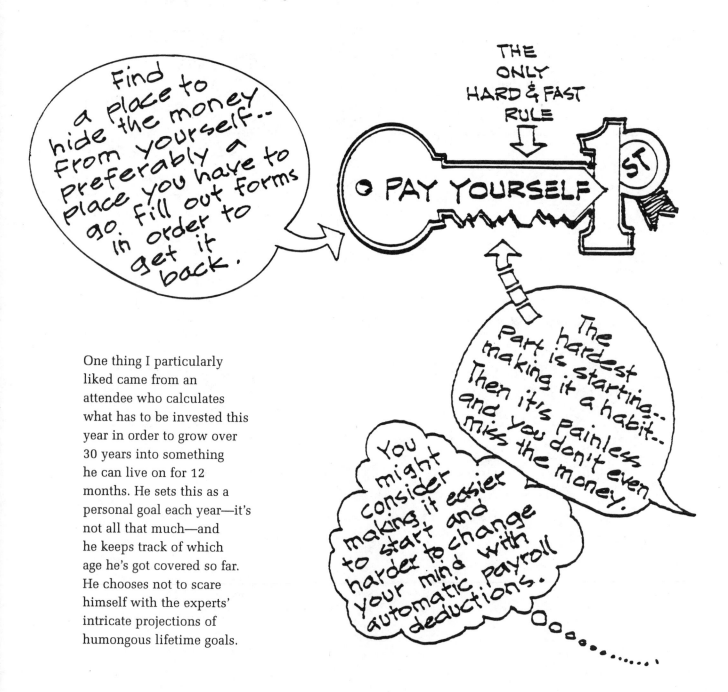

One thing I particularly liked came from an attendee who calculates what has to be invested this year in order to grow over 30 years into something he can live on for 12 months. He sets this as a personal goal each year—it's not all that much—and he keeps track of which age he's got covered so far. He chooses not to scare himself with the experts' intricate projections of humongous lifetime goals.

CREDIT

While there's only one rule--
--PAY YOURSELF FIRST--

There is also one basic attitude to make into a habit. Decide how you're going to deal with credit-- cause none of us can deal very well without it -- your choice:

ON THE ONE HAND

WHILE ON THE OTHER

BREAK GLASS AND USE ONLY IN CASE OF EMERGENCY

CREDIT CARD

DANGER

Use cash to buy when you can. When you can't, don't buy any more.

Using your credit cards and paying 100% of each bill the day it arrives is a great way to build your credit rating.

The secret to having money is to act like you don't.

Just remember, the two things we all know about credit:

1. The prerequisite for borrowing is to not need to....

and

2. Some time or other, we all need to.

OVERHEAD AND PROFIT

An architect in Toledo tipped me to this. He had noticed how contractors make it all into one word—m'ohvrhed'nprofit. For them it's not overhead *and* profit, it's just the one thing, indivisible, under God, with liberty and justice for all. Work with any builder about how to get a project under budget and he'll come up with all sorts of ways to cut construction cost or/time. But m'ohvrhed'nprofit? Never in question—that stays the same percentage of cost, regardless. Like it's in escrow.

Architects can take a lesson. Too many of us act as though overhead is untouchable—a fixed condition of doing business. While profit is treated as a contingency fund—a variable.

Thinking of it that way leads to spending it that way. That's why I like Fred Stitt's suggestion some years ago that we learn to think of profit as just another business expense along with payroll and the phone bill. Even better is the attitude that it's profit that's fixed—it's the overhead we need to make variable

and work at cutting. Might even consider joining the recent trend toward experimentation with automation, outsourcery, and partnering.

Is this just another of Franklin's head trips? Sure thing. Lots of what—and how well—we do, is based on nothing more than our mind-set and the self-image with which we approach the financial side of practice—the way we look at things. So to help us change how we look at the money part here's B school 101 with thanks to friend Ryc Loope, Head of the Durant Group. Harvard calls it a MASE diagram.

Margin
After
Service
Expense

MASE diagram - a way to think graphically about financial management -- make a game of it.

If you can move, swivel, or bend all the lines except the X and Y axes, how many ways can you redraw this same diagram to move point "B" (breakeven) in a southwesterly direction — sooner in the project and at less cost ?

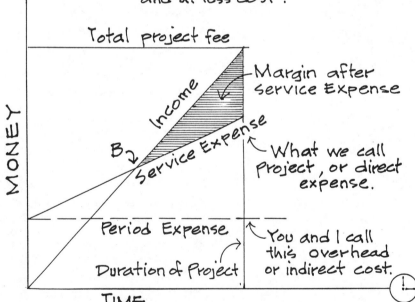

The objective of the game, of course, is to enlarge the area of the margin after service expense triangle.

To a great extent, it's how we think about things—and ourselves—that allows us to change conditions rather than merely complain. Which we do. A lot. The architects' lament about fees that I hear most often concerns the similarity in fees—as a percentage—charged by us versus what real estate agents get. The interesting thing is the tone of moral outrage that creeps in. *It's not fair*—as though to say—*Well, thank God* I'm *at least a* professional.

There is in fact, a similarity between what we and the realtors do. We each make it possible for our clients to acquire the building they need and want. To me the real question is not whether realtors earn their fees—after all, they're simply charging what the market will pay. Instead, I want to know how their mind-set and self-image lead them to profitability in a world where, as Oscar Wilde observed, everybody knows the price of absolutely everything and the value of practically nothing.

So why this time-honored aversion of architects to deal openly about money? For instance—retainers? Credit references? That most architects don't ask for them is not a matter of professionalism—at least not as the world defines that term. Never mind realtors, you have to concede that law and medicine are true professions. But try getting medical attention without a credit check—proof of insurance—ability to pay. Medical services are purchased at time of delivery, and for surgery, advance partial payment is frequently required. We could learn from that. The architects who report they do the equivalent are very matter of fact about it and nobody quibbles. Or we could learn from lawyers. I assume that virtually all lawyers check the credit ratings of their clients, they're just more surreptitious about it than doctors. Nothing covert about their asking for retainers, though—it's simply routine, upfront, a condition of practice.

I agree that we wouldn't want to be lumped in with realtors, lawyers, and doctors, our public image being so much better than any of theirs. But since there's nothing unprofessional about the actual making of profit, of checking credit ratings, of requiring retainers from clients you've never worked with before, I'm interested in how we can do these things in ways to feel good about ourselves professionally.

Hey!
no-brainer....
keep the time the same
and negotiate a
higher fee!

Nah....
cut project time.
Service expense is
mostly salaries
and the slope of
that won't
change

Upgrade
the CAD to cut
Service expense on
this and all future projects.
We'll recover that up-front
bump in overhead in
no time!

Get a
retainer! Start
the income at the
break-even
height!

Let's cut
the overhead--
outsource the part we
don't do well

Let's.
do everything right
the first time--bumps up
the front-end service
expense but it'll cut all
that rework out of
the overhead.

A MASE diagram might bring out some good team discussion. Try it.

Profit. Forget percentages, disregard most of what's published. What's reported typically relates to big firms, where 7 percent of gross is a quantum leap in dollars above the same percentage for the majority of firms. Make it personal and think in dollars. With the back of an envelope, a handheld calculator, and a free lunch for your banker, CPA, or friendly investment broker, you can quickly arrive at the annual profit you need now, in order to meet future needs. College for the kids, occasional vacations, retirement, buying a house—all that. They can help you with those dollar figures to add to the ones you can best foresee needing for new computers, office car, cellular phone, whatever. How to use the total is covered in the *Architect's Handbook of Professional Practice*, page 269—the point here is to think of profit in terms of realistic and defensible needs, not variable and wistful hopes.

Retainers. Talked about this in Chapter 6, but it bears repeating. Ten years ago I'd asked a workshop full of architects for a show of hands from those charging retainers and hope for three. These days it's up to about 20 percent or so, depending on market region. Most architects who get them report that many clients expect to pay a retainer, provided you ask; that none question your applying them to final payment. Alternatives: Break the project into deliverables and ask for payment in advance for each. Or for each phase. Or charge by the hour till the project is defined enough to break it into deliverables.

The architect reported earlier who gets a 100 percent retainer on very small remodeling jobs reported learning it from a dentist who was listening in on the negotiation with his wife, the client. The deal is to offer a 10 percent discount for 100 percent payment in advance. Saves far more than the discount, of course, simply by not having to fool with the invoicing process.

It was Ashley McConnaughey (of MacArchitect financial software, Seattle) who told me of the architect who offers reimbursement of any or all the retainer based on the client's evaluation of performance at the end of the project and agrees to a list of criteria by which the client will judge the quality of professional services. He's never had to reimburse any money but, in addition, there are three other good things about that idea:

- It's a way to help the clients set realistic expectations.
- The architect is getting carefully considered post-project debriefings, a way to listen to clients, which some firms are spending considerable money to get from surveys by consultants.
- And, it's great marketing!

Credit ratings. Any friendly contractor can get one from their bonding company just for the asking. I'm told Dunn and Bradstreet is available on the Internet. Your banker will probably be happy to get it for you. So checking the ability to pay isn't hard, doesn't take a lot of time, and doesn't even require the client knowing you're doing it—though that might not be a bad idea. Your clients take money seriously and expect you to do so as well. In fact, the area in which our public image (and self-image) suffers most is in the perception of how well we deal with money.

So how about full disclosure of fee structures and profit margin to clients? Feds require it and the small firms offering construction management routinely do it. Why not make it standard practice? Only downside I can think of is they'll find out how abysmally low your profit margin is and feel guilty.

PRICING YOUR PROJECTS— SETTING THE FEE

And in that order! These are two separate activities.

What's a poor architect to do? Not being in the widget business, there's no approved textbook process for pricing what we sell:

- No standard projects—they're each different—so no set prices.
- Every firm is different and has unique overhead rates that vary over time.
- Clients and their projects can be problematic for myriad reasons—complicated decision-making hierarchies, weird site conditions, regulatory political process, or complex project delivery, to name a few. Often these can't be readily anticipated during pricing, yet any can determine profitability.

Pricing is only the first step; *setting the fee* is sometimes a very different issue, when you add three more sets of variables:

- Market conditions including inflation or recession, regulatory constraints, and availability of qualified people to do the project.
- The owner's expectations and capabilities.
- All architects not having been created equal: By reason of experience, aptitude, talent, or even reputation, some can bring far more—or less—value to a given project than others.

With that many variables, pricing and fee-setting are as much art as science, and comparing with other architects what fees to charge for projects is not only a violation of antitrust law, it's not even useful. But without comparing *what* architects charge, we *can* usefully discuss *how* to price projects and set fees, and that's what this is about, mainly. We'll also talk here a bit about the *who, when,* and *why*— parameters that can be useful to you in proposing and negotiating fees.

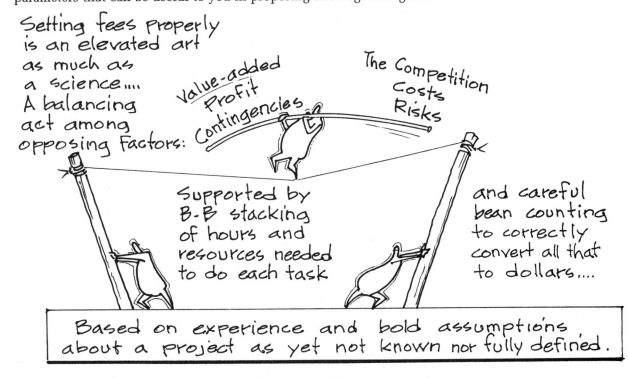

Setting fees properly is an elevated art as much as a science.... A balancing act among opposing factors:

Value-added Profit Contingencies

The Competition Costs Risks

Supported by B-B stacking of hours and resources needed to do each task

and careful bean counting to correctly convert all that to dollars....

Based on experience and bold assumptions about a project as yet not known nor fully defined.

COST-BASED PRICING

Let's begin with how you go about calculating the cost of your services—sounds simple enough—only four components in the equation:

Fee =	Direct project cost	Plus indirect or overhead cost	Plus profit	Plus contingency
Arrived at through:	Breaking it down into, and estimating cost of, separate tasks and phases, which requires assumptions about program, size and numbers of structures, etc.	Calculations based on recent experience for overhead. Don't forget to add the worth of any value-added services or consults you've given previously.	Percentage of cost—and best thought of as just another business expense. Firms that work at "breakeven" go broke when bad things happen.	Percentage of the previous total, using whatever your market will bear—most don't flinch at 15 percent. This is negotiable; overhead and profit are not.
By:	The people who will actually do each of the tasks or phases. Ask them to cartoon each sheet at 8½ by 11 and estimate the hours it will take.	Office manager with help as needed from the accountant.	Your judgment call on what the market will bear— there's no such thing as "obscene profit" in architecture— you'll earn what you get.	WAG—a technical acronym, the first and last words of which are "wild guess."
Based on:	Experience and a data base of job records—or if that's not available, try WAG.	Bean counting, see *Architect's Handbook of Professional Practice*, 12th Edition (AIA Press,1994), p. 269.	A firm resolve that some day you'll be able to retire with dignity.	Extent of unknowns (risk) in scope, site, approval process, etc.
Category	Hygiene	Hygiene	Health	Health

That far right column in the table—contingency—is generally layered into the detail all the way through the process. It's always used, but incrementally and mostly hidden. Sometimes, however, certain unknowns will be such major factors that they need to be openly acknowledged and anticipated with set-aside funding—a virtual escrow account to be invoked if needed.

Obviously, the first two factors in the equation are best based on accurate project records and accounting.

PROJECT RECORDS

The other two take judgment calls -- sometimes intuitive leaps!

Even with a reliable data base on previous project costs, all the factors in that equation for cost-based pricing are

JUDGMENT CALLS! That's scary. There are some things you can do, however, to increase your comfort level.

① GET SECOND OPINIONS

(a) Have your partner or a staff member calculate the time required by the project independently from you. Compare.

(b) The consulting engineers giving you proposals often are in a position to know total fees paid on similar projects. It's in their interest for you to be both profitable and competitive.

(c) Get a second opinion from yourself. (You'll need it for negotiation)

☐ Figure the project cost conservatively. Assume everything will go wrong and take longer -- redesigns, staff turn over, hostile regulatory, cut-throat low bidder, max RFIs, etc.

☐ Now refigure assuming everything goes well. "Count the beans" both ways: Hours, meetings, presentations, site trips--all of it.

☐ You've made a good start at setting the range within which to negotiate. Go one more step. Express both extremes as percentages of construction cost and compare with current market rates. If your lowest number is still high, try working it top down from the market rate. Is it worth doing?

② BUILD YOUR OWN QUICK-CHECK DATA BASE

It's much easier if you do a lot of the same project type. Even if you don't, you need quick approximations -- rough numbers for client interviews -- things like:

☐ Hours per sheet of drawings, per set of specs per project type.
☐ Monthly average cost of total direct expense for projects by size and type.
☐ Total direct hours per square foot of project by type.
☐ Average in-house front-end costs of putting a project on the books and on the CAD system. And, of course .....
☐ Fees for past projects as percentages of construction costs. This, of course, is the universally used quick-check. Pick and choose among the others -- or invent your own quick-check method -- simple enough to keep updated and useful -- accurate enough to rely on.

Most firms price projects based on what the phases of work on similar projects cost them in the past, relying on a time-card system to catergorize the hours spent. Some make it as simple as noting hours worked in the margins of drawings to gather hours-per-sheet data. You can post anticipated project schedules in the drafting room and have people note time spent. Many track with computers.

Whatever the system, it only works if it's used throughout the day. Memories go fuzzy overnight, much less over two weeks when the next time card is due. (Tip: Make paychecks contingent on time-card submittal!) Complicate time-card codes only enough to track projects, phases, and whatever categories of tasks you'll actually use to price future projects.

And of course you'll need a project notebook to track direct costs -- prints, consultant fees, long-distance calls, travel expense, postage and deliveries. This becomes a total project record with summary sheets that include time spent (by phase) plus project size, description, and cost data added. Lots more about this in the '94 _Handbook_ (p. 584) and about pricing (p. 469).

Second Opinions

Quick-check methods

DATA BASE

Yes, it's a lot of bean counting, but the more reliable your pricing data base and quick-check methods, the greater your conviction and ability to withstand scrutiny (in the public sector) and attack at the negotiating table (in the private).

The more you can involve the staff who'll produce the project in the pricing of it, the better. When they propose a number of hours be budgeted for a phase, a sheet, or a task, it's like a verbal contract they'll try to honor. Besides, you don't make enough to need to hide any money matters.

Surely you know they already know what everybody earns -- don't you?

Comparative data about what other firms get paid have very limited value. It's your direct cost, overhead, and profit that matter, and yours is a totally unique firm. But then I bet you say that to all your clients.

TIPS ON COST-BASED PRICING

- **Staff pricing their own work.** Letting the people who will actually do the work tell you how many hours it will take makes a lot of sense—when consensus is reached it becomes a de facto verbal agreement they'll try to live up to. On the other hand, what's actually quoted is still a judgment call: Some staff want to price high in hopes of later becoming heroes by bringing it in below budget. Others' reach will exceed their grasp—they'll base pricing on optimism that with all they learned on the last one, the next project can't possibly be as problematic. Pricing and fee-setting are distinctly different activities.

- **Consultants quoting their own fees** to you is only fair—you don't appreciate bid shoppers or lowballers among your clients, either. Rather than just assuming what you'll have to pay consultants, ask for quotes up front.

- **Projected labor costs** are obviously the major portion of the fee—and are clearly dependent on detailed time records. Every invoice primarily is based directly or indirectly on time. How accurate is your data base, really? Yes, we all keep time sheets, but many architects tell me they're embarrassed to charge what they remember to fill out 2 weeks after the fact. Maybe you should consider investing in "organizers" and holding an in-house course on using time management systems?

- **Hourly rates and multipliers.** Having projected the number of hours required for each task, sheet of drawings, phase of service, etc., most firms then price the work according to multipliers—billing rates at so much per hour for project manager, tech I, II, III, and so on. (AIA *Handbook*, p. 269.)

Alternatively, there is one major firm reporting they simply charge the same hourly rate—an average—for every member of the firm! To test the idea, they went back over 5 years of project records to confirm that, had they been using the simplified method, they would have totaled about the same in fees and profit. On the strength of those findings they changed to a single billing rate and have found it works. They say it simplifies pricing enormously and eliminates all sorts of in-house tension and time spent haggling over who works on which project and when! Go figure.

Yes, the biggest factor in figuring cost-based pricing is the time projected--But don't ever believe the CPA saying "All you have to sell is time." What you offer in design is value--at its best--timeless.

COMPENSATION METHODS

Having calculated the fee on the basis of cost plus profit and contingency, there are a variety of approaches to using the information, depending on the compensation method you choose or are asked to propose:

- Lump sum
- Cost/plus with a guaranteed maximum price (GMP)
- Cost/plus with no GMP
- Percentage of construction cost
- Unit cost (dollars per bed, square foot, etc.)
- Stipulated sum per repetitive unit or project
- Hybrid (two or more of the above for different phases of service on a single project)

What follows are three tables for you to use in comparing compensation methods. The *Architecture Factbook* (AIA Press, 1992) reported that the seven methods listed above cover about 98 percent of all projects reported, so the tables below add an eighth column in case you're quoting fees by some compensation method not listed.

An example is when you're charging lump sums on a piecemeal basis—it's pay as you go, but each deliverable and the price for it are agreed to in advance.

In the three tables that follow, read each item in the left-hand column and disregard the X marks I put in the row beside it. Plug in your own check marks under each of the compensation methods that is appropriate, given specific owner need, project type, service, project delivery, or management consideration.

You'll find some rows where multiple compensation methods are appropriate—others suggesting only one or two.

CLIENT NEEDS AND CHARACTERISTICS

The client:	Compensation method							
	Lump sum	Cost/ plus with a GMP	Cost/ plus, no GMP	Percent of const. cost	Unit cost, i.e., per sq ft, room	Lump sums, repetitive units	Hybrid	Other
Must have the total fee set before starting the project	X	X						
Requires disclosure of full detail of project records and accounting		X	X				X	
Is determined to get the lowest possible fee	X	X			X	X	X	
Has extensive experience with this project type	X			X			X	
Is a complex organization with multiple decision makers and interests			X	X			X	
Requires the project be started before it is clearly defined			X	X	X	X	X	
Needs a prototype for replication in multiple locations			X			X	X	

PROJECT TYPE AND SERVICES

	Compensation method							
	Lump sum	Cost/ plus with a GMP	Cost/ plus, no GMP	Percent of const. cost	Unit cost	Lump sums, repetitive units	Hybrid	Other
Unique project without clearly defined scope, schedule or budget			X				X	
Project site, scope, quality and schedule are all clearly defined	X	X		X				
Franchise and other replications—scope and schedule are clear, locations are not	X		X	X		X	X	
School, hospital, hotel, etc., with lots of similar units	X				X		X	
Facility-management surveys, interior design, etc., involving per-piece measurement		X	X		X			
Site adaptation of a prototypical design with full documentation available	X		X				X	
Regulatory or permitting services			X		X			
Construction administration services only			X				X	

These tables are for your use over time -- Add or change project types or check marks as your experience grows -- it can be a resource to your emerging leadership

ARCHITECT'S PRACTICE MANAGEMENT CONSIDERATIONS

	Compensation method							
	Lump sum	Cost/plus with a GMP	Cost/plus, no GMP	Percent of const. cost	Unit cost	Lump sums, repetitive units	Hybrid	Other
Invoicing is easy to do and understand	X				X	X		
Fee adjusts automatically when scope changes			X	X				
Needs greatest definition of scope prior to start-up	X	X						
Requires accurate in-house budgeting	X	X			X	X	X	
Keeps architect's records confidential	X				X	X		
Requires greatest disclosure of records and accounting			X				X	
Entails maximum risk but permits greatest profit	X				X	X		
Can be used to limit possibile losses of architect		X		X			X	
Assures basic profit while protecting against loss			X					
Allows quick start before final negotiation				X	X	X	X	
Can protect architect from "scope creep" by owner			X	X				
Does not penalize architect for project cost savings	X	X	X		X	X	X	

Note: The first table I saw like these was developed by Memphis architect Lee Askew III, FAIA, in 1993 and is included on p. 474 of the *Architect's Handbook of Professional Practice* (AIA, 1994). The Editorial Committee (of which I was a member) came up with ratings that are somewhat different from what I show here. My sense of it is that the market has changed with the times, but you may want to compare this with what's offered in the *Handbook*, then modify it over time according to your experience.

TIPS ON COMPENSATION METHODS

Often a principle of fee-setting, the *when and how* of payment has value and can affect the total amount to be paid. After all, charging for the use of money is how banks and insurance companies get rich:

- **Retainers.** Remember, collections start now—long before you start work! You can get retainers—but only if you ask for them. After all, your clients are used to paying lawyers retainers, and we all pay doctors up front. One way to set the amount is to cover your work during the average time it takes to get an invoice paid—or you might set the retainer to cover your cost for as long as you'd be willing to work without being paid.

- **Administrative setup fees** are an alternative, in case you don't feel right about charging retainers from repeat clients. With a little bean counting you can reliably calculate the average cost up front to get a project on the books and on the CAD. Most firms reported that in recent years it got as high as four figures.

- **A discount for prepayment**—the client prepaying the entire fee—is sometimes offered on tiny projects. How much would it be worth to you to eliminate the in-house cost of invoicing and collection on the very small projects? Ten percent? Fifteen?

- **A schedule of monthly payments,** when included in the contract, can ease cash flow surprises for both you and the client while assuring the basic fee gets paid on time. That leaves you only the reimbursables to invoice in detail—a lot less risk and hassle.

- **A monthly allowance for reimbursables** is sometimes offered on projects that are largely repetitive or very similar to previous ones. This cuts the cost of invoicing and collections and reassures the owner, though for you it entails the risk of in-house overruns.

If you can get some up-front money and calendar the rest for inclusion in the contract, you'll be sitting pretty.

- **Reallocating costs** can leave the owner perceiving they're getting a bargain. Two examples:

  - The owner has direct contracts with engineering consultants you recommend (provided you've covered the costs of coordination in your price).

  - The owner handles certain costs you normally incur, like distribution of bid documents. This tip is increasingly relevant since many corporations—the ones that are constantly building—now hire staff architects as project representatives.

- **Negotiated contracts** with any of your select list of contractors early in design can save both you and the client money and get constructibility and costing input from the beginning. Many small-project architects offer fee discounts for the owner doing so, knowing that, among people who've done lots of similar projects together, the construction drawings required can be far less detailed and defensive.

- **Hybrid fees** are more and more becoming a standard compensation method. For many architects and owners, the equity of the hybrid fee concept is inescapable: Where the extent and duration of professional services cannot be anticipated, it's only fair that the architect be paid hourly rates.

With this understanding, the architect works to clearly define the project—often well into design development—on an hourly basis, then quotes a lump sum for construction documents. Many return to hourly rates for construction administration since no one can foresee all the delays and special problems construction may entail.

Here's how a commonly used form of hybrid fee works!

PREDESIGN -- From the very first, the architect is paid hourly rates with the terms & conditions of the B141 referenced in a letter of agreement. At the end of SCHEMATICS--or even well into

DESIGN DEVELOPMENT -- Only after the project is fully defined, is a lump sum fee agreed to and a B141 signed. The fixed fee covers

CONSTRUCTION DOCUMENTS -- but may or may not include services for

BIDDING & NEGOTIATION.

Payment for services during CONSTRUCTION ADMINISTRATION (at least the site visit time) is once again at hourly rates.

HOURLY RATES

FIXED FEE

HOURLY RATES

In principle, the architect quotes a fixed fee on only those services, for which the extent and duration can be reasonably anticipated. The rest are performed at hourly rates.

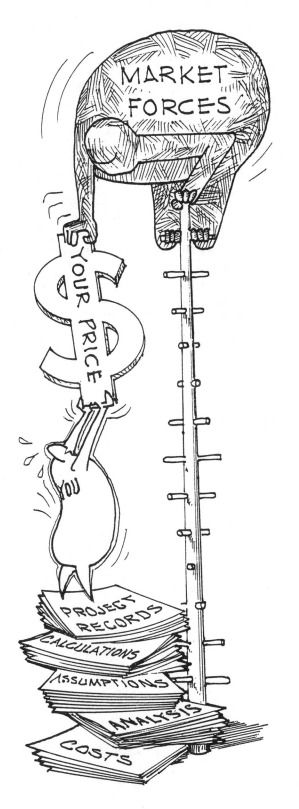

SETTING THE FEE

So far we've talked about the complexities of pricing and compensation strategies. Most of what we've considered centers on calculations for knowledgeably pricing the project based on anticipated costs. That quantification and analysis—much of it intuitive—comes first and requires knowing or assuming a lot about the project in order to price your services. In addition to all that, however, there are market factors to consider in finalizing the fee you'll quote:

- **Market strength** is an omnipresent factor to be kept in mind. How many architects are competing for this project and who are they? What are the odds you'll be chosen for reasons of qualifications or relationship even if your price is higher than that of the competition?

- **Market conditions** including inflation or recession, regulatory constraints, and availability to you of qualified people to do the project may all affect your fee and the compensation method by which it will be paid. There are risks involved in percentage fees in a bad recession just as there are problems with lump sum quotes in times of wild inflation.

- **Market rates** need to be considered, and though antitrust law prohibits your colluding—even discussing fees—with your competition, there are other ways to find what's being paid for comparable projects. Fees paid for public projects are public knowledge and most project types are bought somewhere in the government sector. Finding them out just takes a lot of phone calls.

2.29

CLIENT FACTORS

- **Contacting engineering consultants** who have provided service for similar projects and particularly for the same client can be doubly useful. If you're open to accepting their quotes for the proposed one, they can tell you a lot about ways to approach both the project and the client. When they're under consideration for doing the proposed project they'll want you to be successful, yet competitive.

- **Owner's expectations** are an important factor. However analytical and careful you've been in figuring your costs, your price may be higher or (hopefully) lower than the clients are expecting to pay. Is this a competitive bid situation? Knowing their expectations may not change your price, but it might indicate a need for considering alternative cost reallocations or compensation methods.

- **Factors for clients and other complexities** should be considered and the price increased—or discounted accordingly. Clients come with all levels of capabilities and intentions, sites with wildly varying degrees of problems, and projects with differing arrays of risks and challenges.

- **Speed of delivery** has become more and more a condition of getting the contract. That's because being in operation—or beating the competition's entering the market—is now frequently a condition of, or at least a measure of, the owner's future profitability. It's one case where time actually *is* money. Rushing the schedule is more than cost-added—it's value-added that rightfully should be worth more to them than just the additional cost you incur.

- **Incentives for valued-added service or design** are possible and can be based on such things as speed of delivery or excellence in quality or project performance. At the end of negotiation, one small-project architect reports asking the client to list how they will know at completion whether the architect has exceeded all their expectations. He then asks that they set the amount it would be worth to them if that list were achieved, and helps them determine a fair figure. He negotiates with them their budgeting that amount and setting it aside— as though it's a bonus held in escrow—any or all of which will be paid at the end of the project and solely at the owner's discretion. He reports he always earns his bonus, because he starts with a checklist of specific expectations to be met.

Chapter 8
Don't Manage Time. Manage Yourself.
All Management Is Time Management.

IT'S WORTH YOUR TIME TO TRACK IT

On page 1.24 of this manual I paraphrased management guru Tom Peters's observation that survival now depends on being ultrafast, error-free, and dirt-cheap. To which I added *service* (read instant-access) as a fourth ubiquitous pressure on you to do more, better, quicker. No wonder we all report "There's not enough of me!" so maybe it's time we talk about time. We all fill out time sheets. Architects calculate invoices and set fees on the basis of time. Curiously, only some 20 percent of us carry time management notebooks.

We apparently don't accept the admonition that "time is money," a slogan that must have been invented by a salesperson for toasters or modems or some other "time-saving" device. Or maybe the salesman's CPA explained it that way. But time, like electricity, can't be fully explained. We just know it's a force to be reckoned with, how it works, and that it can either be used to great advantage, or deliver nasty shocks of varying intensity when it gets shorted out or there's a faulty connection. This chapter offers alternative ways to be properly plugged in to managing time by managing yourself.

One sole practitioner says that after hearing me talk about how to put together a simple time management system, he actually did it. Checking back after his first year of use, he reports a $321 average income increase *per month* just from improving the accuracy and reliability of invoices. He finally *knew* what to bill for and had confidence in doing so. This architect feels good about the system as well as his return on investment, because all the components were available at Wal-Mart for about $50. Or Office Depot. Or the drugstore. We're surrounded by them.

Simply put, whatever system works for you works. I know architects happily using sketchbooks, steno pads, 3 by 5 cards—lots of options. I prefer the half-sized three-ring notebook I've carried constantly for 25 years.

WHY CARRY AN ORGANIZER?

 Image! It's the icon of being systematic -- whether you are or not.

 As an information retrieval system. Ideally, you can write it one time and find it again ever after. Even works that way, sometimes!

 To improve your meeting your commitments on time and help you not overcommit yourself.

Showing them a full calendar is the most credible and forgivable way of saying "No."

 To document important decisions, events, agreements, and who said what when. In a land of two million lawyers, your on-the-spot notes can become key evidence.

 To keep instantly available the myriad dates, names, digits, and data all our systems expect you to produce on demand: pin, fax, phone, policy, account numbers, etc.

 To provide a portable marketing system and a way to clearly signal that they and what they say are important enough that you are literally taking note.

2.31

TIME MANAGEMENT SYSTEMS

Use what works and if you're an orderly type who doesn't need one, great! Forget it!

But if you're like some of us and begin to find yourself:

☐ Chronically late
☐ Missing appointments
☐ Overcommitting your time
☐ Forgetting to return calls....

Maybe it's time for an organizer. Only secret to making one work is keeping it with you til it gets to be habit. Discipline yourself to use nothing else.

I avoid big comprehensive systems -- first they're burdens, then guilt trips. And the neat little shirt pocket size -- too small for all I need ready for instant access. The handheld electronics take longer for data entry and limit it to words and digits. Even if they allow graphics, you're still faced with downloading, printing, dating, signing, and filing for the record. Three-ring 9 x 12 notebooks are bigger than I want to carry and look like I'm building a legal case.

I want something simple, just large enough for all I cram in it, small enough to project an image of an informal, thoughtful person.

My notebook system was born when I realized that if my clients wanted to believe me well organized and systematic, who was I to disillusion them? I found that using it really did a lot for my efficiency, information retrieval, risk management, profitability, productivity, and self-esteem. Yes, self-esteem. Every other Friday, I feel more professional and ethical with notes (not just memories) that attest to the ways I've spent my time. Besides, checking off my weekly to-do list is a minor weekend celebration. It nurtures the illusion that I'm in control of my life. The time sheet, you'll notice, by itself sends an entirely *opposite* message. Fill this out, they're gonna check up on me later.

STAYING ON TRACK

The trick is to remember who really *is* in control here and to not be managed by the time management system. Track time; don't let it track you. No guilt trips. (Enough of those get visited on me without tucking another under my arm for constant companionship.) Most architects tell me they track time by the half hour, but it's your choice. Gotta do it some way, so best find an approach that results in optimum value to you and your clients, however you define that.

Your worst option: Track time like your lawyer, then bill it for less than you pay the photocopier repairperson. Lawyers, of course, relentlessly track time to the tenth of an hour. Many endure life in firms that require 2000 billable hours per year. Billable—*not* just reported on time sheets! Poor devils; no wonder some of them become mercenary. Someone said form follows function, but Lily Tomlin may have said it more trenchantly: "The trouble with the rat race is, even if you win, you're still a rat."

At the other extreme, you could charge by the half day as I do. I remind my clients that they're hiring me to be a conceptual thinker, not a clock watcher. My rate, then, is set high to cover minutiae, so I neither track nor bill for phone calls, faxes, normal correspondence, or my preparation and materials for doing their work. My invoices tell what was done substantively and when—with a lot less detail for both parties to worry through.

It encourages half-day blocks spent with intense focus, and since I bill only for work they've authorized, there are no surprises in the invoices. Think about it—it might well lose you clients because your rates would be so high—or it might cull out the bottom-line types if you can afford that. But it may be worth your considering for certain types of clients or commissions.

Point is, clearly there are alternatives within the bean-counting necessity of viewing time as a quantifiable resource to be sold in sequential increments. There are at least theoretical alternatives to thinking that it's necessary at all. Our best designers (and their rates are very healthy, thank you) often seem more time responsive than time responsible—*in* time, rather than *on* time. In 6 years of asking top design architects when during the project their design phase is complete, I've only gotten one answer: "When we hand the building over to the client." Good architecture results from a holistic approach that is consequential, not merely sequential.

PARADIGM PARADOX

What follows makes the punster in me wonder if Tom Peters and I are caught on opposite sides of a pair-of-time shift. To me, there's more to time management in architecture than ultrafast, more to quality than error-free, more to value than dirt cheap. All this paradigm stuff is probably just full of shift, anyway. The world being what it is, however, and architects naturally being to the contrary, next I'll give you a few pages on the straight and narrow version of time management—at least *my* version of it—then an alternative— your old friend the sketchbook.

THE COMPONENTS I USE:

Three-ring half-sized notebook -- good quality so you won't be embarrassed to have and use it anywhere.

Three-ring so you can buy paper for it anywhere: 5½ x 8½"

8½ x 11" or 8½ x 14" -- paper can be 3-hole punched on the narrow edge and folded to fit.

3-hole adjustable punches are readibly available.

Then a set of tabbed alpha dividers to:
☐ provide your filing and information retrieval system.
☐ serve as your address and phone/fax/e-mail directory.

The left page is my record of meetings and events-- decisions by whom and when.

§At the top: "Week of"

But the heart of the system--two sets of two-page spreads-- one, a too-due list and meeting record spread I make for each week -- the other, a set of standard, tabbed "month-at-a-glance" calendars.

Right-hand page is my too-due list I work both ends against the middle--phone calls from bottom up -- errands and hard copy, top down.

Keep these in both--they're forever changing!

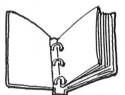

We are so busy doing the urgent that we don't have time for the important.

Confucius (551–479 B.C.)

And I suppose every time management system since Confucius (at least all those I've seen) deal with that same problem. They typically say to make a comprehensive to-do list *first* thing each day, then prioritize it with letters or digits, then do the things both important *and* urgent first, emphatically blacking out the priority symbol to celebrate completion of the task so you can feel good.

I respond emphatically in the negative to such admonitions on several counts:

- I'm a morning person and damned if I'll squander the most productive time of my day making lists! Don't mind at all doing a weekly list on Sunday evening and letting it evolve as it will the rest of the week. Each day I glance at it and decide what's next, and besides, I'm the type who makes lists to change rather than to slavishly implement. I practice organic time management, do what I'm up for next, and anything left on Friday can be starter dough for next week's list.

- *Comprehensive* to-do list? Before I write it I ask—will this take no more than 2 minutes to do? If the answer is *yes* I *do it now*. Should I spend 2 minutes writing and prioritizing and 2 more minutes doing it when its turn comes up? Get outta here!

- Rank in descending order from A to E or 5 to 1 and black out the priority when completed? I want more than this. I want (or may want) to know later:
  - When it was I planned to start.
  - When I really started.
  - How long it took.
  - When I finished.
  - What priority I placed on the task and when that changed en route.

So it is with a hopefully acceptable degree of hubris that I propose you can do all that with an open-faced set of graphic symbols with which to prioritize your too-due list* for the week. After all, there are only four options:

SO DECIDE:

CODE	CONDITION	
	IMPORTANT	URGENT
◇	✓	✓
☐	✓	
○		
△		✓

◇ Is like the ski-slope symbol: Pay attention! Now!

☐ Important but not yet urgent—four-square—just what I want to fill my time doing.

○ Neither important nor urgent yet—but interesting—don't want to lose track of it yet.

△ Apparently makes a difference—though not to me—gotta do it.

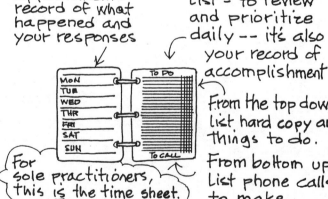

Week's appointments—record of what happened and your responses

Weekly too-due List—to review and prioritize daily—it's also your record of accomplishment

From the top down: list hard copy and things to do.

From bottom up: List phone calls to make.

For sole practitioners, this *is* the time sheet.

---

*On the opposite page, the vertical lines are for the days of the week. That's where I prioritize, then record start, finish, and changes in priority. But I also use the graphic codes in lots of other places—like to triage mail and bills I owe.

A SAMPLE WEEKLY CENTERFOLD

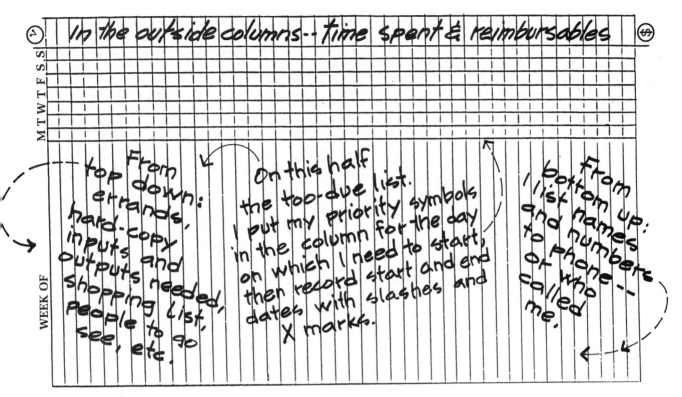

Here's a copy of the actual page I use—reduced on the photocopier by 15 percent so as to fit the margins here. The next page is a clean copy if you want to blow it up, make double-sided copies, cut them in half, and three-hole punch them for use in your half-sized organizer notebook.

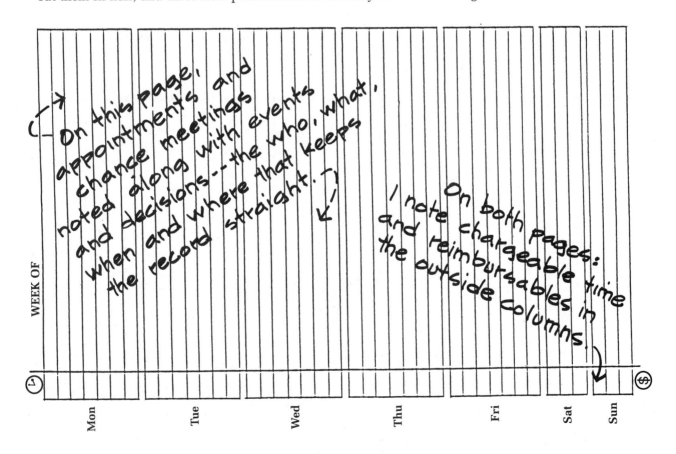

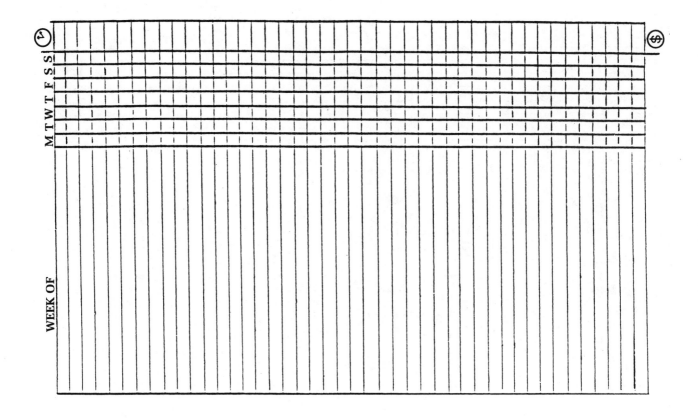

WEEK OF

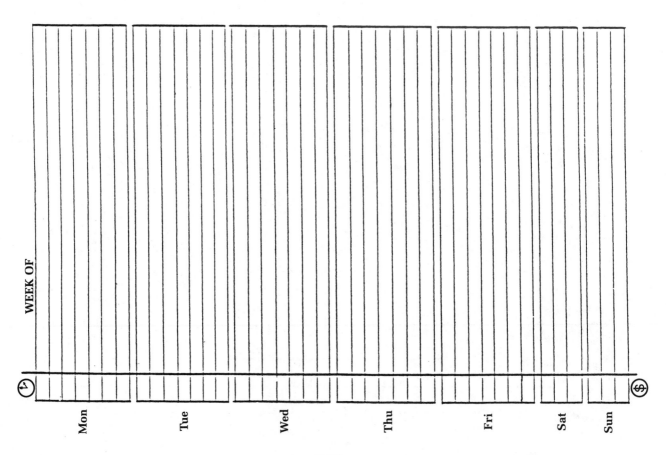

WEEK OF

Mon

Tue

Wed

Thu

Fri

Sat

Sun

THE SKETCHBOOK/JOURNAL REVISITED

I have a commonplace book for facts and another for poetry, but I find it difficult always to preserve the vague distinction which I had in mind, for the most interesting and beautiful facts are so much more poetry and that is their success. They are translated from earth to heaven. I see that if my facts were sufficiently vital and significant—perhaps transmuted into the substance of the human mind—I should need but one book of poetry to contain them all.

Thoreau.

This is a time when the architecture profession—seeking to emulate the successes of the computer and entertainment industries—is proclaiming the need to reinvent itself, aligning itself more closely with its clients. We do this periodically, generally confusing the fact that architecture always responds to its clients with the mistaken idea that the proper response is for architects to copy their clients' business practices. At least the information revolution has now pushed the profession into changing its selection of role models from widget makers to digit makers, which is certainly progress of a kind.

This is written in full appreciation of the importance of digitization, and in no way argues with the success to be found in it, so long as that doesn't become *all* we do as architects. Woodrow Wilson said the business of America is business. I hold that the business of architecture (including digit making) is ancillary.

In my search for ways to help us keep a proper balance, I'm currently investigating the efficacy of using sketchbooks in a new way and I invite you to join me in the experiment. There's lots of precedent for keeping a sketchbook/journal. Back in the olden days (before word processors) an overwhelming majority of creative and significant people—those we still read, quote, admire, try to emulate—all kept sketchbooks/journals as a matter of course.

I'm finding my return to this seemingly anachronistic practice helps me capture more of the wondrously creative discoveries which the mind constantly surfs and seldom tarries long enough to seriously consider. The mind is naturally a far richer resource than the Internet, yet we force it to act like a machine with single-purpose programs to be booted up and run. What with all this computer analog, you're probably wondering why I don't just use one instead of a sketchbook. It's because though I can *thoughtlessly* draw—and thereby discover what the mind is thinking—I can't thoughtlessly compute.

Some thoughts on using a time-honored tool for a reflective and creative life-- an alternative to the burden of using an organizer for those of us who're left brain challenged!

or right brain enabled!

Even the finest notepad computers—much less word processors—are at root binary. They remain left brain tools for linear listings of words and numbers, each keystroke required in exact sequence.

Use of them, for me at least, is necessarily premeditated, on purpose, and by *their* rules, rather than at my whim. For all of us, the processes of creativity and design occur primarily in the right brain land of *both-and*, *what-if*, and *now*, rather than in the left brain, linear domain of *yes/no*, *either/or*, and *next*. Art and discovery—in fields all the way from nuclear physics to fiction writing— are reported as immediate enlightenments—spontaneous, joyful, and intuitive insights into an inclusive synthesis.

The sketchbook/journal can be a tool, a venue, for dialectic dialogue between designer and project that allows the holistic solution to spring full-blown into awareness.

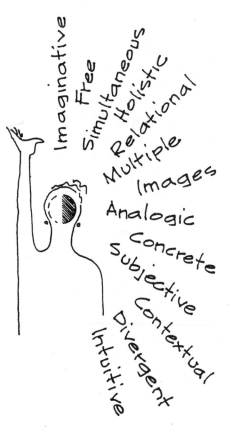

THE SKETCHBOOK/JOURNAL: WHAT IT'S NOT

It's not an organizer—unless you want it to be. I've taught time management enough years to concede that 80 percent of practicing architects will never use a hard-copy system long-term. Even in a profession where all services are priced and invoices calculated on the basis of time spent or projected. Apparently, the left brain categorization and priority setting that is the basis of all organizers becomes first a burden and then a guilt trip for most of us, so we refuse to fool with it.

What I'm proposing here instead, is the possibility of improving our design and marketability through a return to using the sketchbooks we've all carried at one time in school. I'm proposing we practice ways to easily combine—switch back and forth between—the functions of right and left cerebral hemispheres within the covers of the same volume. As a spin-off, I'd expect such a practice to improve client, risk, and project management, to increase profitability. But the immediate and primary objective is to free your creativity by encouraging right brain activity—giving it equity. You've heard the colloquialism, "I'm of two minds on this issue." Truth is, we're all of two minds on *every* issue. In *The Tao of Psychology* (Harper, 1979), Jean Shinoda Bolen, M.D., writes:

> *The left cerebral-hemisphere contains our speech centers, controls the right half of our bodies, and uses the logic and reasoning of linear thinking to arrive at assessments or conclusions. It focuses on what is tangible and measurable. . . .The left hemisphere sees the "bit" or "parts" and the cause-and-effect relationships between them, rather than the whole interacting picture. Its relationship with the world is to see the world as being separate from itself, something to use or dominate—its style is active. . . .*

> *The right cerebral hemisphere is quite different: Images, rather than words, are its tools. It knows through intuition what the totality of a picture is, and also experiences a sense of what something emerged from, what it may become. The right brain can contain ambiguities and opposites. It takes in the whole of an event at once, rather than focusing on what it takes in. The right hemisphere compares through metaphor rather than measurement. Its style is receptive and reflective. . . .*

BOTH/AND ⟵————————⟶ EITHER/OR

Actually, at this point I carry both a left brain time-management system *and* a right brain sketchbook. I find them equally essential, but very different in function and intent.

Trouble with using both a sketchbook <u>and</u> an organizer, of course-- doing so provides lots more places to lose your critical notes and data

For years I had doodled and diagrammed a lot in my organizer, kept it as loose as possible, but I always found my left brain analytical mind clearly in charge there. As an experiment, I put my organizer aside for a 3-month period and carried only the sketchbook, using it for time management also.

In fact, it worked very well. With Post-it tape, I flagged a centerfold two-page spread at the beginning of each week to use for planning and record keeping of appointments and important decisions or meetings. In between flags, I kept the equivalent of a ship's log—a running commentary of notes and diagrams of projects and people and thoughts.

Took a long time for me to appreciate the—for me—single flaw in the system. Information retrieval eventually became a problem. Over the years (it happens to all of us) I had come to rely on my organizer to supplement faltering memory. Things would come up that I'd *know* I'd already considered and made note of, yet couldn't dredge up the exact answer to. So now I've made a deal with myself; I keep both.

When it's appropriate to really free up and give myself permission to use right brain creativity, I send my unconscious a clear signal by opening my sketchbook. However, that's precisely why I find myself dealing with important projects in the organizer as well as the sketchbook. Staying in the budget and on schedule is organizer work, but the main reason I hang onto it is to have access to 20 years' worth of names and addresses and all the digits I'm expected to have available instantly on demand.

There's clear consensus among authorities from lots of disciplines, however. The decisions you can live with come from your intuition and feeling functions—right brain activity.

MY SKETCHBOOK/JOURNAL IS

- A private place where the right brain artist in me is encouraged to sketch, explore, discover, and evolve vivid images—to emote, whine, or exult, without fear of reprisal or ridicule—to start from the middle of a page and work in all directions at once.

- A place to simply observe and note (when at my best, without judgment, fear, or greed) what the left brain "parent" in me keeps harping on. When I can do this with enough detachment and repetition, eventually that left brain part of my mind acknowledges that it has been heard and cuts me some slack. Interestingly enough, what works best for me in making this happen is to attempt wherever possible to avoid the use of the words *I, me,* and *mine.* Cuts down on the ego interventions and leaves me in a more detached, third-party observer position.

- A place to gather—without concern for order or hierarchy—the rich disarray of data (much of it subjective and little more than hunches) that eventually will find its way into the underlying reality that my work seeks to express, to which at least respond.

If I had to pick between them right now I'd keep the sketchbook!

I'm convinced that data gathering is best recorded in freehand graphic form. Words work for Thoreau, but they require a lot more pen strokes than an ideogram and I need a simple, visual, information recall system—get the picture? And photography? I gave up on that some 25 years ago. Happened when, in trying to organize a filing system for my thousand or so 35-mm slides, I realized I had no idea what they pictured. Could remember only a few of the images and precious little of the reality. With that realization I told myself:

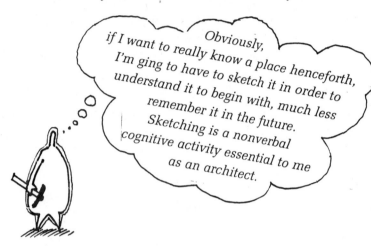

Obviously, if I want to really know a place henceforth, I'm ging to have to sketch it in order to understand it to begin with, much less remember it in the future. Sketching is a nonverbal cognitive activity essential to me as an architect.

Nor will I accept the excuse that you're not good at drawing. Often, the graphics we like and find most meaningful are thirty-second thumbnails or quick gesture sketches—no more than immediate and direct records of impact and feelings evoked—subjective data gathering, graphic communications. We're all used to communicating graphically, all have our favorite tools. So it's just the book that needs discussion here.

Only advice I've got about drawing implements: Keep them simple and portable. Keep them always with you. Keep using them. George Hasslein, beloved teacher at Cal Poly, likes to tell architecture students: "The worst thing that can happen to you is that you'll graduate, get a job, do well at it, and quit drawing."

THE BOOK

What I want is a book that is:

- Presentable enough for me to unabashedly carry with me and use anywhere.
- Of good quality paper with enough tooth for pencil, felt-tip, and my ubiquitous fountain pen.
- Cheap enough for me to not begrudge myself the use and misuse of it. That's to help guard against catching a case of the dread FOWP (fear of white paper—from Cathy Johnson—*Sketching and Drawing*, Northlight Books, 1995).
- Hardcovered and tough enough to take some abuse without the pages getting dog-eared.
- Wire ring–bound so it opens totally flat without blowing pages at me when the wind picks up.
- Dimensionally right for photocopying those pages I choose to share.
- A book with neither front nor back, so I can flip it to work both ends against the middle.

What serves me best is a hardcover, blank, artist's sketchbook—7 × 10 inches—ring-bound (Canson, Bienfang and Cachet Classic are three brands).

It's really two books in one. Taken from one direction, it's my sketchbook and project log, full of notes that record discussions, directions, and alternatives considered. The edge is a tatter of 1½ × 2-inch Post-its to mark crucial entries and I'm happy to share it with anyone, particularly when we each remember a distinctly different meeting of the minds about the same issue having to do with the project. Helps to show them chapter and verse, each entry with date, location, those present, and project issue title.

Left brain stuff, except that lots of it's in the form of cluster diagrams, mind maps, and ideograms with notes. Scattered liberally among all this are sketches—scenes, people, and buildings with no relevance to the project other than to prove we're talking to a real design professional here—*Come look, Maude! Feller draws pictures by hand!* When most people can run a computer better than I, and all have full access to the same software, it doesn't hurt to have an edge.

By now, my sketchbook is generally accepted as a slightly eccentric, though somehow reliable, project log. Little do most people know that, when flipped upside down and opened from the other side, it's suddenly become a journal, a private world, my place of inner dialogue.

Not that it's just a playground in which my right brain inner child can squander valuable time with no discipline. There's a rule for its use that requires serious commitment—one I borrowed, in modified form, from Julia Cameron's *The Artist's Way* (Putnam, 1992).

The rule is easy to say and hard to carry out: *Write a centerfold of two pages, first thing every morning, in longhand, stream-of-consciousness script.* First thing. Nonnegotiable. The reason to be so emphatic about the rule is that my left brain "parent"—what Cameron calls *the enemy within*—finds endless clever reasons why I don't have time for this today, why it's a silly pointless activity anyway, and why my writing doesn't make any sense. To get past this, I simply acknowledge and note down each left brain comment, often marveling at its ingenuity in disparaging and belittling what I'm doing and why. Again, it works best when written without using first-person singular pronouns or possessive forms.

This is when it becomes of critical importance to have made the serious commitment—with both cerebral hemispheres—to write a two-page centerfold for the day, every day. This is when the two pages often become filled with heated dialogue between the two halves of my mind. Not that it matters what I write, and it's not particularly helpful to read it afterward, though every month or so, I usually scan back over it to become aware of changes taking place in my life. I just write whatever the mind brings up and if nothing comes up, I fill two pages reporting that fact and how I feel about that. It's the act of writing that counts, not what's written, though occasionally poetry comes out of it, or insights important to my life.

Then there *is* such a thing as stream-of-consciousness drawing. I use any round flat object (a coffee mug does fine) to scribe a rough, lightly penciled circle. Closing my eyes, I then "let" my hand do a graphic that intends to fill the circle. Focusing on the results, I look for any design composition hidden within that I can elaborate on, shade in, draw out—at least wonder about. It's a rough variation on a ancient and respected art form found in virtually every culture from medieval rose windows to eastern mandala painting.

Whether you find all this totally radical, or just what you've been looking for, is equally fine with me. Feel free to ignore, use or perfect this for your own path. Two things:

1. *Here I've shared my personal version of processes reported by great and respected thinkers and artists over the centuries.*
2. *Use of them can result in extreme redirection in one's life and career path.*

C. G. Jung—daddy of Myers-Briggs typology—worked with mandalas for the better part of his professional life. He attributed many of his wonderful breakthoughs in philosophy and psychiatry to having done so. As usual, my version is only a quick-and-dirty exercise, but still pays attention to—has me spend quality time with—that cerebral right hemisphere which the world keeps telling me to ignore.

Alan Watts observed that in order to have any meaningful intellectual life, one must be capable of emptying the mind—stopping the mind from all thinking—for at least 20 minutes a day. He was talking of meditation in which one "centers" and becomes acutely aware and receptive. I find that stream-of-consciousness writing and sketching can approximate the same thing, when I can get my left brain to shut the hell up. But it still takes commitment and about 30 minutes a day. So I set my clock early.

The reason to make, much less go through with, such a cockamamy commitment? It's the changes in conscious actions, in personal behaviors, energies and values, that take place over time subsequently and as a clearly attributable result. I know people who have made abrupt career changes as a result of journal keeping—in each case, to their betterment. There are countless cases of people curing artist's block, discovering hidden talent, redirecting their lives through the simple act of journal keeping.

Cameron has run workshops and counseling sessions for years that have helped people become creative or to rediscover their energy and ability to be so. Ira Progoff [*At a Journal Workshop* (Dialogue House Library, 1975)] spent years researching what famous people have had in common. The results led him to develop a journal-keeping method that has helped thousands be better able to succeed.

All of what's reported here are vastly simplified versions of eclectic gatherings from many sources—all of which I've personally tried over 20 years. These are merely sharings of practices I have found useful. Don't have any answers—still looking. All that's proposed is a place to start for developing your own best ways to return to your intuitive side greater voice and equity—ways to return to your work a better balance between synthesis and analysis—ways to return to your clients more design value for fee earned.

If, along the way, you happen to become remarkable (at least in the perceptual sense, and only by reason of still using one of those quaint sketchbooks) then even being remembered is at least a marketing edge. Lot of value in name recognition in this analytical and digitized world.

CAD literacy no longer gives you any appreciable edge in today's market. *Anybody* can do that, but sketch? Communicate quickly through diagrams? A picture is worth a thousand keystrokes.

ON THE USES OF HUMOR AND GRAPHICS

Part 1 of this book—Making Projects—seeks to equip you with extroverted ways to reach out to your market and serve clients better on terms right for you.

Part 2—Core Stuff—goes introverted, looks at tools and mind-set, not just in-house, but internal to you. Three reasons to focus the previous pages on your personal efficiency and right brain enablement:

- It can improve your capabilities in the design and practice of architecture.
- It can change your sense of personal joy and fulfillment in practicing this profession.
- It's what's most readily marketable.

The critically unique contribution that architects bring to built-environment projects—what's most easily perceived by our clients as being value-added—is our right brain, holistic, imaging vision and design. When asked why they hire us, architects' clients consistently have reported in AIA surveys over the years that the first, most obvious reason, is to have us design their projects. They then go on to list secondary reasons having to do with the architect's managing the people, technologies, and processes necessary for successful project implementation.

The clients for the majority of projects simply assume management is a given and not that extra something which prompts careful selection and hiring of an architect. So sure, first design—also management—but what kind of management? Management of what? I believe that, in a major way, they hire us to manage the vision and the envisioning process, to safeguard both from all the erosion that's inherent in the niggling details of expedient implementation of the project.

What's useful to consider about vision (as either a verb or noun) is the importance of *context* to the efficacy of that vision. As we found out the hard way through the Modern movement, you can draw an object in space, but you can't build one. Paul Laseau, Professor of Architecture, Ball State University, pointed out to me that the three important components of any architectural project are *needs*, *context*, and *form*. He contends that architects too often assume that needs and context are givens—that form is their only domain of action. Not so, he says—you needn't deal with only one—what you do with form can change the other two. I'd put it more strongly. You cannot *not* change the other two, and while clients may ostensibly hire us to mitigate their needs through designed form, they also require that we respond to and mediate the context.

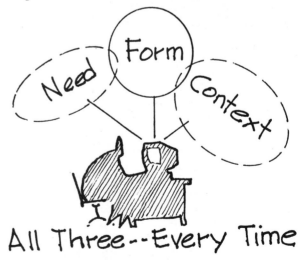

More to the present point, clients come to us—engage us—in order to engage *their own* context/visioning capabilities. After all, the findings (Myers-Briggs, Keirsey and Bates),[*] are that 80 percent of all managers are sensate/judging (SJ) in temperament—left brain people ensuring that the world they control is left brain dominated.

When it comes to acquiring work/living environments with 30- to 50-year life-cycles, however, they know they need help with the big picture. My findings—supported by those of Bill Ronco and Hugh Hochburg[†]—are that some 70 percent of architects are intuitives—big-picture people—right brain typologies.

For the last 25 years,[‡] split-brain research by eminent specialists has held that the right hemisphere of the brain, though nonverbal and nonsequential, is essential in creating art—in the act of design. Their findings are that the right hemisphere deals in analogs, images, holistic understandings. That the left hemisphere, dealing in words, numbers, and sequences, dominates our culture, our lives—, *and* its right-half silent partner. When you can't talk, it's hard to argue.

More recently—in perhaps the best work yet on the subject of brain hemisphere functioning—Robert Ornstein[§] summarizes it very clearly and somewhat differently:

In the end, the question of who's running the show seems to depend on which of the shows we mean. Clearly for the point-to-point links between entities, be it strict logical analysis, or a surgeon's touch, or a writer's hand movement, or the precise movements of the human tongue, it is the left side of the human brain that provides the lead. The right side takes the baton when the large elements of the world need to govern what to do. . . . It handles the components of the large view. . . . The right seems to provide the overall set or sets of alternatives from which to choose, the overall framework of the world, what's connected to what, what is possible here.

In essence, Ornstein is saying that the left hemisphere processes *text*, the right *context*.

---

[*]D. Keirsey and M. Bates, *Please Understand Me* (Prometheus Nemesis Book Company, 1978). Actually, the statistics are reported by Consultants Psychologists Press.
[†] Hochburg heads the Coxe Group, Seattle, WA. William C. Ronco heads Gathering Pace, a consulting firm in Bedford, MA. The three of us use Myers-Briggs typology in consulting and have occasionally confirmed our findings with each other.

[‡]Bogen, Sperry, Gazzaniga, et al. For perhaps the most popular exposition of this view see Betty Edwards, *Drawing on the Right Side of the Brain* (Putnam, 1989), p. 26.
[§]Robert Ornstein, *The Right Mind: Making Sense of the Hemispheres* (Harcourt Brace, 1997), p. 176.

Ornstein describes case studies of patients with right hemisphere brain damage being unable to get the punch lines of jokes,[*] since understanding humor involves abrupt shifts in one's sense of the context, of understanding multiple meanings of words or phrases, double entendres—right brain stuff.

Those findings shed fresh insight on our time-honored admonitions to preface business meetings, sales pitches, negotiations, and public speeches with a joke. Rather than telling the joke to impress people with your flair for humor, it's a matter of telling them something to activate *their* sense of context. Each of those personal interactions is best served when the participants have activated, and are prepared to use, that hemisphere of the brain which deals with context.

Along with form and needs, we architects are hired to manage context and the client's perceptiveness of it, their ability to access its nuances. Toward that end, many architects find humor a powerful tool. And the more relevant the joke is to actual project situations and our efforts to contend with them, the more effective it is. Moreover, jokes on ourselves send clear messages of full disclosure, hence trustworthiness. Brings to mind the old truism, *The reason angels can fly is that they take themselves so lightly.*

The other important tool for helping our clients engage their sense of context is our basic skill at sketching. Here, I'm talking about personal graphic skills of immediacy and power—the diagrams, doodles, and sketches that are second nature among designers—yet sheer magic to our clients.

---

* Ibid., p. 106.

Two overt reasons that impromptu graphic skills are so essential: The first is that they are compelling—it's almost impossible to not watch somebody sketching out ideas. Second, it activates our clients' right brain activity—gets them thinking contextually.

There's a third, covert reason: I believe immediate graphics send a very positive subliminal message. We all could draw until about the age of 6, when we began to be taught that graphic communication was childish, compared to dealing with words and numbers.

As adults, the subliminal message we communicate with quick graphics is that, by drawing, we are daring to be vulnerable—that we are being totally open and communicative with a childlike directness. Again, full disclosure, which implies trust on our part, and therefore trustworthiness.

After all, how many people are there to whom those clients would reveal themselves by impromptu sketching?

To most people, moreover, being able to talk and draw at the same time—much less upside down from across the desk—is a clear sign of incredible talent and intellect. This in no way denigrates the importance of technical drawings as the most efficient means to transmit certain data, but face it—anybody can buy AutoCAD or PowerPoint. The key, then, to successful reviews or presentations of pre-prepared graphic materials, I believe, is to use hard copies and energetically annotate them on the spot with a graphic record of comments, questions, suggested alternatives, and proposed changes.

Quick graphics and notes can be the ultimate feedback. When what people say warrants being made a poster—or scrawled on a finished presentation board—they understand they've been understood—the first step toward consensus.

So draw fast (rather than well). Use rapid pictograms, bubble and adjacency diagrams, traffic signals, clouds around notes, arrows, boxes, flags, check marks, doodles—anything that's relevant. When you can do this and all the while be giving feedback, asking the open-ended questions, reflecting on the current situation with humor, and deferring judgment till your graphics prove that everyone understands clearly what's been said—that's interpersonal skill!

When you note their comments all over a presentation drawing they'll know they're important to you.

When you can draw, letter up side down, and discuss the project-- all at the same time-- they'll know you're brilliant.

If they see you've lettered what they said in bold felt-tip they won't need to say it a third time.

Remember this is no art contest--just draw to communicate as fast as possible. The epitome is fast rough sketching while commenting on the humor in it all.

CHAPTER 9: INTERPERSONAL SKILLS FOR

This chapter is about skills. I sandwich them here in the middle of the book because they are central to effectively doing all the rest of what's covered. They may not be the first things you need to know about all those practice areas or activities listed in the illustration, but success in any of them largely depends on using good interpersonal skills.

THE CORE SKILLS

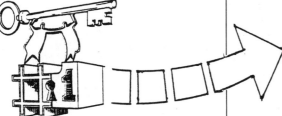

Like all skills, interpersonal ones need direct transmission—training rather than education. Yes, there is some theory—a body of knowledge on which to base effective use of these skills. And in typical western, cause and-effect style, what's offered here starts with that—which makes for complications. William Buckley once wrote verbal instructions for playing "Chopsticks" on the piano to illustrate the complexity of talking about simple skills. About as much fun to read as a computer manual.

You could go at it the other way, since it's arguably a Zen sort of thing. Just get in the habit of using good skills until enlightenment eventually comes. If you're convinced of the need for interpersonal skills and committed to improving yours, you might skip to page 2.59, titled Skill Set: One-on-One. If you want to know how it works and why it's important, stick with me.

All I'm saying is that like most other skills these are best learned by doing. They are easier done than said—yet require constant practice till they become second nature—habits we consistently use. Having them doesn't guarantee we'll win, but not having (or not using) them often means we won't.

MARKETING
NEGOTIATION
EFFECTIVE MEETINGS
MANAGING RISKS
LEADING PROJECT TEAMS
REDUCING REWORK

BEHAVIORS
SKILLS
AWARENESS
UNDERSTANDING
KNOWLEDGE BASE

So why the hard concern about all these "soft skills"? What's the big deal?

If you factor in the increasing number of stakeholders at the table in today's projects, then the opportunity for conflict and poor personal interaction goes up exponentially. Project managers on big projects report their primary design challenge is devising a way for all those people—each with a different vested interest—to make reasonable decisions in a timely fashion.

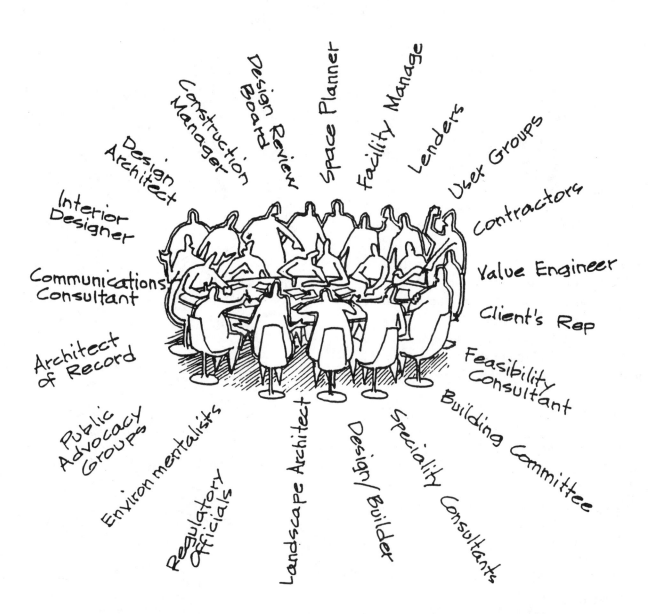

But the need for—and value placed on—good interpersonal skills goes up exponentially, as well.

Nor is technology the answer. When every stakeholder in the project has the same software—and therefore access to the same information—that you have, takes a lot of good interpersonal skill to justify your presence, much less lead them to discover the difference between architecture and just building. Not only that, as Henry C. Beck III recently said, "All this wonderful technology gives me the ability to be misunderstood *a lot faster*.

In fact, it's precisely because of information technology that there is a higher demand for good interpersonal skills than ever before in history.

WIIFM *

POP QUIZ

1. Estimate what percentage of your work time, on average, is spent interacting with other people.

2. Estimate what percentage of *that* time is value-free. It doesn't help the project at all, but it's necessary in order to avoid or fix misunderstandings, to defend yourself, or for blame storming. Or it's those weekly meetings with the same agenda issues that never get resolved. Whatever. Take a guess.

3. Now multiply those two percentages together and the product of that times the 50 hours a week you work on average times 50 weeks per year times your hourly billing rate.

The average, among architects I've asked, comes out something like this:

$$60\% \times 20\% \times 50 \times 50 \times \$95.00 = \$28,500$$

Amazing, isn't it? There's a lot at stake in improving these skills you invest so much of yourself in using.

My modest goal for your improvement is that by practicing what's here, you decrease your value-free interactive time by merely 10 percent and improve your profit by some $3000 this year.

And the only way to improve any skill is through mindful practice. Lots of it and on a regular basis. As an analogy, consider golf pro champions. They spend countless hours perfecting skills to hit the little white ball a few extra yards in the right direction. A matter of simple skills and a certain mindtrip. Mastery—mental as well as athletic—takes lots of practice.

Problem here is, it's not inanimate objects you're dealing with, it's people—all with their individual head trips going into the game. The lie of a golf ball is child's play, by comparison. Nice thing is, practicing the skills you need here requires no clubs, carts, courses, or afternoons off. You can work constantly with only the original equipment we each were issued. You can continuously hone and perfect your skills on staff, bosses, spouses, children, even lesser mortals.

Best of all, like design, you never really master these skills. Finding joy in the practice is the ultimate goal—again, it's a Zen sort of thing. When practice becomes its own reward is when you're really on the road to mastery.

That's when you're ready for the hard stuff, with interactive skills to use whether the going is smooth or rough. Showing good form even when they don't want to play the game—when they're resistant, or cynical—when the competition is tough. It's then the soft skills get so hard—and so essential.

SKILLS involve learning by doing

Lots of practice--

Using the best tools at hand--

supported by consistent and good technique-- a sound knowledge base

---

*Rather than being a descriptive term for a golf stroke, WIIFM is a business acronym for "What's in It for Me."

THEORY

Basic principle: The mind-set with which we approach dealing with people tends to become a self-fulfilling prophecy. We go into meetings or negotiations with mental and emotional baggage about how tough this is going to be—so it is. Or we decide we will get a lot out of talking with this person—so we do.

There's been a lot said here already about mind-set—your basic intentions and attitudes essential for success in marketing/negotiation. Just as with Olympic stars, it takes *knowing* you're gonna go out there and do your best that makes it possible.

This next part—about how our minds work—will start out sounding like a detour into design theory. But the architect in me believes that everything relates to design and vice versa. Bear with me.

MIT philosopher Donald A. Schon is known for his seminal research on what happens in an architect's mind while designing (*The Reflective Practitioner*, Basic Books, 1983). Schon says that design (*like interpersonal skills*) may be something that can be learned but not taught, and that the design process starts with *experiential* imaging.

He says we develop an experiential image of how great the project is going to be, then learn from the project itself as we're designing—that we enter the virtual world of the project sketches while we're making them. When our experience of that virtual reality matches the excellence of the experiential image we had before we started sketching, then we know we're getting there.

Personal interactions can become the same sort of creative process.

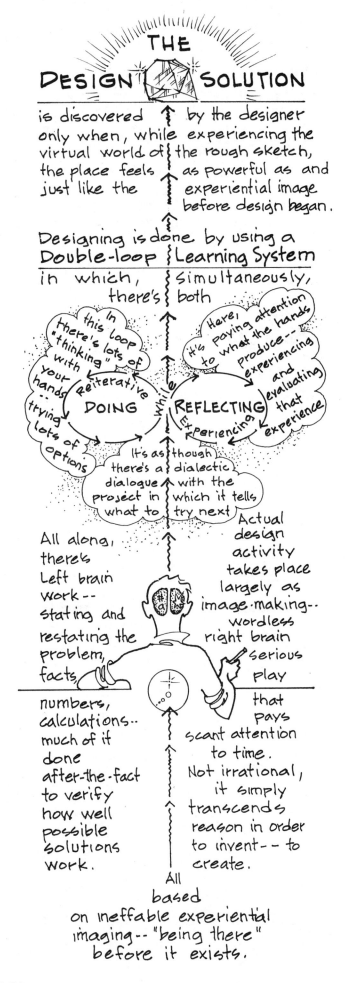

In these days of information overload there's more coming at you than you can deal with.

In response, you tend to screen out all except two kinds of data:

① What matches or confirms your inner truth. (See! I was right!)

② What denies or threatens your inner truth. (Whoa! No way..... gotta change that!)

The rest we tend to ignore.

THE WORLD Out There #Data #Words #Diffs

PERCEIVES
SORTS
DECODES
DRAWS ANALOGIES
EVALUATES
DECIDES

THE CONSCIOUS MIND

THE SUBCONSCIOUS tends to lots of things you don't consciously think about (like adjusting heart rate or breathing). It also contains your inner "truth"--an operative "computer software."

Your subconscious only operates in the present tense. (You never dream in past or future tense.)

It can be reprogrammed with new positive inner operative truths.

When reality doesn't match your inner truth, your **creative subconscious** goes to work in highly inventive ways to change reality.

Well, they can't all be great projects, or meetings, or negotiations, nor am I suggesting you approach every one with ebullient optimism. There are ways to reprogram your subconscious for better performance, however—realistic ways to use experiential imaging for benefit to you, the client, and the project every time.

Lou Tice, of the Pacific Institute in Seattle, describes the same phenomenon as Schon, but in different terms and not about architecture. He calls the experiential image a present-tense, subconscious *truth*. Rather than the absolute TRUTH, this is a lowercase, operative truth. We all have one as the basis of who we feel we really are, what's acceptable to us, and how we behave. Tice says that when reality—what's happening out there—doesn't match our inner truth, a cognitive dissonance is set up. Our creative subconscious (there it is—design talent!) kicks in to change reality to what we *know* it should be. We become wonderfully creative in making the outside world meet our expectations.

Point of all this is that we can experientially image—reprogram our subconscious inner truth to include three operative principles:

- That the operative truth of everyone we deal with (however weird to us) is valid to them and very valuable to us to know.

- That no one gets up in the morning vowing to make this the worst project ever—they all aspire to be the best at whatever they do, and getting a good project contributes to that, at least according to their inner truth.

- That our best interests are served by using our skills to help them achieve their aspirations.

It's important to note that *aspirations* (in negotiation they're called *interests*) are usually mutually acceptable, but seldom shared. They're very different from *expectations* (in negotiation jargon, *positions*), which are often mutually exclusive and stated right up front.

We know (at least those of us who are or have been married) that the only person you can change is yourself. When effectively used, straight talk and active listening—the communication skills covered on the following pages—can influence others for positive change. But to be effective, these skills must become habitual behaviors.

It's very hard to change your behaviors (much less those of another) by sheer willpower. Which is why weight control businesses are so lucrative—they mostly rely on willpower which guarantees lots of repeat customers. Far easier to modify your behavior by reprogramming the subconscious through imaging.

Lou Tice teaches that when you want to change ineffective behaviors, or problematic situations, create self-affirmations. Describe what things are like, now that the problem no longer exists, and image the enjoyment of that virtual reality until it's your operative truth. He carries these descriptions with him, written on 3 by 5 cards, and frequently reviews them, plays them like commercials to himself. These positive personal affirmations, over time, become reality.

Though vast and complex, the subconscious is most effectively influenced by your conscious mind in somewhat the same ways you use to communicate with a small child. For instance:

- Keep the message in the present tense, since the subconscious only functions in the *now*. Your dreams (subconsciousness speaking to you) are never in past or future tense.
- Give it lots of positive reinforcement but remember the subconscious doesn't differentiate between positive and negative reinforcement. Lots better to tell Little Johnny *We always play in our own yard* rather than *Don't play in the street*. Johnny wasn't even thinking about the street till you mentioned it.

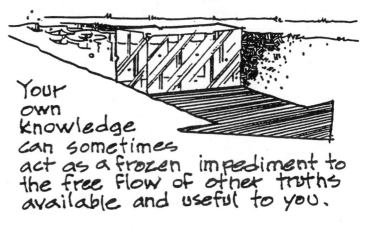

THERE ARE MANY TRUTHS
Perhaps none of them absolute.

Your own knowledge can sometimes act as a frozen impediment to the free flow of other truths available and useful to you.

EXPERIENTIAL IMAGING

The first key to good interpersonal skills, then, is managing your own mind-set—your inner truths and aspirations—through experiential imaging, so that you can:

- Not only acknowledge, but accept that their inner, operative truth is very different from yours. Knowing that their expectations and quantifiable objectives are all outward clues to perceived best interests, you can work to affirm and make those inner aspirations explicit.

- Be aware of—and responsive to—not only what's being said, but also what's happening in the interaction while it's happening— second attention, body language, behaviors, etc. Don't hesitate to openly discuss and improve process as well as content.

Use good communication skills to help them disclose—and to confirm that you understand—the interests and aspirations that are the underlying basis for their stated positions and expectations. Listen actively to what they say they want, so that you can help facilitate joint discovery of what they really need.

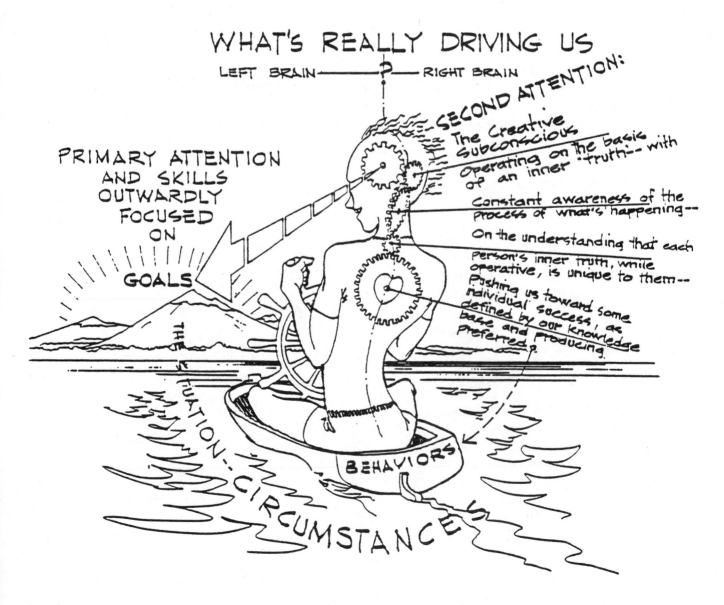

INFLUENCING OTHERS*

ENERGY	STYLE	BEHAVIOR
PUSHING →	**PERSUADING** X+Y=Z →	**PROPOSING:** Ideas, suggestions, recommendations, questions suggesting proposals **REASONING:** Facts and logic in support or opposition, argument for or against, rhetorical questions
	ASSERTING	**STATING EXPECTATIONS:** Needs, demands, standards, prescriptions **EVALUATING:** Positive or negative judgment, personal and intuitive **USING INCENTIVES/PRESSURES:** specifying ways and means under your control to damage or help the other
PULLING ←	**BRIDGING**	**INVOLVING:** Soliciting views, information and ideas from others. Encouraging input. **LISTENING:** Paraphrasing, summarizing, reflecting other's feelings, giving feedback. **DISCLOSING:** Revealing interests, feelings, uncertainties, making yourself vulnerable, asking for help.
	ATTRACTING	**FINDING COMMON GROUND:** Pointing out common values, beliefs, aspirations, synergy. **VISIONING:** Viewing future with optimism, picturing ideal outcome using positive images, metaphor or analogy using emotional words.
MOVING AWAY ↓	**DISENGAGING**	**POSTPONING:** To a future time **PROCESSING:** Standing back to review what's happening -- methods, procedures **CHANGING THE SUBJECT:** Including the use of humor to defuse tension **TAKING A BREAK**
	AVOIDING	**AVOIDING:** Backing down, dismissing real differences; discarding objectives withdrawing from the situation

* This from Boyce Appel, Appd Associates, who puts on a great professional development workshop several times each year where you learn to use all this. They're headquartered in Atlanta.

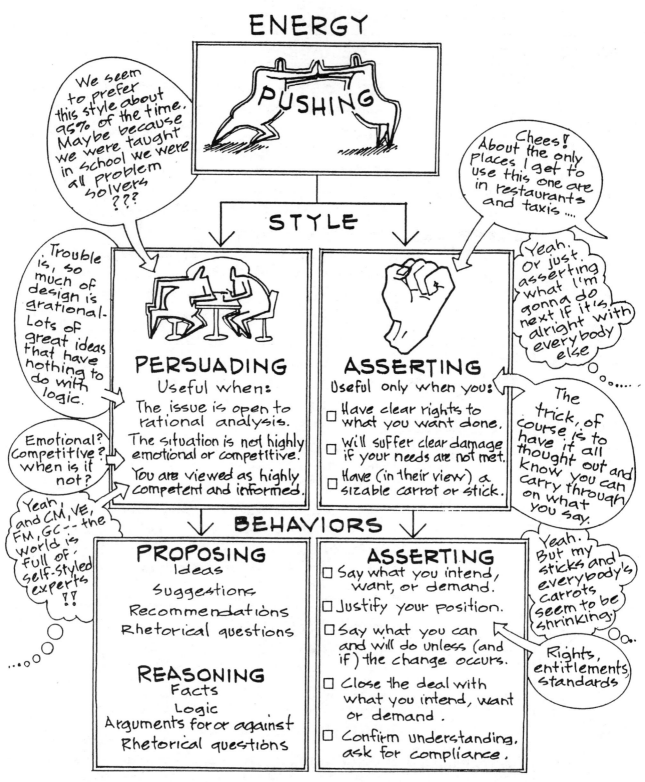

These pages of charts—each presenting energies, then styles, then behaviors—comprise most of my theoretical knowledge base about how to influence others. Three energies, six styles, fifteen behaviors—that's what you've got to work with.

It comes from Boyce Appel in Atlanta, who puts on workshops where you practice the skills (behaviors) in role-play exercises in front of an (ugh) camcorder and then are forced to watch yourself on TV. The first thing you learn from it is that you bore the hell out of yourself because you spend 95 percent of your time using pushing energies. Which might be fine if you were a mathematician or lawyer.

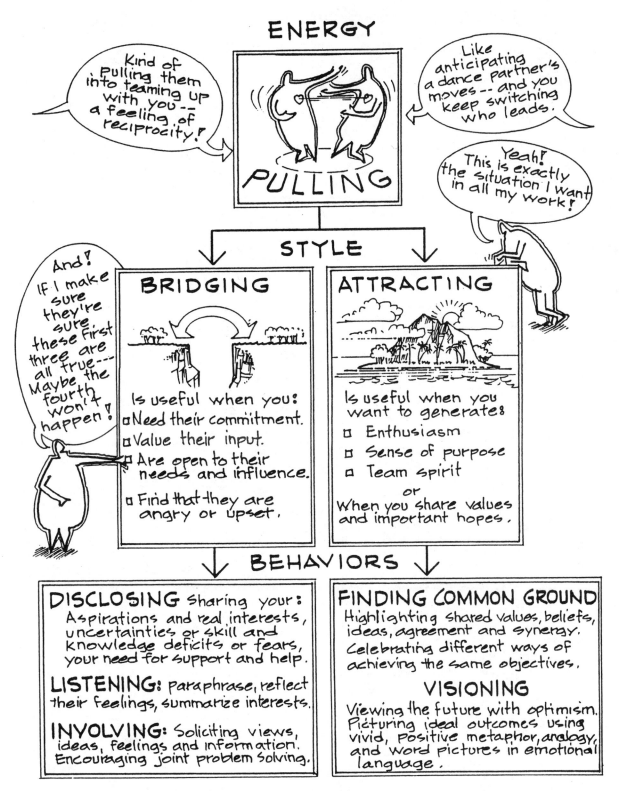

Old adage: *Maturity is nothing more than increasing your repertoire of available behaviors.* Except for *maturity*, read here *success*. Each of the 13 behaviors is clearly appropriate in certain situations. Problem is, how do you know when to use what and remember to even think about all this in the midst of a project meeting? Answer is, be aware of what's going on while it's happening. The clue is experiential—which of the three energies are you *feeling* at the moment in any given interaction? Requires a lot of focus and on-top-of-it awareness. If you're feeling pushed, chances are they are also, since we tend to mirror each other's behaviors. Voila! Change the game—switch to the pulling style—now which behavior shall I use?—etc., etc.

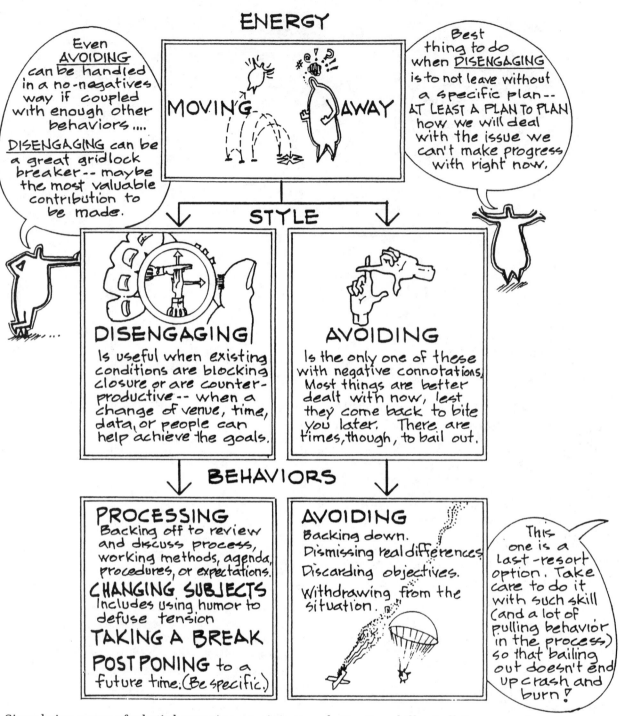

Since being aware of what's happening *now* is a second attention skill-set all its own, you can only learn by doing it, and the hardest part is reminding yourself to do so. I don't know what more to say to you here than to let you know it's available to any of us and incredibly useful.

One thing I've found helpful is trying it all out premeditatedly in situations where there's not a lot at stake. I know it sounds calculated and manipulative, but you really can do a lot to hone your skills by using them to interact with desk clerks and waiters. The other option: Burnish your *pulling* behaviors; commit to using them excessively, and note the positive reinforcement you get as a result. Steep odds are that you've been *pushing* all along like the rest of us.

Good luck, and if you figure a way to polish your skills at using all this stuff without the humiliation of watching yourself on TV, please let me know.

SKILL SET: ONE-ON-ONE

Finally. We've come to the actual skills, which are really very simple—at least to describe. Mostly just listening, and talking—same communication skills you've been using forever. Actually, for architects, it's listening, talking, writing, and drawing. But the greatest of these is listening.

Question is, how much do you choose to hone the effectiveness of your skills? With time, attention (and the accepting mind-set we just talked about), you can carry them to incredible levels. Top counselors, trial lawyers, theologians—all these are professionals who live well by the use of verbal communication.

Every school of theology requires students to learn to use *I statements* as part of a professional obligation to "Do No Harm." Putting your sentences in the first person singular allows you to say almost anything with the least possible offense to the listener.

The simple habit of starting your sentences with "I" instead of "You" instantly avoids a lot of judging and solution sending. Architects seem especially prone to these primary roadblocks to communication because we've all been taught we were to be professional problem solvers.

We each successfully survived the jury system and were taught to take pride in critical thinking. Many of us behave as though, being certified project problem solvers, we're now entitled. As architects, it should be just a matter of clearly articulating our criticisms, judgments, and solutions for them to be immediately accepted and acted upon. Right? Wrong! It's not what I say so much as how I say it. One easy way to think of this is to remember the design crits of your past. We all have vivid memories of the best and worst crits we've gotten. In architects' jargon, the difference between crit and criticism is often a fine line between help and hurt.

Of course, using the first person singular isn't all there is to it. To say, "I think that's a dumb design" is more a personal attack

STRAIGHT TALK

We each can only speak for ourselves. For example, straight talk works best for me when I:

1. **SAY WHAT I SEE & HEAR:**
"What I hear us saying is...."
"What I see happening here is...."
Just state facts and verify as appropriate:
"Did I misunderstand?"
"Have I got that right?"

2. **SAY WHAT I THINK:**
"So that makes me think...."
"Which indicates to me...."

3. **SAY HOW I FEEL:**
"And that excites me because...."
"I fear that others will...."

4. **SAY WHAT I WANT:**
"For me to be effective in this, I'll need...."
"I will fully support this, provided...."
"By next Friday, we'll have to have..."

DESCRIBE MY ACTIONS AND INTENTIONS:

Past: "I couldn't come by so I e-mailed...."
Present: "Let's go over it again now, so...."
Future: "As soon as they respond, I will...."

than it is an *I statement*. Real effectiveness demands being truly open to the other's operative view of things, making sure we understand—*and that they feel understood*—before giving the crit. Skillful preachers, priests, rabbis, and counselors are adept at *I statements*. The good ones report facts—often the fact that they have perceived something in a certain way. They then report what those perceptions lead them to think, how that thought makes them feel.

Given time, skillful counselors are stopping all along the way to confirm your understanding *that you've been understood* as they go. Only then do they say what they want, expect, or advise. The gifted ones also take pains to affirm you as a person—and your validity as a person—at least at the beginning and at the end. We can learn a lot from those professions.

ACTIVE LISTENING

For this one, let's learn from police interrogators and trial lawyers. Questions are to those guys like drills are to dentists. They use them to get down to the rotten stuff. The objective in their work is to learn everything they can about the facts, and your position or intentions regarding those facts, before revealing their own.

They're in a tough, competitive, win-lose business; I don't envy them. But if you remove the competition—the goal-oriented, manipulative part—you can use the same skills for mutual discovery, joint problem solving, and facilitation. Do no harm.

The key is to be sure everybody gets heard and keeps talking openly til everything is out on the table. With no hidden agendas or relevant data overlooked, you can work creatively together on the problem. That means others have to be convinced that you have no hidden agenda, no ulterior motive.

You wouldn't want to be mistaken for a lawyer! A good way to avoid that is to disclose, openly and up front, your own interests—what you really need in terms of outcomes from the discussion. Tell them what you hope to accomplish by listening.

Then really listen. Notice I didn't say *just listen*—that would indicate that it's easy and it's not. Listening is a highly valuable, difficult, and energetic skill. Which is why shrinks and trial lawyers get paid so much. And why we call this listening active.

ACTIVE LISTENING

(Check their body language)

(And check your own)

① OBSERVE: Watch, as well as listen, for what they:
- ☐ THINK
- ☐ FEEL
- ☐ INTEND
- ☐ DO

② ACKNOWLEDGE: Paraphrase-- play back in your own words what they just said, with a question mark at the end.

NO JUDGMENT OR PROBLEM SOLVING TIL THEY ACKNOWLEDGE THAT YOU'VE FULLY UNDERSTOOD WHAT THEY'VE SAID.

③ ENCOURAGE: "Tell me about it." "Wow. So?" "And then?"

④ CHECK YOUR UNDERSTANDING WITH OPEN-ENDED QUESTIONS: Questions starting with <u>Who</u>, <u>What</u>, <u>When</u>, <u>Where</u>, <u>Why</u>, or <u>How</u> can't be answered yes or no. Keep them talking.

⑤ INTERPRET: Ask yourself what they left out about thoughts, feelings, intent, actions. Fill in the blanks for them out loud, watching, listening, or asking for verification you're right.

The rule is that, while listening, you not judge or problem solve—again, the hardest part for architects, since we've been professionally brought up to do both incessantly. Instead, keep giving feedback. Just tell them what you are hearing. When you can, give them a summary of what you've heard. You can say what that makes you assume—the thoughts, feelings, even conclusions, that would have come to you, were you in their place.

How to do it? For clarity, what follows is broken into parts—again, a sequence. But it's important to remember that earlier stack of five links and add this lot to it—just another part of that jumble of things good facilitators do holistically, consistently, and by second attention.

1. **Use good body language** and constantly read theirs. Research shows that some 90 percent of the message transmitted in a conversation is not in the content of the words used. Rather, it's in the expression, tone of voice, speed of delivery, posture, eye contact, gestures—all. those nonverbal ways we communicate.

The message you want to send is one of being sincerely interested in, and *open to*, their input. Nothing is more insulting than to have someone mechanically use all the right skills on you while their first attention is obviously somewhere else.

The real trick of good nonverbal communication is not to be tricky. It's that matter of mind-set, again. Given a genuine and lively curiosity about the issue or the other person, your body will handle its own language, if you'll relax enough to let it. You have to *be present* to win, using the skills *with*, not *on* people. Let the message generate the mechanics, not the reverse.

LISTENING SKILLS

ATTENDING SKILLS
A posture of involvement
Appropriate body language
Eye contact
No distractions

FOLLOWING SKILLS
Door openers
("Want to talk about it?")
Minimal encouragements
("Un huh .... Sure .... Oh?")
Infrequent questions
("So then? .... And?")
Attentive silence.

REFLECTNG SKILLS

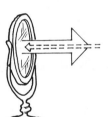

Paraphrasing
("So you're really saying ....")
Reflecting feelings
("Which suggests you feel ....")
Tying feelings to content
("And the frustration pushes you to ....)
Summation reflections
("So in a nutshell, what happened that Tuesday is going to cause ....)

TWO KEYS TO ACTIVE LISTENING:
→ No Judging
→ No Problem Solving
(That comes later.)

Lean toward them a bit—don't slouch a message of retreat, defensiveness, or apathy with your posture, crossed legs, or twiddling thumbs. Don't signal you're:

Defending your space (folded arms)
Frustrated or mad (rubbing your neck)
Somewhere else (jingling your change)
Lying or bored (avoiding their gaze)

If someone continues to dominate a discussion I may smile broadly, invade their space a bit, paraphrase their litany to make sure I've got it right—then ask what they want me (or us) to do—where we're headed with all this.

Open your eyes, smile, and maintain eye contact without staring fixedly. Normal blinking signals thoughtful attention. They'll be watching your face and eyes—we all do that.

Provided it's not an affectation, you can use squints, eyebrow raises, smiles, jaw-drops, winks, nods, and eye movements to signal your responses to their messages. Almost nothing is too hokey, so long as it's sincere. Disney didn't make it on drawing mice—the secret was animation.

Use inclusive, open-handed gestures. We all know how to read neck-rubbing, clasped hands, thumb twiddling, pocketed change jingling, and pointed fingers jabbing at us. The worst one that architects use is seemingly being unable to talk without brandishing sharp implements at people—pencils, our weapons of choice!

IT'S FAR LESS WHAT YOU SAY....

Posture, Expression, Tone of voice, Gestures, Speed of delivery, Eye contact

THAN HOW YOU SAY IT.

2. **Avoid nonsequiturs**—those questions or answers that stop further discussion or action. Nonsequiturs can be positive as well as negative. *Yes* ends the discussion just as effectively as *No* or *Whatever.* Worst design crit I ever got was *That's great! You got it!* Having achieved perfection leaves you no place to go—any statement of judgment invites closure. If you want to keep them talking, simply report what you see, hear, are experiencing, or perceiving. No solution or decision implied. Our best decisions are made jointly and *after*, not while, actively listening.

3. **Use open-ended questions.** Every aspiring lawyer is taught to ask questions that can't be answered *yes* or *no*. The easy rule: Any question that starts with *who, what, when, where, why*, and *how* is open-ended.

To answer open-ended questions, people only have four options. They can:

- Make a declarative statement.
- Hide behind a return question.
- Say they don't choose to answer.
- Confess they don't know the answer.

Their choice among these four provides useful information in itself. So keep them talking, focusing your primary attention on what they're saying. But all the while, be mentally phrasing that next open-ended question that really needs an answer. Not only that, a part of your second attention needs to be tending to your nonverbal signals and reading theirs.

4. **Paraphrase.** Just repeat what they said using your own words with a question mark at the end. Or request confirmation—*Have I got it right?* Paraphrasing is very flattering— shows you're really working at clearly understanding their full meaning explicitly.

5. **Parroting.** If all else fails, you've always got the court witness trick (taught to them by their lawyers) of simply repeating back the last three words said to you and ending it with a question mark. You might use parroting when what they've said is complicated, aggressive, or rambling. Actually, I prefer to apologize for being slow and ask they try me again. *Can you say that a different way? I don't think I follow.*

Police interrogators use parroting constantly to get alleged perpetrators to incriminate themselves. Which shows how nearly irresistible our urge is to "straighten people out." *Dummy can't understand plain English. Read my lips, Fuzz.*

Here endeth the lesson customarily given on communication skills. However, I contend there is yet another at which all architects are proficient. Graphics are consistently used in our profession for basic communication. Skills at sketching and diagramming are so ubiquitous among us as to be assumed negligible. Pure second attention stuff. We all can sketch two-dimensional indications of three-dimensional objects. No big deal.

Yet graphic skill is a riveting attention getter. You can't not watch it, and the more rapidly and poorly you draw, the more the observers are sucked into participation—*What's that going to be? What should I make of this? Oooh, added another squiggle! To draw in public!*

FOR DRAWING OUT LOUD!

It's something we all did till school forced us to conform and put away childish things like crayons. The subliminal message now is, that by drawing, we are daring to be vulnerable— that we are being totally open and communicative with a childlike directness.

Implies trust on our part, therefore trustworthiness. After all, how many people are there to whom those clients would reveal themselves by drawing? To most people, moreover, being able to talk and draw at the same time—much less upside down from across their desk—is a clear sign of incredible talent and intellect.

Graphics with quick notes can be the ultimate feedback. When what they've said warrants being made a poster, they understand they've been understood—the first step toward consensus.

So draw fast (rather than well). Use rapid pictograms, bubbles, adjacency diagrams, traffic signals, clouds around notes, arrows, boxes, flags, check marks, doodles—anything that's even halfway relevant. All the while giving them feedback or asking the open-ended questions.

If you're jotting down headings for categories of information needed, how can they refuse to help fill in the blanks? If you then note—better yet, diagram—their answers, how can they possibly not have been understood?

From what's in these pages, you'll have already picked up on my having a second attention repertoire of pictograms that I draw without thinking. Signs of a misspent youth—by now they're a shorthand way I illustrate or summarize ideas, thoughts, and conclusions.

I've used them countless times in discussions and seminars without any one ever stumbling over the meaning. Whereas San Francisco's David Sibbett (he teaches this stuff) or Ken Bussard, FAIA (Renaissance Design Group, Des Moines), uses different pictograms for the same meanings, no one stumbles over theirs, either. For that matter, maybe we all got them from architects like Bill Caudill and the early CRS bunch. The list of architects who use diagrams to communicate is constantly growing. Keeps on like this, you may find yourself with a credibility gap if you don't sketch upside down graphics in meetings!

INTERPERSONAL SKILLS

ACTIVE LISTENING

Check their body language

And check your own

① **OBSERVE:** Watch, as well as listen, for what they:
- ☐ THINK
- ☐ FEEL
- ☐ INTEND
- ☐ DO

② **ACKNOWLEDGE:**
Paraphrase-- play back in your own words what they just said, with a question mark at the end.

NO JUDGMENT OR PROBLEM SOLVING TIL THEY ACKNOWLEDGE THAT YOU'VE FULLY UNDERSTOOD WHAT THEY'VE SAID.

③ **ENCOURAGE:** "Tell me about it."
"Wow. So?"
"And then?"

④ **CHECK YOUR UNDERSTANDING WITH OPEN-ENDED QUESTIONS:**
Questions starting with Who, What, When, Where, Why, or How can't be answered yes or no. Keep them talking.

⑤ **INTERPRET:** Ask yourself what they left out about thoughts, feelings, intent, actions. Fill in the blanks for them out loud, watching, listening, or asking for verification you're right.

STRAIGHT TALK

We each can only speak for ourselves. For example, straight talk works best for me when I:

① **SAY WHAT I SEE & HEAR:**
"What I hear us saying is ...."
"What I see happening here is ...."
Just state facts and verify as appropriate:
"Did I misunderstand?"
"Have I got that right?"

② **SAY WHAT I THINK:**
"So that makes me think."...
"Which indicates to me...."

③ **SAY HOW I FEEL:**
"And that excites me because...."
"I fear that others will ...."

④ **SAY WHAT I WANT:**
"For me to be effective in this, I'll need...."
"I will fully support this, provided...."
"By next Friday, we'll have to have..."

DESCRIBE MY ACTIONS AND INTENTIONS:
Past: "I couldn't come by so I e-mailed...."
Present: "Let's go over it again now, so...."
Future: "As soon as they respond, I will."...

DRAW

CHAPTER 10: GROUPWORK

Used to be, architects had individual clients, but that rarely happens these days. Now, most projects seem to have a cast of thousands. Project meetings and design reviews with multiple special interests in contention get more frequent and larger. So much of our time is spent in meetings now, that making them useful, productive, and efficient is essential to all of us. Making them effective, creative, and enjoyable is the stuff of facilitation and you can add enormous value to the services you provide by facilitating—making meetings easier. It involves little more than learning a few simple tips about meetings to go along with the interpersonal skills we just covered in previous pages.

But those interpersonal skills were all one-on-one, you say, *and here we're talking groupwork.* My point exactly. As Lyndon Johnson said about politics, *It's all retail.* To do well at groupwork takes a lot of mindful practice til you can use the basic skills effectively with several people simultaneously. And do so while maintaining a heads-up peripheral awareness—a second attention analysis—of the interactions in play within a group dynamic as they're happening. Ideally, your virtuosity with the entire repertoire of interpersonal skills will have every other member of the group feeling you're taking a special and personal interest in them. And they'll be right.

In terms of the group getting things done, however, the best interpersonal dynamic between you and each of them might be beside the point if the other participants in the meeting can't interact well with each other. When that happens, and provided you've got the skills and inclination, you can find yourself being the interpreter or interventionist, playing back to all of them your paraphrasing of what each of them is saying. Notice that none of this scenario is predicated on your having a given position in the group—leader, member, boss, participant, chair, consultant, visitor—titles make amazingly little difference, given the right skills. Before you know it you're a facilitator.

Groupwork—how to facilitate meetings—is included in this manual for several reasons:
- Most projects of any size these days require weekly project team meetings. With so many people all now claiming a voice in project review and approval, and so many committees to work with, facilitation skills are at the core of transformative practice.

- Beyond use on specific projects there are incredible opportunities to serve community, school, club, AIA, church or temple through facilitative abilities—and at the same time enhance your market position enormously. Obviously, it can also lead to diversification into a practice of urban design, programming, community planning, etc.

- Numbers of architects have asked me how to facilitate, since from time to time I make a living doing it. While I'm unaware of any rules for facilitation, in these pages I simply give you thoughts and tips on how it happens to work best for me, in hopes you'll develop your own best ways to improve your meetings, diversify your practice, add value to clients and projects.

One final thought on approaching facilitation. There is great personal power to be had through facilitating. If control is something you're into, I say that's fine, cut to the bottom line and go into politics now. Otherwise remember the old adage, *There's almost no limit to what you can accomplish, provided you don't need to take credit for it.*

THE FACILITATOR'S ROLE

MANY HATS

DISCLOSING

TRANSPARENT

NONJUDGING

AFFIRMING

ENTHUSIASTIC

PROCESS ORIENTED

PROTECTIVE

Process, not content: Rule is, you can't be a facilitator and a participant simultaneously. Secret is: True facilitation requires you have *no* vested interest, beyond a deeply felt commitment to the continued well-being of every participant. You have to go into the meeting with *absolute* faith that they'll know the best answer to the problem, provided you bring them the best process for their discovering it. This may well be the most important thing I can tell you about the facilitation trade.

Be transparent: In project meetings, of course, you have compelling interests at stake. Best thing to do is be open—utterly transparent—about those areas where you feel that way. Where you have authority and intend to use it, they need to know in advance. Where the transactional power resides with them, acknowledge that also, along with your need to influence their use of it. Having your own agenda is fine, so long as it's explicit—nothing hidden.

In my work as an independent facilitator, I generally tell them up front that I'm there for process, not content, that where I need to break that rule I'll warn them by literally changing hats. I put on my baseball cap: *OK, I'm changing hats now. Gotta tell you what I really think.*

Keep them safe: The next role important to facilitation is that of keeping participants safe from one another. In extreme cases this involves getting in an aggressor's face—literally. When they become overbearing and dominating I invade their personal physical space, pleasantly and nonjudgmentally asking exactly what they want me to write next on the flipchart—what it is they want the group to do. I write whatever they say and return it to the group to deal with in subgroup work, dot-polls, or to be deferred to a future time by shifting it to a "to-do" chart for future meetings—whatever seems appropriate to the group.

Keep it focused: I use the same interventionist tactic as needed to keep us focused on meeting objectives. When a digression strays us out of our flight plan it goes on the to-do list. The flipchart record of it stays posted, however, to assure the digressor that what he or she needed to say has been heard and duly noted. It's good form to return to that list at meeting's end to assure that issues perceived to be urgent won't be ignored forever. Or to let the group decide it really doesn't want to deal with them at all. Or to plan to plan a response and when.

Keep it in context and keep it up: And finally, the facilitator's role is not only to manage the immediate physical and psychological context but to keep the participants mindful of the larger context—working with the big picture. If wordsmithing is required, either flipchart it yourself and propose it, or break people into three-to five-person subgroups with a short-fuse deadline for plenary report-backs. Keep the meeting as fast-paced and context-oriented as possible.

MEETING PREPARATION

Lots of rules around for holding successful meetings. Good stuff to read, and if they fit the groups you work with, fine. I've never found any rules that work consistently since, for me, planning and preparing for a meeting is a design problem. Like architecture projects, meetings are one-off events, each different from the rest.

Even a weekly management meeting routinely involving the same people will always be impacted by the constantly changing context within which the organization operates. Then there are the variations in personal pressures for each of the participants at work and home, the residue of new interactions and events since last week—all that and more. The Taoist saying is that you can never step in the same stream twice. If it's important enough to call a meeting about, it's worth designing the meeting to accomplish it well. Here are the categories of things I tend to do to set meetings up to succeed.

The meeting notice—if one is needed—ought to briefly cover the who, what, when, where, why, and how or how much—but be written like a cross between an invitation, a demand, and an advertisement. I do not distribute a premeeting agenda. For me, a standard meeting agenda distributed in advance is more than a missed opportunity for teamwork. It's a clear signal to beware constricting coils of encroaching bureaucracy. It means I'll have to search outside the meeting for the true reason it was called and the meaning behind what went on there—-the real power and structure that runs this place,

To those who welcome a standard format and agenda as a sign of stability and as reassurance there's no change in the organization, I say that's a false and malicious rumor. Reality is as the I Ching warns—when you think nothing is changing it only means change is taking place at levels you are not yet perceiving. Odds are, you won't like some of the surprises that come from not paying attention, so you can look at putting a meeting together as a good chance for finding out what's really happening.

PREMEETING
The intended outcomes that have surfaced in getting the meeting notice put together furnish the beginnings of a project design program. The rest comes from huddles and caucusing with as many participants as possible, to try fashioning a comprehensive list of issues to be dealt with. If I am to facilitate the meeting, I try to collar as many people as possible, typically asking, *In the best of all possible worlds, what would be the outcomes of this meeting? What would happen as a result?*

For a meeting involving people I don't know, it's important to find out all I can about their demographics, histories, roles, practices, and assumed expectations for the meeting. If all of us know each other, I noodle around with scenarios about the participants, anticipating their preferred behaviors and processes.

From all this, processes come to mind for getting the intended results—a meeting plan. On the basis of that, I'm generating any handouts or presentation materials needed and worrying away at the logistical needs, including—for in-house meetings—a last-minute reminder by e-mail or phone.

TOOL KIT
I keep a supply of all these on hand.

- Flipchart—the stiff-backed facilitator's kind with spare pads of blank or grid paper.
- Poster paper—a 3-foot-wide roll in case I'm going somewhere they don't have flipcharts and it's too far to take my own. Often I simply roll sufficient flipchart sheets as an airline carry-on.
- Ledger-sized photocopy paper, 11 by 17, makes terrific mini-poster paper for subgroup work and still large enough for show-and-tell time in groups up to 20 people.
- Masking tape—for posting stuff on walls, windows, bookcases, whatever.
- Post-its—3 by 5 size and several decks. These work great on flipchart paper, though not on walls. They're large enough to capture the gist of a thought and small enough to force people to one-liners or keywords. What's great is to have input from everyone that can be posted and rearranged by category or priority.
- Index cards—blank 3 × 5 cards are large enough for brainstorming lists to be passed around or turned in.
- Tape-dots—several colors of Avery Label ¾-inch round file labels. The color codes are useful to distinguish input from different categories of participants, or to indicate a best/worst priority, differentiate subsequent priority-set reallocations—second thoughts at the end of discussions that changed people's minds, etc.
- White, self-adhesive file labels, 1 by 2¾ , for correction of egregious errors on the flipchart and for use as ad-hoc name tags.
- Felt-tips—four kinds:
    - Boldest washable chisel points I can find—currently Sanford Mr. Sketch—which can be read the length of very large rooms—except for the yellow and orange ones, which fade to illegibility even across small rooms.
    - Crayolas Classic or Bold colors—a box for each subgroup table.
    - Washable Vis-à-Vis overhead projector fine point felt-tips for scrawls, annotations, and recording of their comments while I'm using view graphs. Gives it more immediacy and they pay attention better.
    - Permanent view graph markers for making last-minute diagrams, lists, or sketches to illustrate key points.
- View graphs—and these have become a serious problem. I've got several hundred (you've been looking at some of the pictograms as illustrations in this book), they're all hand-drawn (I hate it when people put up typed lists and then read them to me) and I've found no logical way of organizing them.

The set of view graphs for any given facilitation is custom picked hopefully to allow covering whatever the group might agree on the spot will be our agenda. The right-hand margin of each view graph is tabbed by having folded a standard white self-adhesive file label in half with about ⅛ inch of the view graph edge sandwiched front and back by the label. The tabs are noted so I can pick view graphs out of a stack. Each view graph has an 8 ½ × 11 backing sheet on which I can felt-tip bold cues or reminders. So far it's working, but barely. I've spent many an evening littering the floors of hotel rooms with view graphs, then rearranging them in probable sequence of use for tomorrow's sessions. What's useful about the process is that I can walk the floor mentally rehearsing in my mind all I want to cover, using the view graphs as visual cues to remind me.

LOGISTICS

Details, details, details. I am a relentless stickler about the particulars of room layout, setup, lighting, and air-distribution system controls. I invariably go an hour early to move furniture, get my materials laid out, and spend some quiet time with my own premeeting mind-set—that's even for an in-house meeting. If it's a workshop in a distant city, I go a day in advance to work with setup crews and logistical staff, and to be sure any handouts have arrived safely.

I'm rather rigid about room layout, typically demanding to be centered on the long wall of a rectangular room. If you spread your hand, I'm at the center of your palm and participants are along rectangular tables oriented like your fingers—long axes aimed at me or the projector screen behind me. I pull the tables as close to me as is possible and still have room to walk among them; I want to talk with people—not at them.

I strongly avoid round banquet tables. Be reasonable—having dinner at a round table, who talks? Only those next to each other. Facilitating a roomful of round tables means one or two loud ones per table speaking up and the rest very quiet or mumbling to a neighbor. Probably why King Arthur lost in the end. I want these participants in each other's faces for subgroup work and getting their heads together to look down the long axis of the table when they need to see what I'm writing on the flipchart.

For any meeting of more than five people I'll be on my feet the whole time. That's unless I'm using an overhead projector, in which case I sit facing them so as not to block anyone's view.

I consider a head table—much less a podium—to be a barrier between us. Roving talk show host is more my style when facilitating large groups. For team meetings, football huddle is the apt metaphor, if you can picture a flipchart included.

If there are to be food and beverages, I try to head off there being any sweets offered—I've watched too many heads nod from metabolic sugar lows. I remove any glasses, beverages, or snacks that hotels and conference centers like to clutter participants' tables with. I see that they're available on a table along a rear wall so that, although participants can access them, hopefully we can maintain alert focus on the issues at hand instead of munching and lounging. Facilitation—making it easy—is best accomplished by making your role appear effortless, which demands relentless attention to every detail until the first participant walks in the door.

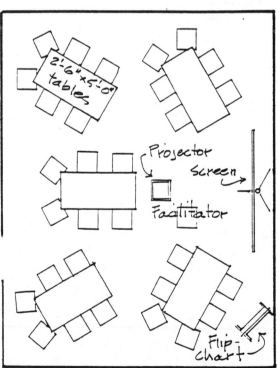

This diagrams how 30 people can fit into an 18' x 24' room and work as 5 subgroups or in plenary session.

GETTING MYSELF READY FOR THE MEETING

MEETING DESIGN

Having said all that, you might expect me to have meticulously planned all that's to be said and done, by whom, minute by minute. Just the reverse. None of this has led to a fixed agenda in my mind, much less on paper. The only part of the meeting I design and mentally rehearse is a strong beginning—typically involving some quick brainstorming, often zany enough to get them thinking *If this guy is this crazy I might as well relax and have fun at this.*

Whatever the opener, I *know* what will happen in the first few minutes. Beyond that I'm careful to plan no more than an inclusive set of options we might pursue together, and how I might facilitate any of them working best for the participants. I do, however, develop a rough outline of a default agenda in case they all sit down and stare stoically at me—even though that's yet to ever happen.

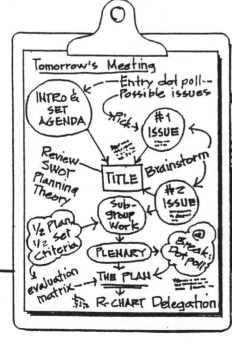

THEN, USING QUICK BUBBLE DIAGRAMS, I IMAGE TRUST & TEAM-BUILDING EXERCISES, SEQUENCES, ISSUES AND HOW THEY'RE BEST DEALT WITH, etc., etc., etc.

> *If the issue is Urban Design, for instance, I will have walked, sketched, and map-studied the area enough to be able to make quick recognizable diagrams of what they talk about.*

- It's important that I know all I can *about the content* they may want dealt with, and to see that it includes issues I believe need to be covered.
- It's also important to my impromptu style that I stay open and flexible about precisely how those issues will be dealt with and when.
- Perhaps most important, I spend lots of energy experientially imaging the best it can be, how well it's going to go, and what that feels like, present tense. Lou Tice stuff. I sometimes tell people that I can't wait to hear what I'm going to say, though they always think I'm joking. No joke—if I *really* feel that way, and expect them to as well, they probably will.

For most events I'll have arrived with little more than my kit of tools and a bubble diagram of topics to be dealt with. The bubbles might be numbered to indicate generally the sequence in which to introduce them. For important events I go so far as to storyboard a sequence in my organizer or sketchbook, using a rough version of Disney Imagineers' design process. Mine has none of their sophistication. It's a labyrinth diagram of hasty pictograms and key words or one-liners. It gives me cryptic (to others) graphic cues about what might be dealt with next and it's readable from 3 feet away. I may have flagged it with red to remind me of interactive exercises I had thought of and where they could happen.

While I'm facilitating, the notebook is propped open on the seat of a chair in front of me. I take my cues where possible from the group dynamics and input, but if there's the least lag experienced I can resort to my default mode by walking past that chair.

While they're doing interactive exercises, the notebook also furnishes a good checklist to make sure we're not leaving out anything important.

By the time the meeting starts, I've taken all reasonable steps to assure it won't be derailed by physical, technological, or logistical roadblocks. I then relax and focus on enthusiasm—it's infectious. Typically, as they're arriving, I'm smiling in the doorway like a gracious host and privately working very hard at putting names together with faces.

MEETING PROCESS
Here are a few things virtually always applicable about my meetings, though how they get carried out varies greatly depending on participant demographics and numbers, meeting purpose, etc.

Name-calling. Responding to people by name is incredibly important, and I've never been good at the word-association method for recalling names. With a crowd I don't know, I'm introducing myself while looking them in the eye as I repeat their name back to them, then using it two or three times in the next few sentences. I work hard at inventing open-ended questions I can ask on a first name basis. Yes, I truly *am* interested in learning about their practices, how business is going, their role in the firm, how far they've traveled to get here—all that—but at the same time it's a way of preparing myself to call them by name throughout the meeting to come.

If there are intervals between arrivals, I use the time to scan the roomful of people already present, calling off their names mentally.

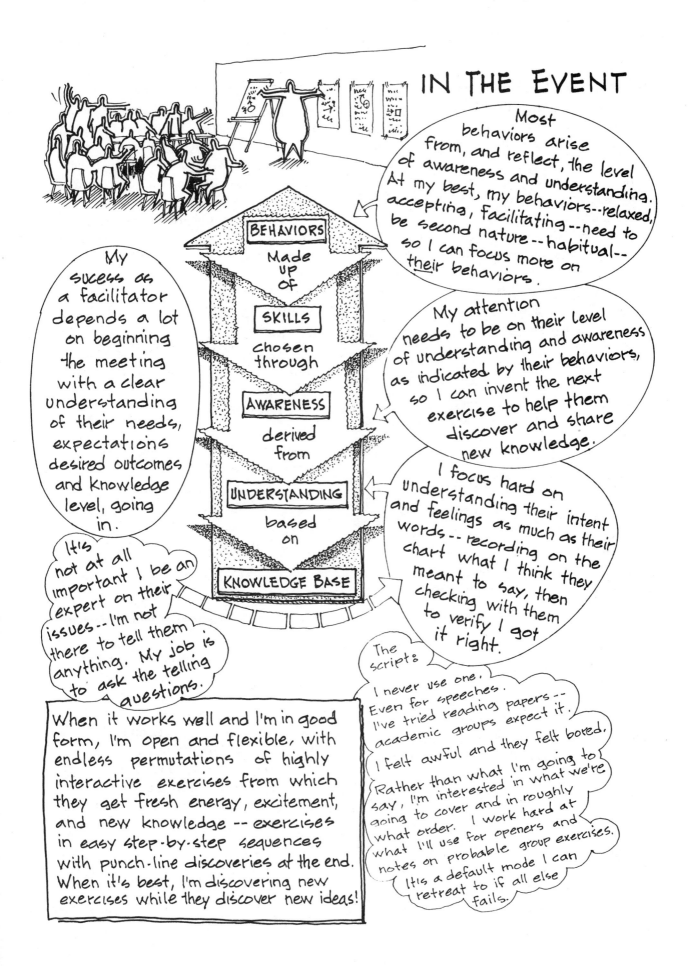

IN THE EVENT

Most behaviors arise from, and reflect, the level of awareness and understanding. At my best, my behaviors--relaxed, accepting, facilitating--need to be second nature--habitual--so I can focus more on their behaviors.

My success as a facilitator depends a lot on beginning the meeting with a clear understanding of their needs, expectations desired outcomes and knowledge level, going in.

BEHAVIORS
Made up of
SKILLS
chosen through
AWARENESS
derived from
UNDERSTANDING
based on
KNOWLEDGE BASE

My attention needs to be on their level of understanding and awareness, as indicated by their behaviors, so I can invent the next exercise to help them discover and share new knowledge.

I focus hard on understanding their intent and feelings as much as their words -- recording on the chart what I think they meant to say, then checking with them to verify I got it right.

It's not at all important I be an expert on their issues--I'm not there to tell them anything. My job is to ask the telling questions.

The script: I never use one. Even for speeches. I've tried reading papers-- academic groups expect it. I felt awful and they felt bored. Rather than what I'm going to say, I'm interested in what we're going to cover and in roughly what order. I work hard at what I'll use for openers and notes on probable group exercises. It's a default mode I can retreat to if all else fails.

When it works well and I'm in good form, I'm open and flexible, with endless permutations of highly interactive exercises from which they get fresh energy, excitement, and new knowledge -- exercises in easy step-by-step sequences with punch-line discoveries at the end. When it's best, I'm discovering new exercises while they discover new ideas!

I insist on first-name name tags and carry papers of self-adhesive file labels to use in case the organizers of the meeting haven't provided the proper kind.

Actually, I prefer it when we make out first-name name tags on the spot. The process of making those is another chance to gain, temporarily, instant recall of participants' names. Temporarily, because by tomorrow I'll remember faces but not the names—a fact I laughingly disclose when people congratulate me after a 60-person workshop on my ability at having called everybody by name all day long.

Introductions. In the arrival process noted above, not only have my self-introductions already been made, but to the extent possible I have introduced participants to each other— gives me another way to practice using their names and gets them comparing notes on practice issues. Depending on the size of the group and whether the participants know each other, I structure it differently but the objective is the same—to create an operative level of mutual trust and acceptance. This is particularly important among architects, since they're mostly introverts.

I never put them through the ordeal of having people stand and say their names and where they're from and what they do, etc., etc. Introverts suffer such anxiety, faced with the prospect of their turn coming up, that they can't listen to or retain the data about anyone else. That often means they'll further isolate themselves for the rest of the day, being embarrassed to ask about something they might previously have been told.

Instead, for large diverse groups I try to have tape-dot poll charts mounted on the wall and give them tape-dots as they enter.

I ask that before the meeting starts they flag the posted statements most closely depicting their current situation. Much of the data can be indicated by putting dots along a continuum from always to never, or best to worst. Some are yes/no choices. Others are gotten at in multiple-choice offerings of five or so statements ranging between two extremes, and I always use this format to get at how they feel about, or relate to, the topic for the day's session.

Other than that, the data I try to surface generally includes:

- Their firms (by total number of staff, project types, disciplines, services offered, etc.).
- Their roles in the firms (principal vs. not yet).
- Their average number of workweek hours and utilization rates.
- Their previous year's personal billing rates.
- Their percentage of work time spent interacting with others (because at some point in the day I'll get around to the core stuff—the people part).

When I'm working with small groups for team building or strategic planning it makes an amazing difference in the quality of meeting process and outcomes to do a timeline exercise.

Give them a minute and a half (it really takes about 3 minutes) for each person to fill a 3 by 5 card with a list of important watershed events (Dag Hammarskjöld called them *markings*) in their lives over the last decade. I first volunteer my own, flipchart style, to demonstrate, and I include personal career, medical, and domestic problems to show how totally transparent we can be with each other in the work ahead. They then make their lists and take turns reading them out to the group.

Invariably, even people who've worked together for years learn new things about each other in this process. That allows previously observed and inexplicable behaviors and responses to suddenly fit into a greater context and make sense. I've used this process with groups as large as 15, when we were going to work intensively together for 2 days. It's proved to be well worth the half-hour or so required, considering the mutual trust and openness it has always engendered.

As soon as they trust the people they're with, introverts act like extroverts—and they need to have fully participated, if the meeting is to have been a success in their view later.

Ice breaker, trust building, agenda setting.
I always try to start by revealing something about myself with at least a touch of wry humor. As noted before, Ornstein's mind research finally tells us *why* it's useful to start with jokes—it's to engage *their* right brain intuition in taking a larger view of why we're here and the potential inherent in this collective context.

Best not to deliver a long, involved, and memorized joke—that can be taken as a performance, which automatically sets a stage for *me vs. you* instead of *us* perception. A couple of puns will do, especially if they are disparaging about yourself to indicate that you trust them and the situation enough to disclose at a personal level. Encourages them to reciprocate.

If it's a small group, and particularly one that considers itself a team, it's often just as effective to proudly and warmly reiterate the mutual trust that exists—or at least why we have nothing to lose by trusting each other here today.

Along the way I'm telling them my expectations of them—high-energy interactions, inclusiveness, open communication, and teamwork.

Whatever size group it is, one of the very first things to do is to ask them to set or revise the agenda. When I've already had them flag agenda issues on the entry tape-dot poll, I read the contenders back to them. When in top form, I can flipchart them a list in approximately the order we might undertake to deal with the issues and ask for their approval. If we've had no tape-dot poll, I may well ask them to brainstorm completions of statements such as:

- *By five o'clock today we will know (have decided, learned, developed, become able to, etc.). . . .*
- *For the good of my firm, the five most important issues for me to work at today are. . . .*
- *In the best of all possible worlds, and as a result of this meeting, our company will. . . .*

Sometimes it's appropriate to do almost the reverse of that—start the session by breaking into subgroups, each with one of three quick-list assignments: Describe what it's like to live (or work) in this (company, industry, city, college, etc.) in the year (5 years out) if:

- The worst happens.
- We do nothing and "business-as-usual" continues.
- The best happens.

What actually results from this exercise is that the first two lists are so similar, everybody gets urgently motivated to develop an agenda to see that the best happens.

Even when the meeting has been called in order to have the group decide one issue or develop a specific product, I propose a general process and ask for better ideas.

Point of all this is to turn the meeting over to them, to get them to take ownership of it. I'm there for process and to capture the proceedings graphically for the record. It's their meeting.

From plenary to individual to subgroup to plenary. After introductory and agenda-setting exercises—often as part of them—the group is well served by rapid changes of pace. After plenary discussion of what we're up to, typically I have them do brief individual assignments followed by quick report-back sessions of the full group. Works for all types. Introverts get to fret, purse their lips, and make cramped notes on a 3 by 5 card—think before they talk. Extraverts get to dash something off and finish thinking while they talk during the report-out session.

Even in a group of six people it's frequently helpful to follow individual exercises with some subgroup work before the plenary report. Everybody can free up more easily with four or five others than with the entire group, and when it does get reported, no one person has to take responsibility—*The group made me do it, don't blame me!* Subgroup reports, by the way, are required to be in poster format and stay on the wall as contenders for the exit tape-dot poll of most important things for the day.

Actually of course, the plenary session is carried out in an inclusive, nonjudgmental way in an effort to get as much diverse thought and data up on the wall as quickly as possible. Demonstrates that, in this meeting anything goes. Add-on comments and questions for clarification are fine, and if there are dissenting comments I simply note them elsewhere as fresh and different thoughts. But I walk all over the lines of anybody who wants to debate.

Next step might typically be to gather a quick tape-dot poll while I hurriedly make clumsy tents naming as many front-runner choices receiving dots as there are tables. Participants are then asked to self-select where they choose to sit for subgroup work on the table topics named.

In large-group continuing education events I feel I have failed as a facilitator when participants have spent less than a third of our time in interactive or personal work. In small-groupwork, I want to be listening and quietly recording at least half the time. We learn best by doing, so I work to keep them doing with lots of wall graphics and exercises.

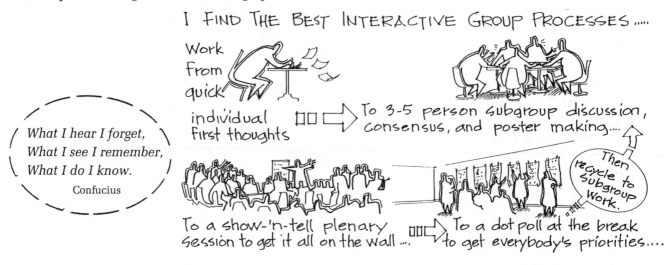

I FIND THE BEST INTERACTIVE GROUP PROCESSES.....

Work from quick individual first thoughts

To 3-5 person subgroup discussion, consensus, and poster making....

Then recycle to subgroup work.

What I hear I forget,
What I see I remember,
What I do I know.
Confucius

To a show-'n-tell plenary session to get it all on the wall ....

To a dot poll at the break to get everybody's priorities....

2.76

Work from the general to the particular. I'm a firm believer in being all-inclusive at the beginning, getting every possible option up on the wall for consideration. I then facilitate the group's finding consensus on priorities, working to develop first individual, then subgroup scenarios and proposals.

I've already explained much of what I ask of participants aims at widening the scope and enlarging the context of the issues at hand at the beginning of the session. Here are a few more.

EXERCISES TO ENLARGE THE CONTEXT

List making. Having them individually make quick lists is the easiest, of course. It's more interesting and they're more productive if you don't put them through the same exercise twice, however, so here are variations on the list-making theme. I may use two or three of these in the same meeting.

- They fill up a 3 by 5 card (or list no less than five entries), then read their lists out loud while I record on the flipchart. The only rule here is that when they take turns reading out their lists as plenary input, they don't reiterate what someone else has already said and that I've previously captured on the chart. We want this comprehensive, not redundant.
- Using big felt-tips, they put as many options as they can think of in 1½ minutes on 3 by 5 Post-its—one option per Post-it. Then two or three members are asked to arrange the Post-its on wall charts *in categories* and *without talking to each other* while the rest of us do something else.
- They're asked to make lists in bold felt-tip poster format on 11 by 17-inch paper and put them all up on the wall. As in the previous variation, you can quickly see the redundancies—a form of prioritization of what to deal with next.
- They make and share lists for subgroup discussion and synthesis, the most useful form of this being the "Pass 'n Cull" exercise explained in the illustration on p. 2.80. In large groups, I may use "Pass 'n Cull" to reduce the subgroup's list to one item per member. With *very* large groups I may ask each subgroup to dot poll its own list before providing the plenary group with only three top choices—or their single first choice.

Brainstorming is very different from list making in that it's a formal exercise with definite rules to follow. On the chance that my use of the two terms here makes them sound interchangeable, illustrated pages 2.78 and 2.79 detail how to really-do a brainstorming exercise.

Fishbone diagramming is not quick nor easy and requires lots of discussion and analytical thinking—probably why I haven't had much success using it. I include a page (2.81) on it in case you're faced with working with left brain types. It also can be helpful as a beginning to systems thinking, because it forces categorization that shows interdependencies among parts of the system that previously had been thought unrelated in cause and effect.

BRAINSTORMING

is not a bull session. Done well, it is a structured problem-solving process that is tremendously effective.

Statistical proof from research and countless workshops is that groups make better decisions than individuals -- provided the groups decide by consensus.

Other critical skills -- active listening, straight talk, selling, negotiation, etc. -- are elsewhere in the book with the idea you'll practice them on clients, then use them to set the same tone of collaboration in-house. Same thing here, but in reverse.

Practice brainstorming with staff so you can learn to use it with client groups. It can become a powerful tool for getting all stakeholders heard and in agreement.

Consensus, of course, is not the same as unanimous.

Consensus occurs when every stakeholder is absolutely convinced:

(A) Everything they feel and have said on the issue is fully understood by all.

(B) That they fully understand what every other stakeholder thinks about the issue.

(C) That they will be able to actively endorse and support the group's decision.

To reach consensus, it's worth using all your interpersonal skills, and even then, it takes a long time. Brainstorming is a good shortcut.

① EXPLAIN THE RULES

As Leader, your job is to:

- □ Present the problem
- □ Explain the rules
- □ Record on flipchart
- □ Keep time
- □ Keep the group focused
- □ Keep energies high
- □ Keep the participants safe from one another
- □ Help them hazard being totally open + forthright.

Ideally, the facilitator is not a participant

② DESCRIBE THE PROBLEM

Explain the issue, giving full background and context. Record all immediate answers or recommendations without judgment or debate.

- □ This makes sure the participants realize they've been heard and are taken seriously.
- □ It also gets the pat answers out of the way of the creative process to follow.
- □ While you're at it, start a separate wall chart for "off-the-subject" issues.

The working flip chart

The "you-were-heard, we'll-tend-to-it-later" List.

③ STATE THE PROBLEM

Everyone needs to agree on the problem statement -- which can take longer than any other step, but can also be the most important. You're looking for a simple question that starts with "HOW CAN WE...."

④ BRAINSTORM

Give the group "1½ minutes" (they'll take 3) to list as many answers as possible.

Tell them to work for quantity and speed -- forget quality or even making good sense.

Keep time. At the end of the first minute (or when they start to lag) tell them to "get crazy".. list the wild funny most impossible solutions they can -- forget all restraints.

⑤ RECORD THE RESULTS

Have the first member read their list, which you record in quick headlines on the flipchart. Everyone else then takes turns adding only those ideas not previously listed. The rules are:

- ☐ No discussion
- ☐ No judgments
- ☐ No humor or ridicule
- ☐ No criticism
- ☐ No questions other than for clarification

 Now ask for and record any additional ideas that may have occurred to people while listening to each other's lists.

If it's a large group, ask two members to take turns capturing the gist of each idea in bold felt-tip on Postit memo notes. One idea per Postit, which you put on the flipchart in categories.

⑥ CLUSTER DIAGRAM

Discuss, clarify, summarize, categorize. Record it all on

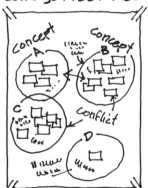

wall charts, but only for as long as it takes to satisfy them they've all been heard and all are understood.

⑦ PRIORITIZE

To avoid skewed results from peer pressure or politics, ask each to designate their three top priorities -- thumbs up or down -- as you poll them on each choice. Alternatively, take a dot poll.

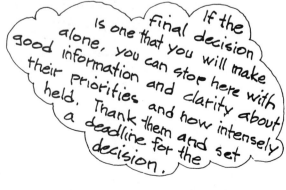

If the final decision is one that you will make alone, you can stop here with good information and clarity about their priorities and how intensely held. Thank them and set a deadline for the decision.

The PASS'N CULL exercise is a variation on brainstorming.

PASS
'N
CULL
IS
USEFUL!
{
◻ As an agenda setter for large groups of people who haven't worked together before.

◻ If you're short on time and need quick results from brainstorming

◻ When the group needs to set initial priorities among a multitude of options -- to get decisive.
}

Distribute 3×5 cards. Start as in brainstorming, EXCEPT: You assign the question and how many options each person is to list. Works best to assign one more item than there are people at each table.

FROM THE LISTS OR POSTERS THERE ARE MANY WAYS TO GO-- plenary or subgroup discussions, dot polls to prioritize, breaks to reform into new subgroups of shared interests, etc., etc., etc.

Everyone! pass your list to the person on your right. Take the card from your left and read the other person's list.

Now, with a single line, strike out the LEAST important item on their list. Pass that card to your right.

PASS
'N
CULL

①
②
③
④
⑤
⑥
⑦

Do the same thing again. Strike out the least important item now remaining on the list you've just been given.

By now, you should have your own card back, with input from your colleagues about what is most important.
But it's your list and your decision -- pick one. In each sub-group, someone self-select to be scribe. Make a poster that lists each person's one item.

Keep doing this till there is only one item remaining on each card. Do not strike out the last item of a List. Return the card to its originator.

EXAMPLE: FISHBONE DIAGRAM

Example Fishbone Diagram: Why we redesign late into Design Development

LATE REDESIGN

PROCEDURES

- In-house red-line reviews late in the game
- Client decides to go V.E. or CM
- Can't get reliable cost estimates til it's all drawn.
- Design Review Board forces change

PEOPLE

- Partner designs & sells what we can't make work
- Client's decision making
- Their power plays; conflicts; New client rep. assigned
- Dumb or hostile regulatory officials
- Junior staff get great late design ideas
- Our staff turnover
- Project Managers reassigned

POLICIES

- Client's users not on the team -- design hell when they finally see it. raise it.
- Consultants are selected late -- get D.D. "over-the-wall."
- Client's Review Process drags but to meet deadlines we have to keep working

TECHNOLOGY

- Client's funding hits problems based on schematic cost estimate and we aren't told
- Inadequate clearances assumed for mechanical in schematics
- Material and systems selection changes
- Publicity about Project alerts vendors to sell clients on using new technology
- New materials
- We lose a zoning code battle.
- Soils Test Report requires it
- Structural and M.E.P. conflicts discovered late

2.81

EXERCISES FOR NARROWING THE FOCUS---MAKING DECISIONS

The first part of a typical session, having focused on being as inclusive as possible, comes to a time to start homing in on what we're going to do about it. It's in the last half we must design a course of action and draw up a plan.

All the work that's gone on to this point has been overwhelmingly verbal, fully preoccupying our left brain. Meanwhile, perhaps our right brain has quietly been snatching opportunities to design solutions to the agenda issues all along. That's the only thing I've come up with to account for some of the breakthrough solutions I've seen groups quickly produce once it's time to design one.

I'm no Robert Ornstein, just an architect who's known for years that once having stated a design problem to be solved, it's then best to "sleep on" it. Seems to me all the preceding exercises to expand the options while deferring judgment are in some ways a quick equivalent of that. Point is, don't allow the press of time to force you to stint on exercises to enlarge the context and widen the scope of inquiry. It's the meetings that I've seen lunge from agenda to solution to implementation plans that have bogged down in endless discussion and are left defeated.

One more warning: Expect a "hump" somewhere in the beginning of the last half of a planning session or retreat. It's typical, even with careful attention to the previous steps, to "hit the wall" soon after starting to focus on specifics and decisions. Perhaps it's because in the first half we've been working at exercises that all aim at general *effectiveness*—the right things we might do. Second half—during which the "hump" occurs—aims at *efficiency* or the best way to get things done. Is it the realities of implementation that threaten us, or the realities of the system within which we work? Calls to mind Lily Tomlin's wonderful one-liner: *Reality is the leading cause of stress today, for those in touch with it.*

Whatever the causes, the facilitator's role becomes highly crucial when they hit the wall. It's the groups that have built their momentum and worked out a maximum list of potential options who seem to have most easily coasted through this lag time and rediscovered their creative energy. Even then, you may find them looking at you with that *Whatta we do next* question in their eyes, or worse, the *Just tell me what to do and I'll do it* look. That's when you need a bag of tricks to build back their enthusiasm, so included here are three tools that can help:

• Johari boxes and other matrixes

• Flowcharts

• R-charting

Finally though, when all's well that ends well, they make choices and plans. They self-select and publicly commit to assignments and deadlines. As a group they decide what the follow-through will be and how they'll know they've succeeded. That's when it's time to declare victory and help them all leave with a high level of excitement and motivation. That's best done by reviewing all the charts still mounted on the wall, affirming them and asking for their evaluation of the progress made. If you're out of time for this—as I always seem to be—a very fast substitute is an exit dot poll of the three best (or most important) things to have come out of the groupwork.

JOHARI BOXES & OTHER MATRIXES

You can spot when a group of right-brained architects is going into their left-brained analytic mode -- the matrix shows up. Matrixes are useful for getting to specifics and making comparisons. Here are some easy examples.

There are four things every firm works to provide. In the column marked "You," number them in their order of importance to your firm. "1" is least important.

	YOU	CLIENTS
QUALITY	2	4
SERVICE	1	3
DELIVERY	3	1
COST/PRICE	4	2

Now number them in the order of importance to your client base.

A Johari box is a four-box matrix used to evaluate or characterize based on two variables. You can make up your own. Here is an example.

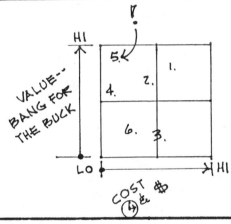

Competing proposals can be numbered in the order discussed, then rated by consensus or during the break by dot poll or felt tip.

One use of a matrix is to have the group reach consensus on three or so verbs that summarize the mission of the organization.

These become criteria for evaluating plans of action proposed. A dot poll during the break can help decide which proposal to hone & tweak.

Each attendee gets two dots per column of criteria

PROPOSALS	serve	grow	excel	#
1	o	c oc		o o
2	o	oo o	o	o
3		oo o		oo c o o o8
4	oo o oo	o	ooo oo o o	o
5	oo oo o o o	oo o oo	o oo o o	o o o o
6	oo c	c		o

2.83

R-CHARTING

Jointly developing a responsibility chart is a good way for a team to:

- ☐ ANALYZE TASKS REQUIRED TO MEET GOALS
- ☐ SELF-DELEGATE EACH MEMBER'S ROLE
- ☐ CLEARLY ESTABLISH WHO'S RESPONSIBLE FOR WHAT.

R-charting involves publicly negotiating verbal contracts within the group. Agreements are especially binding when they are recorded on large flipchart or poster paper in a group session.

STEP ①.

The team discusses the process or system that is at issue and agrees on an intended outcome -- the goal.

- ☐ Brainstorming
- ☐ Fishbone diagrams
- ☐ Cluster diagrams
- ☐ Pareto charts

Any of these can be useful in identifying the sequence of tasks needed or obstacles to improving performance

PEOPLE   METHODS   Problems   GOAL   Technology   Policy

PARETO   #   CAUSES

TASK   TASK   GOAL   TASK   TASK   CLUSTER DIAGRAM

STEP ②.

Members develop the R-chart by agreeing on actions and decision making necessary to carry out the process successfully. These are listed down the vertical axis of a matrix -- all in sequential order.

Cluster diagrams of ideas about what has to happen to make it all work can be numbered to show the sequential order.

DECISIONS OR TASKS	Name	Name	Name	Name	Name	Name	Name	Name	Name	Name
Task	R	S	S				I			S
Task	A/v	I	S	R		S	I		S	
Task	I	A/v	R		S	S	I		S	
Task	I	A/v		S	S	S	S	R	S	S
Task	I	A/v	S	S	R	I	S		S	I
Task	R					I				S
Task	A/v	A/v	S			I		S	R	
Task	I		A/v	R	S	S				S
Task	A/v	A/v	R			I		S		S

TEAM MEMBERS

STEP ③

Each team member's name is listed across the top. Intended roles and responsibility for each task are agreed to, using these rules:

- ◼ There can be only one person with the R -- responsible for a given task. In cases of disagreement there are two options:
  - (a) Split the task into smaller tasks, each having a different person with the R.
  - (b) Kick the original task upstairs to a person to whom those disagreeing all report.
- ◼ Minimize the A/v role -- more than one has the "R" reporting to multiple bosses.

LEGEND: R-CHART SYMBOLS	R = Is Responsible	I = Must be informed
	A/v = Must approve or veto	S = To furnish support

EXAMPLE: A FLOWCHART FOR PREDESIGN OF A PROJECT

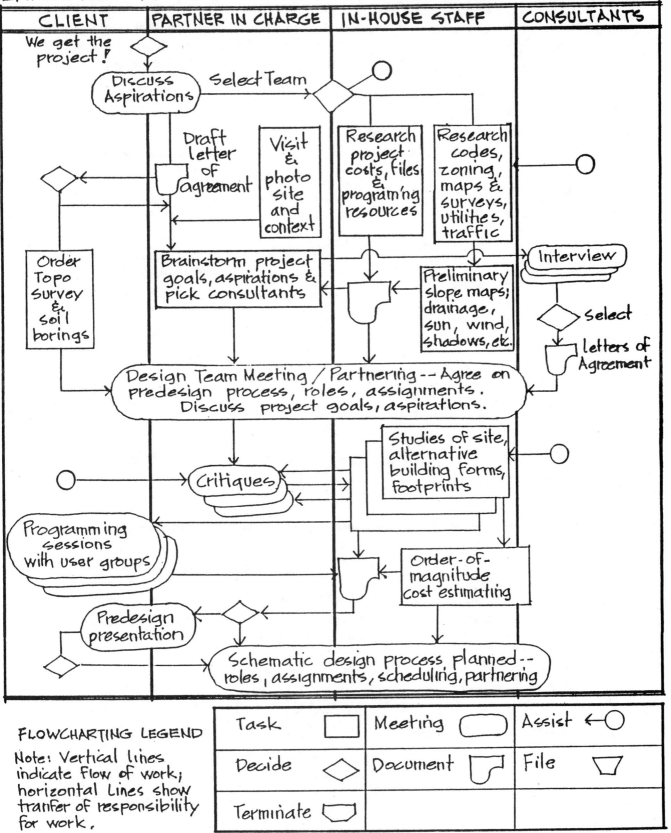

FLOWCHARTING LEGEND

Note: Vertical lines indicate flow of work; horizontal lines show tranfer of responsibility for work.

Task	□	Meeting	⬭	Assist	←○
Decide	◇	Document		File	▽
Terminate					

2.85

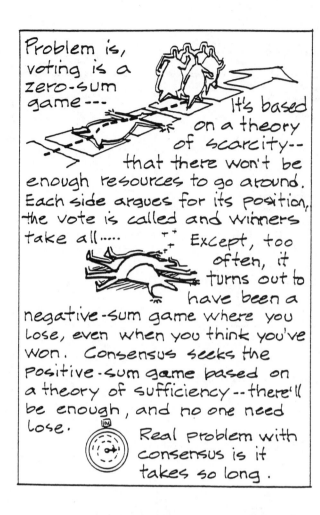

Problem is, voting is a zero-sum game--- It's based on a theory of scarcity-- that there won't be enough resources to go around. Each side argues for its position, the vote is called and winners take all..... Except, too often, it turns out to have been a negative-sum game where you lose, even when you think you've won. Consensus seeks the positive-sum game based on a theory of sufficiency--there'll be enough, and no one need lose. Real problem with consensus is it takes so long.

Yes, I know not all of what they say they'll do will actually get done, frequently not much of it at all, once they return to their now-piled-high desks and project pressures. I do believe, however, that what has been accomplished already is truly significant —

- They've come to understand each other better.
- They've honed their abilities at teamwork, and improved mutual trust.
- They have practiced decision making with no voting.

No small matter, and I'm typically ready to celebrate with them—particularly about the no-voting part. That one rates going into in greater detail, not only because it's the core stuff of groupwork, but because I've got a few more tricks to share with you for getting them past the reality hump.

VOTE-FREE DECISIONS

We all know voting is a lousy way to make group decisions. Well most of us know. Problem is, it's a zero-sum game based on the assumption that somebody has to lose. Yet when stress builds, old tapes play again in our minds and, *Call for a vote* comes the strident cry. When it does, my immediate response is to want to leave (and I frequently do) whereas if I were smarter and more detached, I'd hang around to figure out the politics behind it all. Truth is, I don't really want to be part of any organization, much less a meeting, where Robert's Rules of Order are the norm. In addition to the fated somebody, the organization always loses. Asking for a *team* to vote is an oxymoron.

OPEN CONSENSUS BUILDING
The ideal form of group decision making, of course would be unanimity, but the world's not like that, so the next-best thing is consensus, meaning:

- Every member fully understands the position of each other member on the issue.
- Every member is morally certain his or her position is fully understood by every other member.
- Every member is fully prepared to accept and work to support the decision of the group.
- The group documents the decision in an agreed-to consensus statement.

Problem with this process is that it takes too much time, so try any of the three shortcuts that follow:

DOT POLL

Been using this so many years with so many groups of architects, it's become almost a standard ploy in lots of AIA meetings. I'm not sure where it came from; it may even have been my own invention. After the group has apparently surfaced all suggestions and options and everything has been recorded on flipchart paper and posted on the wall, take a break. But first give out colored Avery Label ¾-inch file folder circular tape-dots to the participants with the instructions that during the break each is to put a limited number (3? 5? you decide) on the best ideas. Sometimes I give out two colors of dots and ask them to flag the three best and the three worst options.

Looking back, I'm amazed by the fact that people have never seemed hurt, frustrated, or angered by the group's dot poll choices. Urgent imperatives to the group may only have gotten the originator's own dots, while other options are covered up—yet the losers never seem to show signs of pursuing the matter and always actively work with the others at dealing with the group's choices.

Other advantages of dot polling:
- It's quick and easy because there's as much culling as choosing—we all can decide immediately what we don't like. Getting three choices also means not making a final decision.
- Although people could be watching where you put dots, it somehow feels anonymous and tentative—you're not faced with saying anything to be possibly held to later.
- It's an equal opportunity exercise, all dots being identical (though I sometimes color-code by categories of participants if that will help the group; I never color-code an individual).

- It's the introverts' chance to reflect before deciding and to be heard without talking.
- After the break it's much simpler to work only with the options that got the most dots rather than bounce among the total number of choices we had noted inclusively before.

The disadvantage of dot polling is, you're still left with synthesizing the top priorities into a coherent and acceptable consensus statement.

THE FIVE-FINGER COMFORT CHECK[*]

Best shortcut I've seen came from a group of some 20 naval personnel (of a wide variety of ranks and all in civilian clothes!) meeting as a committee at NAVFAC offices outside Washington, DC. Had a guy at a flipchart, of course, but if he were a facilitator, he certainly was the quietest one I've ever seen. I'd say that, instead of interpersonal skills, what had singled him out for this duty was an uncommon ability to synthesize disparate comments onto a flipchart in a single coherent statement. Which he did. Silently. With lots of cross outs and page flipping.

Finally, when discussion lagged, he began to ask for help in editing what he had written and of course the extroverts gave lots of directives while the introverts quietly considered the issue—a complex matter that would direct the future actions of everyone in the room. I sat waiting for the ranking officer—so far I had been unable to identify him—to make the decision.

Instead, the flipchart synthesizer abruptly asked whether they were ready for a "five-finger comfort check," counted "one-two-three," and everyone in the room (except me) held up from one to five fingers. Seeing my confusion, they quickly explained what I've shown on the accompanying illustration.

The exercise was repeated—with my participation this time—then the synthesizer personally and quietly asked those who had held up less than three fingers to say how the flipchart statement could be rewritten so that they could hold up three fingers. Quick strikeouts and discussions of amendments, two more five-finger comfort checks, and we were out of there. In 20 minutes, *and* with an agreed-to consensus decision recorded for future reference!

I'm quite certain that every member of that team was keenly aware of how many fingers the ranking officer(s) held up, but nonetheless it was an elegant display of consensus building. There was no discernible pulling of rank, no show of regret or dissatisfaction with the outcome. All of them had been included in the making of the decision, each seemingly felt heard.

I've gotten terrific results using that process working with even so divisive a group as college faculty redesigning their curriculum. Faculty groups are notoriously addicted to Robert's Rules, however, and finally I made it a condition of my agreeing to continue to work with them that they'd agree to abandon ole Robert and abide by any consensus they could reach. Which they promptly agreed to by solemn and formal vote!

Even then, by end of day when they were faced with final commitment, I had to resort to the next alternative that's slightly more formal, but even more inclusive. While it's still vote-free in a strict sense, it allows an illusion of voting.[†]

---

[*]East Coast Naval Facilities Command, Alexandria, VA, Committee to Minimize Project Error (1994).
[†]Though reported in a column by management consultant Don Maruska in the San Luis Obispo *Herald-Tribune*, July 1998, I believe both Don and I got the rated poll method from Art Stevens, former parliamentarian for the U.S. Congress, and now an Episcopal priest based in Los Osos, CA.

The five-finger **COMFORT CHECK** helps a group reach consensus quickly

1. After enough discussion so that rehashing of positions begins to become an obvious barrier,

   the facilitator writes an attempt at a consensus statement on the flipchart.

2. When group editing begins to die down -- or when when the one holdout finally quits trying to edit -- the facilitator calls for a "COMFORT CHECK." The rules of the exercise are demonstrated.

3. Asking if everyone is ready, the facilitator counts 1 -- 2 -- 3! In time with the count, each member fists one hand into the palm of the other. On the count of 3!, each holds up from one to five fingers, meaning:

5: **GREAT!** Don't change a single word.

4: **GOOD.** It's fine.

3: **OK ....** Wouldn't have said it that way but I can buy in.

2: **PROBLEM.** Let's talk.

1: **NO WAY!** I've got serious problems.

4. The facilitator then asks each one- or two-fingered respondent (by name) "OK, what should I mark out or write in up here, so that you can hold up three fingers?"

5. Recycle as necessary. Comfort checks are not final votes so they avoid the hurt of losing a vote. When you are the dissenter, you can see how far apart you are. So long as you speak up, and your proposal is recorded, amended, and discussed, there's no chance you weren't understood. And the process is enough like a childhood game to put humor into things!

THE RATED POLL

1. Through full and open discussion, consensually agree on what options are available. This is not difficult since it is totally inclusive of all positions. List and alphabetize the alternatives or decision options on the flipchart and post.

2. After sufficient discussion, ask the members to grow quiet, jot notes to themselves, brainstorm privately all the reasons against accepting option A. Then circle the group, each in turn listing reasons for possible opposition to that option. The rules: no debate, no discussion, no repetition of reasons previously given. Questions for simple clarification are permitted so long as they are not leading questions. Any member can "pass" with no reason given. All reasons voiced are recorded on the chart.

3. Again, grow quiet to reflect, then give all possible reasons in favor of accepting option A. Same rules, same procedure.

4. Proceed to voice and record pros and cons for each of the other available options or choices in exactly the same manner.

5. When each option has been dealt with and both pro and con given by every member of the group, each member writes on a 3 by 5 card a "score" between 0 and 100 in favor of *each* available option.

6. Total scores are tabulated and discussed. In my experience using this procedure, there's always been acceptance, with discussion limited to next steps, given the decision made.

There's actually a step #7 in properly using the rated poll.

Ask how they feel about the process and the results -- if each is prepared to implement the decision. Gives them a chance for self-affirmation. as a group.

The rated poll is powerful and effective but takes time -- save it for major decisions.

What's good about this decision-making process is there's adequate structure to the process to assuage all those parliamentarian devotees. Yet it cuts both time and power plays from the unstructured dialectic consensus-seeking process, and is actually more inclusive.

That's four methods for no-vote group decision making, none of them the single best solution.

- I spent 15 years in a firm using the unstructured consensus-building method. Decisions took *forever* to get made, and, turned out, not all of them were the wisest, only politically expedient, given the filibustering of the extroverts in the crowd. Everybody got tired of the number and length of meetings required to get things done.

- Using tape-dots helps, and remains the simplest and most useful ploy I've found to cut through the time-intensive dialectic posturing that sometimes builds on itself in groupwork.

- The five-finger comfort check is a big time-saver, but people get bored quickly and some find it too cutesy.

- The rated poll method is excellent for the really tough or important decisions, but seems a bit ponderous for lots of issues.

PART 3:
DOING PROJECTS

As much as anything, this part of the book is about the mind-set with which to approach management—it makes no pretense of being a comprehensive work on all that has to be done to manage either firms or projects. Instead, it's a collection of tips on:

**Fine-tuning your firm management
to orchestrate—**

Doing projects that really "cook,"
through—

**Managing them in ways
that embrace the paradoxes,
and allow—**

Recycling of all you learn
for continuous improvement
along a path of mastery.

PART 3. DOING PROJECTS.....

This makes no pretense of being a comprehensive list of how to manage either firms or projects. It's merely an eclectic gathering of learnings from talking with (and facilitating for) good architects. It's a collection of their tips, nothing rigid about it, but taken in aggregate, hopefully it'll yield insights on ways to approach project and firm management and processes useful to you. Started to call it Exemplary Practices, meaning "worthy of imitation," but I'll let you be the judge of that.

Many of the practices listed here are routinely reported by (or by staff of) a dozen or so architects that the profession collectively agrees have done lots of great projects over the years. They've all won plenty of design awards, have been frequently published and interviewed. I also include a bunch of good ideas from lesser-known practitioners who nonetheless share a commitment to constantly improving their practices and their projects. Don't we all.

Everything here comes from direct reports by those who've done it—none of this is my invention, though I've personally tried a lot of it. As my firm got busy and then big, I became fascinated with the how-to, project process part. That was a personal defense mechanism in order to remain a design architect, to avoid being turned into a business manager. So I got active in the AIA Practice Management Committee and found if I'd openly disclose my hot tips first, everybody else would share theirs. Learned a lot that way about minimalist and participative management—which was what I needed.

1st Tip: Some of this I began picking up many years ago by inviting my local competitors to dutch-treat lunches where we compared notes on how we ran our offices..... Then in 1989, Weld Coxe and I put together

The Signature Firms Roundtable

Robert Buford, AIA
  Robert A. M. Stern
Frederick Clarke III, AIA
  Cesar Pelli & Associates
Warren J. Coxe, FAIA
  Hartman Cox Architects
David Denton, AIA
  Frank O. Gehry & Associates Inc.
Peter H. Dodge, FAIA
  Esherick Homsey Dodge & Davis
Joseph Esherick, FAIA
  Esherick Homsey Dodge & Davis
Graham Gund, FAIA
  Graham Gund Architects Inc.
Charles Gwathmey, FAIA
  Gwathmey Siegel & Associates
Peter E. Madsen, FAIA
  Graham Gund Architects Inc.
Robert Packeard, AIA
  Zimmer Gunsel Frasca Partnership

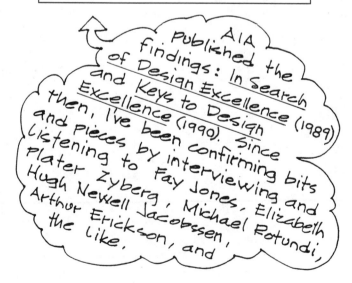

AIA published the findings: In Search of Design Excellence (1989) and Keys to Design Excellence (1990). Since then, I've been confirming bits and pieces by interviewing and listening to Fay Jones, Elizabeth Plater Zyberg, Michael Rotundi, Hugh Newell Jacobssen, Arthur Erickson, and the like,

WHERE I'M COMING FROM WITH THIS.....

One can think of practice -- firm and project management -- as a bit like carefully tending a supersaturated solution to induce the sudden crystallization of design excellence.

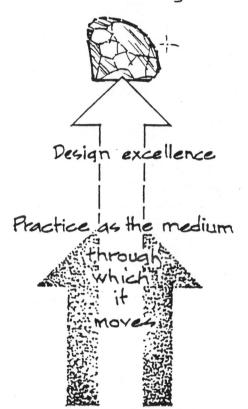

Design excellence

Practice as the medium through which it moves

Trouble with that analogy is the implication that adding more by-rote layers of management might assure consistently excellent design. On the other hand, there are the Howard Roarks among us. Both make the mistake of assuming good design and good practice are two separate things. It's like Weld Coxe told us... "For too long we have worried about the design of design and the practice of practice. There's only the one thing. Architecture."

My worst fear about all this? That some damn fool will misunderstand and think this is prescriptive, that the whole sequence is mandatory, that it has to be undertaken all at once. Wrong. My hope is that you'll simply surf through what's listed here to see what might work for you, or be adaptable for your firm's needs, then:

- Pick any tip(s) that makes sense within your current workload and given methods of producing projects— hopefully something relatively easy to implement.

- Try it, but not before—or without— tinkering to customize it to fit your unique needs, style, and practice. In our profession, nothing is one-size- fits-all.

Whether to adapt, adopt, or ignore is your judgment call. You might well decide that your firm—like any other organic body—would reject too alien a transplant. Or that, for your firm, the cure would be worse than the curse. But hopefully you'll find here:

- Ideas to discuss within the firm.

- Principles that prompt you to tweak your practices.

- Tips—or combinations of them—to use in changing your firm's culture and project performance for the better.

Before talking about project-specific processes, in this part I offer some tips about firm management, then deal with challenging paradoxes inherent in management. I end with what I learned from top designers about predesign, and add a proposal that you bookend your projects between that and post-occupancy evaluation.

CHAPTER 11. GETTING THE FIRM OUT OF THE WAY

The title comes from exemplary design architects I've interviewed over the years. When asked what it takes to do great projects, they generally attribute some 40 percent to teamwork and synergy among project members, then another 40 percent to individual design talent and ability. That leaves only 20 percent attributable to the firm as the venue, the support mechanism, the launch platform. They agreed that for them the secret of good management is to keep the firm out of the way of doing projects well.[*]

One neat way to look at that is to realize some 60 percent of what it takes to achieve design excellence (the team plus the firm parts) is stuff that can be managed and obviously, as it's presented here, management is hardly rocket science. Not only that, we've all got *some* design ability or we wouldn't be in architecture. Add whatever percentage of that we can bring to the 60 percent that's manageable and WOW! Design excellence is within reach of any of us!

Though she didn't put it quite so bluntly in her book,[†] in 1989 Dana Cuff was saying that from her findings there are no excellent firms, only excellent projects—that no one does great projects every time and that most of us can do one every now and then.

The not-so-neat part is somehow managing in ways that keep the right balance—that make the firm the stable work platform that supports project teams doing good work—instead of the other way around. No easy thing. Good management (leadership, really) is like architecture. You're always changing things to make them better, and systems theory is right—you can never change just one thing.

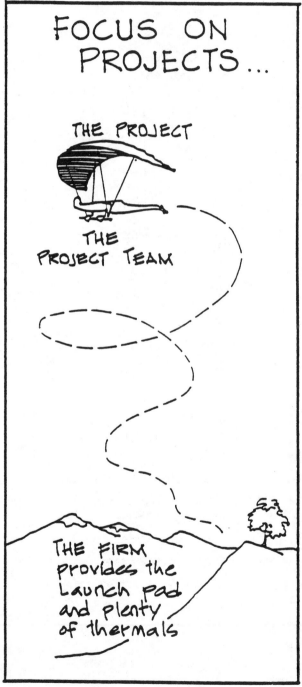

FOCUS ON PROJECTS...

THE PROJECT

THE PROJECT TEAM

THE FIRM provides the launch pad and plenty of thermals

---

[*]This principle was articulated first for me at the 1989 AIA Signature Firms Research Roundtable facilitated by Weld Coxe and reported in my *In Search of Design Excellence* (AIA Press, 1990).
[†]Dana Cuff, *Architecture: The Story of Practice* (MIT Press, 1992), p. 234. In 1989 Dana and I put on some research seminars together as part of the AIA In Search of Design Excellence program.

Sixty percent of what it takes to get good design can be managed....

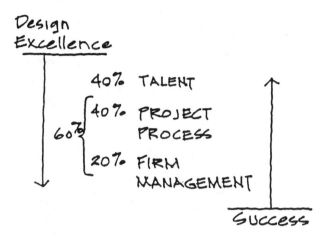

Design Excellence

40% TALENT

60% { 40% PROJECT PROCESS
      20% FIRM MANAGEMENT }

Success

Provided you take care to never micromanage.

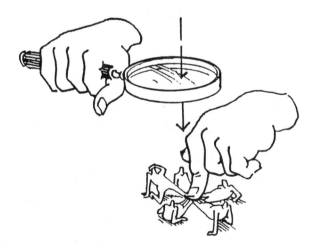

Say for example that management sets challenging quotas of billable hours, then monitors and rewards utilization ratio performance. Very good business, except it's sending messages over time that maximizing one's utilization ratio is the real path to success within the firm. The obvious response (even if only subconsciously) will be for staff to maximize the chargeable hours and therefore the bill.

As David Maister[*] points out, it won't take long for clients to know what's happening: *A provider that is not efficient in spending the client's money soon loses the client's trust and confidence.* I'd add to that, *word gets around fast.* So minimizing the bill—working with top efficiency to solve problems on behalf of the project and the client—is not only the right and ethical thing to do, it's clearly the best business practice as well.

Another example: Business 101 says *maximize the leverage*—use the lowest-paid employees capable of the task, push decision making to the lowest possible level, flatten the firm, and cut the overhead of supervision. This is one that architects are especially prone to—after all, *we* all had to learn by the sink-or-swim method, didn't we? Yet as professionals we owe the client due diligence—and the overhead of mentoring is a wise investment, long term.

David Maister again:[†] *What you do with your billable time determines your current income, but what you do with your nonbillable time determines your future.*

I'd add, *and your firm's future, as well.* I once pushed my firm to boost the utilization ratio and delegate more—times being hard. The immediate response from project managers was a polite but very firm prohibition against my giving any more design crits after schematics. Said my time was too expensive for their projects to afford, given my own new rules. Knowing what I know now, if I were given it to do over, I'd start some in-house design classes so the projects wouldn't need as much of me.

---

[*]David H. Maister, *True Professionalism: The Courage to Care about Your People, Your Clients, and Your Career* (Free Press, 1997), p. 26.
[†]Ibid., p. 46.

Maister's premise—and mine—is that management quickly gets down to core principles and values—that doing the right, ethical, professional thing is also good business. Nice to hear that good business and architecture are not mutually exclusive, but when we're in the dialectical throes of simultaneously meeting payrolls, paying the rent, and affording the next software upgrade, it gets hard to remember.

Which is why I never recommend bringing in someone with a purely business background to manage the firm. Most times, I've seen one of two things happen—either the firm's culture and core values change or the businessperson leaves soon—not much of a choice. My choice? Instead, make the business of the firm everybody's business.

Here's a quick assessment tool from Likert—a Michigan guru from the 1960s. He worked out a typology of organizations based on the way decisions get made. One useful application is to have the boss do a quick self-assessment, while the staff do an independent and anonymous report of their perceptions. Then discuss the differences in the two. Most architects think they're consultative and participative while staff see them as autocrats or benevolent autocrats.

Try it out. List the issues that get decided in your firm by each of the four following ways:

Autocrat	"I'm the boss, I'll decide."
Benevolently autocratic	"I'm the boss. I'll decide, then convince them that they did, or at least that it's the best decision."
Consultative	"I'm the boss, but before I decide, I'll ask and seriously listen to all the people affected."
Participative	"We'll decide."

Decisions rated on a scale of 1 to 5

Autocratic	Speed	5
	Ease	5
	Consistency	5
Benevolently autocratic	Speed	4
	Ease	4
	Consistency	3
Consultative	Speed	2
	Ease	2
	Consistency	2
Participative	Speed	1
	Ease	1
	Consistency	1

Impact on staff rated from 1 to 5

Autocratic	Potency*	1
	Morale	1
Benevolently autocratic	Potency	2
	Morale	2
Consultative	Potency	4
	Morale	4
Participative	Potency	5
	Morale	5

*Potency is Likert's term for the self-empowerment staff feel in order to handle problems on their own rather than kick them upstairs or over the wall.

From Likert's findings--and from my own experience -- I found that once I got past the illusion I was a lone cowboy hero stomping out brushfires as soon as they happened....

And the one about being the quick-draw troubleshooter who had to make every decision.

Too many times I was acting the autocrat while actually providing the prime bottleneck, keeping good staff blocked from doing what the project needed, and when.

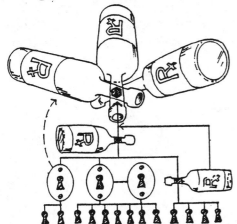

My advice?

Practice full disclosure. Share far more information than you would have thought wise—at least make it accessible. In my 85-person firm this included openly disclosing anything staff wanted to know about—fees, contracts, utilization ratios, profitability—anything except confidential personnel files and information protected by law. The reasons you may want to do this:

1. All firm members, as stakeholders, are expected to unilaterally work to improve the quality of the firm and its projects, so they need access to current information—virtually full disclosure—in order to act responsibly. If you want staff to act as professionals, you'll need to treat them as such. Making data available on such issues as financial, marketing, and project performance, works to create a culture of mutual trust, respect, and collective purpose.

2. They already have access to the information—always have had—and it's a waste of time and energy for staff to surreptitiously dig for data, or for management to attempt to safeguard it from them. Besides, even big-firm principals don't make enough salary to ever be embarrassed—what do you have to hide?

3. But the most important reason: We need to disclose fully and repeatedly our true (espoused) values. Keep telling the story—almost a tribal thing. Through the generative power of language* we can invoke group commitment and collective action to align real-world management activities (values in action†) with what we say we believe in—professionalism and a conviction that it is possible to do well by doing good if we have the courage for it and find joy in what we do—which is projects.

---

*Peter Senge, A. Kliener, C. Roberts, R. Ross, and B. Smith, *The Fifth Discipline Fieldbook* (Doubleday, 1994), p. 27.
†The terms from Chris Argyris as quoted by Maister, op cit., p. 6.

THE FIRM ORGANIZATION

Work on (and from) relationship. Virtually every design firm has a relational rather than rational structure. The two are not mutually exclusive or necessarily opposites, and *relational* certainly is not synonymous with irrational. *Relational* refers to things getting done—decisions made—through personal interaction and relationship, rather than through company policy, rules, and standards. Only reason to bring it up—since we're all the way we are—is just to remind you to remember it when times get rough.

Unfortunately, in relational organizations when things go wrong, the temptation is to attempt a quick fix by becoming "more businesslike." Too often we resort to big corporation management controls, bureaucracies, and other encumbrances—which industry now acknowledges are anachronistic and counterproductive, even in rational organizations.

Better we think of the firm along the lines of an extended family and, as any family counselor can tell you, the hope for any dysfunctional family is improved communication, open (but also compassionate) confrontation—creative abrasion, even—when it's needed.

Basically, says friend Stu Rose, there are only two types of organizations:

① The **RATIONAL**, like an efficient machine, is made up of parts (people) carefully selected and assembled to run smoothly according to precise performance specifications (job descriptions). When the machine malfunctions, you get out your tools and either redesign and respecify, or you can swap, relocate, or replace defective parts.

Architectural firms don't work that way, and in fact, the big widget-maker corporations are all trying hard to learn to operate the way we always have worked -- as

②  **RELATIONAL** **ORGANIZATIONS**

When asked for an organizational diagram, top design architects most often draw something like this

CLIENT

DESIGN PARTNER

MANAGING PARTNER

ADHOCRACY

of course, that's just a diagram. Lots of days, it feels more like this

OUR PRACTICE

YOU

Pick the team based on:

(A) The project leader's evaluation of what the project needs in terms of:
- □ Expertise
- □ Talent
- □ Interest
- □ Personal chemistry

(B) AVAILABILITY

(C) The
- □ Preferences
- □ Enthusiasms
- □ Interests, and
- □ Professional growth needs of available staff.

PROJECT TEAM

Work in adhoc, project-specific teams assembled through dialectic in-house interaction. Project team membership is typically based on two things:

1. Leadership's assessment of individual capabilities, anticipating the needs of the project and the probable relational chemistry among the clients and other members of the project team, both in-house and out.

2. Available firm members' preferences and professional growth needs. We know that maximum motivation and optimum morale come from having some say in what projects one works on and how the work will be done.* Having a say is not the same as a vote—and enormously different from having the *final* say. But it still matters a great deal.

The corollary is that, once formed, the team needs to remain virtually indissoluble until completion of the project. That it be empowered and charged with carrying the project through from beginning to end. One of the biggest complaints we hear from designers and clients alike is that, too often, team members representing the other party (or our own) get changed midproject.

---

*In countless surveys on job satisfaction, money consistently ranks way down the line below these two. In my experience, money has virtually always been a symptom rather than the cause for staff complaints.

Decide—don't vote. Chapter 10 covers the how-to part of the vote-free decision-making process, but the question here is, when to use it. Yes, the consensus-building process takes more time. Yes, there are always decision makers with the final say. But we know (at least statistically) that groups make better decisions and fewer mistakes than individuals; that leaders make their best decisions if first they listen to stakeholders with an open mind; that consensus-based decisions produce ownership and therefore wholehearted implementation by all involved. We also know—each of us by personal experience—that in every vote, somebody loses. Do that enough, the projects will too. Keep it up, next comes the firm.

The other side of that is the judgment call every project manager is endlessly making as to which decisions really require the team.

Teamwork is a no-brainer we all learned in kindergarten—it's always required. But as Katzenbach[*] points out, teamwork is not the same as having a true team, and much of what we do demands what he calls a *single-leader work unit* operating with peak teamwork. It's not a nonteam—it just knows when to not operate as one. Point here is that voting is an anti-teamwork activity. Either go with a tacit agreement to abide by an individual leader's decision or take the time to get consensus—but don't vote.

Specific goals, common approaches, a need to join forces

SHARED COMMITMENT

REAL TEAMS HAVE:

COMPLEMENTARY SKILLS — A large enough number of members to provide all the capabilities needed to do all that the project requires and to do it well.

MUTUAL ACCOUNTABILITY — A small enough number of members for each to be fully accountable to each of the others and all to feel mutually accountable for the success of the project.

EXCELLENT PERFORMANCE · EFFECTIVE WORK PRODUCTS · PERSONAL GROWTH

Have only an implied internal hierarchy. Firm size permitting, other than *principal* or *partner*, titles should be only for the duration of the project and used only at the interface with those outside the firm.

Inside the firm, capability and experience levels of fellow members are always common knowledge. Formal titles can get in the way of doing projects, and usually are invoked only to settle disputes on the basis of position rather than merits. Yes, general project responsibility (e.g., project designer, job captain, etc.) needs be agreed to at the outset, but these roles—and certainly project task responsibilities—are best assigned through consensus or implicit agreement, and on an as-needed basis within the team.

An apt analogy might be a good jazz combo. The leader selects the music and sets the beat. After that, every member of the band is not only empowered but obligated to improvise—extrapolate—do whatever it takes to achieve total satisfaction and delight for themselves and everybody in the audience. The lead keeps shifting among the members— almost intuitively, by mutually understood minimalist signals, even gestures. A good project team's like that.

---

[*] Jon R. Katzenbach, *Teams at the Top: Unleashing the Potential of Both Teams and Individual Leaders* (Harvard Business School Press, 1998), p. 11.

Sure, we all got into this profession to do great design, but there are also hard-core business reasons to inculcate a design culture in your firm -- Like lowering staff turnover, or differentiating you from all the competition. Being technically competent is now only the price of admission.

Nurture a design culture. This is a matter of values and, like all quality management, is best inculcated by walking the talk. This one can be hard to pull off, depending on the core values of the founding principals. If their overriding concerns are about service, or production, or being competitively priced (all good concerns to have, of course), project team priorities will correlate. Staff naturally respond to the values in action that leadership demonstrates, so if your goal right now is to upgrade design quality, then demonstrate it. Start every staff meeting with a discussion of what we're doing design-wise. Discuss every project question first (though not only) in terms of design intent and how well those can be met by the options available.

In 10 years of asking top designers when, in the course of the project, their design activity is complete, I have gotten only the one answer: *When the project is turned over to the owner at completion.* Doesn't mean they don't have deliverables and sign-offs at schematics and design development, or that conceptual redesign continues all during construction phase. Just means there's a subtle but powerful difference in their mind-set and semantics. For them, drawing a wall section, writing a specification, observing construction—each is an act clearly as integral to the process of achieving design excellence as schematic sketching. They demonstrate this conviction by their own actions and by their responses and communications to staff.

COMMON SYMPTOMS OF A FIRM'S DESIGN CULTURE

Design is first on the agenda-- in informal chats, in project reviews

Staff organize off-hours, impromptu field trips to see:
□ Admired designers'
□ The competition's
□ Ours

All-staff celebratory presentations are held at the end of schematics

Design crits-- never prescriptive--
□ Always begin with shared understanding of intentions and aspirations,
□ Can be offered by any firm member at any time and are taken seriously,
□ Are a routine at Friday afternoon pinup project reviews among staff.

The same team carries its project through from beginning -- to end -- no handoffs

Theory, published work by others, and personal goals for projects--all get talked about a lot.

Sketchbooks and study models are in common use --and as a matter of personal initiative.

3.11

DEMAND FOR QUALITY

PREDESIGN | DESIGN | DESIGN DEVELOP. | CONST. DOCS. | BID & NEGOTIATE | CONSTRUCT'N ADMINISTRATION

Doing good quality design -- like any other form of quality program is more a way-of-life issue than one about means of Livlihood.

Top design architects were talking -- and walking -- it that way long before the global quality movement. Their value system becomes a matter of firm culture -- of belonging.

Doesn't mean they don't have the same Monday morning project planning and resource allocation meetings you have -- what some call "Didja" meetings -- "Didja finish that yet? Didja budget and schedule that? Didja call them?"

We all have such meetings. It's how they get carried out that often makes it obvious you don't have a design culture in the firm.

Even of it doesn't come top-down, there's lots that any team member can do to inculcate a design culture. Some symptoms of a firm's having one are commonly reported to include:

- Staff organize field trips on weekends to inspect their own projects, critique the work of admired competition, sketch renowned (or just plain pleasant) places.

- Everybody in the firm feels free to offer design critiques, does so, and is taken seriously.

- Formal design reviews—sometimes with visiting jurors and celebratory wine and cheese—are often held at the end of the schematic phase.

- Routinely, staff (not management) hold Friday close-of-business pinup sessions to informally review design and talk design theory.

In large firms weekly design reviews may be done within project teams with interested others dropping by. In small firms it may comprise the entire staff. In some of the more exemplary design firms these sessions are reported to go for many projects well into the construction documents phase. It's important to note that the agenda for these informal staff sessions is restricted to discussion of design issues. These are get-togethers in addition to, not replacements for, the typical Monday morning meetings at which project management allocates resources and reports on project schedules and budgets.

Track time spent on, and categories of, rework. You've already got job codes to track projects. If you're like most firms, you have prefixes or suffixes for job-codes in order to track phases of services on the time sheets. Adding digits to track rework will layer on yet another level of complication, but it's one you can soon get used to recording.

The purpose is to provide a way to later look for systemic patterns, so your codes will need to identify the category of origin, i.e., clients, contractors, subs, consultants, regulatory officials, technology changes, and yes, in-house mistakes and changes of heart or mind. No finger-pointing—this is done for the purpose of looking for what, not whom, to blame. The goal is that—by identifying the origin (and the increase or decrease) of the need for rework—you can identify important changes needed in the system and redesign how certain portions of a project (or how whole projects) normally get done.

Perhaps the biggest challenge of this (and of any) design problem, is in stating the real problem to be solved. The *what is*, and *what ought to be* parts of the design process too often get preempted by *what if* quick fixes.

Let's say my job codes show a high level of rework coming from contractor RFI submittals. Systemic responses conceivably include a wide array of options:

- Different scheduling for—and attitudes about—redlining and project review.
- Different project deliveries.
- Getting interested bidders in for prebid constructibility reviews.
- Partnering sessions with low bidders.
- Providing in-house continuing education.

- Holding weekly job-site coordination meetings with all subs.
- Changing pricing and negotiation to cover value-adding costs.
- Including get-tough contract clauses that make the contractor reimburse the owner for time lost answering unnecessary RFIs, etc., etc., etc.

Question is, what really needs to get resolved? Til I've looked at the whole system, all the *what ifs* are only a clutter tempting me to lunge at ready-fire-aim solutions that fix the immediate problem but don't cure the causes of them. RFIs are the symptom. What are all the systemic causes and which of them can we deal with effectively?

What's sometimes tough to remember is that it's *the system* rather than the people you're out to fix. Fifty years in this profession, and I'm yet to meet a contractor who gets up in the morning, proclaims it's yet another beautiful day, and vows to spend it screwing up another project, big time.

Wouldn't be in a contractor's interest to do that. They want repeat work, referrals, and good, troublefree projects at least as much as you do. Over the years I worked with a few who had bought into the bid-low-and-make-it-up-in-change-orders strategy, but even those didn't want a bad project to result. In recent years the AGC has worked so hard at teaching partnering, and the market has swung so far toward design/build, that the hard-line adversarial strategies are far less prevalent these days among contractor managers. In my experience, they never extended to the workforce. Innately, we all want to be as proficient as possible at whatever it is we do.

So yeah, it's like those TQM people say. Maybe 15 percent of project problems comes from inept, corrupt, misguided, or generally dumb-ass people. But as any of us who've ever been married can testify, you can't change anyone but yourself. So focus on the things you *can* change and that are causing 85 percent of the problems. As Bill Clinton might better have posted on his wall—*It's the system, stupid.*

Speaking of changing yourself, keep in mind that when you expect the worst of people, you frequently get it. Expectations of others have a way of becoming self-fulfilling prophesies. Old sign in an automotive shop of long ago: "If you want it done bad enough, you can probably get it done bad enough." They didn't mean it the way I now read it but a new and deeper truth to it still haunts me. The entire design and construction industry in now encumbered by a huge legacy of reactive forms and defensive procedures from 50 years of largely self-inflicted risk-management crises. To what extent does the system of project forms that you currently use exemplify an expectation of the worst? How can you begin to temper that with practices and communications of high aspirations for the projects, the processes, and the people that produce them?

WORD-ASSOCIATION QUIZ

What images come to mind as you read the following list?

☐ Cop
☐ Street repairmen
☐ Politician
☐ Used car salesman
☐ Lawyer

It's nearly impossible to even hear the job titles without imaging

STEREOTYPES

Same thing in the design/construction industry:

Code Official
Value Engineer
Developer
Interior Designer
Construction Manager
Contractor

And the more negative the stereotypes -- and the expectations -- we carry into a project meeting, the more likely they are to be proved true. People have a way of meeting our expectations.

DON'T CALL IT QUALITY MANAGEMENT

I purposefully use the dread QM words here so that those of you who are adamantly opposed will know to skip this. Quality management got short shrift in the design professions long before the inevitable backlash in corporate America. In a sense you're stuck with it though, whether you'd like to skip this or not.

By now both big business and government have invested so many billions in training itself that the movement continues under a series of constantly changing names. As Joel Barker says in his book on paradigms, *Quality is no longer a corporate goal, it's the price of admission, in today's market.*

In 1997, Charles Nelson predicted* *Within 2 years, evidence of your having a continuous improvement quality system will be prerequisite for obtaining projects of any considerable size.* That's already the case with many corporate and government clients.

One thing is certain: Even if some clients don't give points for quality management, none of them count off for it. So even if you don't believe there's a market mandate, you may not want to ignore the potential benefits available through working for continuous improvement by any other name:[†]

- A marketing edge, as perceived by the marketplace.
- The potential for real increases in profitability.
- Real, perhaps dramatic, reductions in the risk of practice.
- Increased accountability, both professionally and personally.

Designing and implementing a continuous improvement program by any name is no easy matter and certainly no quick fix, however. AIA Corporate and Public Architects Committee[‡] members told us that one of the easiest ways they have for seeing through your marketing pitch and knowing you really *don't* have a quality program is when you tell them "We've designated Joe as our quality assurance manager." They know (from doing it) that it's not a project phase nor job description, nor organizational department. It's not something someone's managing, it's what everybody is continually doing. Like tackling weight loss by changing your lifestyle, as opposed to periodically going on crash diets. Since neither one's fun, you may want to figure the odds on which is most effective, long term. And all of us—with the apparent exception of people who produce checkout stand magazines—know the answer to that.

The exciting possibility is that perhaps the timing is right for our professions to provide a creative breakthrough. Frankly, the marketplace is giving no clear direction currently whether to go ISO or TQM. The message is: Pick either but have some way to prove you're doing it. What's encouraging is that we're being told to act like designers, enhance our cherished individuality, and design our own enlightened quality systems. Beats all those previous management experts telling us we had to repackage ourselves in their prescribed generic business model of the month—or else.

---

*Charles Nelson, in a presentation to attendees at the AIA Convention in Minneapolis in 1996.

[†] Charles E. Nelson, *TQM and ISO 9000 for Architects and Designers* (McGraw-Hill, 1996), p. 5.

[‡] At symposiums I facilitated in Denver and Indianapolis in 1993.

TREAT QUALITY IMPROVEMENT LIKE ANY OTHER PROJECT

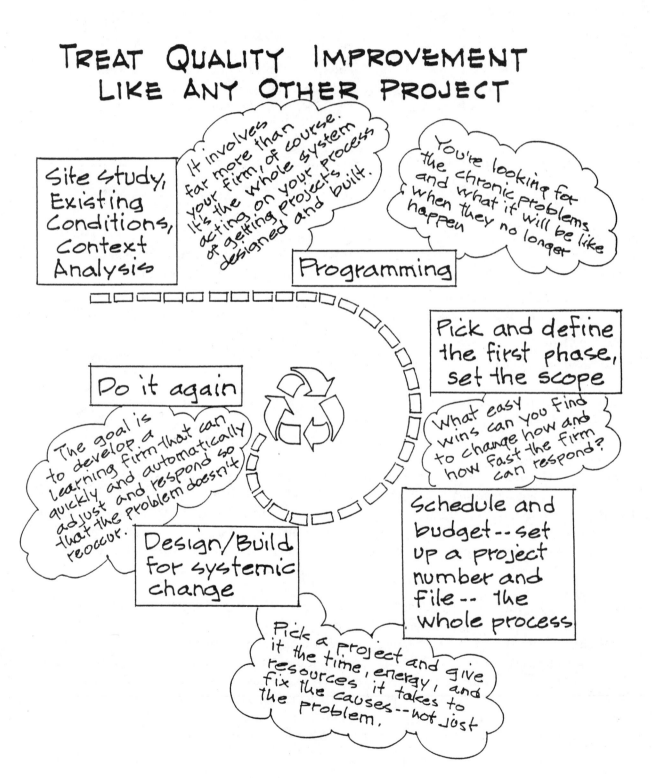

Site Study, Existing Conditions, Context Analysis

It involves far more than your firm, of course. It's the whole system acting on your process of getting projects designed and built.

Programming

You're looking for the chronic problems and what it will be like when they no longer happen

Pick and define the first phase, set the scope

What easy wins can you find to change how and how fast the firm can respond?

Do it again

The goal is to develop a learning firm that can quickly and automatically adjust and respond so that the problem doesn't reoccur.

Schedule and budget -- set up a project number and file -- the whole process

Design/Build for systemic change

Pick a project and give it the time, energy, and resources it takes to fix the causes -- not just the problem.

Assuming you buy into the substance and intent (*And face it, we're all in this for* quality *in the built environment*), this is clearly within your field of expertise—a design project! In order to make a creative design project of it, here is a dangerously oversimplified sequence of steps for a process you might undertake. As the language implies, the principle here—the most useful tip—is:

TREAT QUALITY IMPROVEMENT LIKE ANY OTHER PROJECT

1. **Site analysis**. Acknowledge and document what it is that you say the firm does now for quality, how well you think it's being done, and how important you think it is for the future. Find out what staff, clients—all the other project stakeholders—perceive *really* gets done, how well, and what they think is needed. Analyze the perceived gaps between what you're doing and how well, versus your intentions and the levels of importance you assign to them. Acknowledge or at least proceed as if the problems are not the people. They—like you—are doing everything possible to become the best they can be at what they do. The system is the project. Here are some tips—and a gap survey form—to help you go about all this.

If your practice is large enough to afford independent client, consultant, and builder surveys, wonderful—go for it. There are good consultants to provide such services, or perhaps you know an off-for-the-summer school teacher, or someone doing temp work, who's capable of undertaking the effort with some coaching and a script from you. If none of that sounds doable, consider other ways.

One young midsize firm I know books a meeting room once a year at a nearby resort for a Saturday morning and invites important clients—or prospects—in to speak honestly to the entire staff. Sure, they don't get to hear all the negatives that might have been said in a confidential survey, but the clients are amazingly open and tremendously flattered to be asked.

Like everyone else you know, they have been reading about (and trying to implement) quality management programs, and so are truly impressed with the firm's intent and relevant questions. They take their responsibilities seriously, allude politely to many of the firm's weaknesses, and pointedly say what it is they don't like and don't want from architects in general.

Some firms simply call or visit past clients—the best are combining this with post-occupancy inspections of past projects. I'd settle—as is covered in Chapter 14—for that plus a POE survey mailed out. However you do it, it's a perceived value to the clients, you learn a lot, and it's great marketing.

Open exchanges of evaluation with your consultants and contractors ought to be easy to arrange. Each of them wants to do more work with you in the future, and so has a real interest in your being more successful and a better firm with which to work.

The real cost of such efforts comes from honoring the implicit (but serious) obligation that, once begun, you'll keep up the relationship and provide follow-up. But the benefits of the information you may receive—the strategic partnering relationship you can build—the marketing edge you definitely will get—all this far outweighs the cost of time, meals bought, etc.

GAP SURVEY

From: (Your Name)   Date:

Please rate each of the following 53 statements listed here in each of the two boxes provide

(Note: The difference between the two is the Gap column.)

5. Strongly Agree   4. Agree   3. Neither Agree nor Disagree   2. Disagree   1. Strongly Disagree   N/A   Not Applicable

THE JOB

#	Statement	Current Conditions	Preferred Future	Gap
1.	My job is challenging and interesting.			
2.	I am paid fairly for the work I do.			
3.	I have autonomy and control of my work.			
4.	I am encouraged to innovate and make improvements.			
5.	My talents are used effectively for the good of the firm's projects.			
6.	I am satisfied with the employee performance evaluation system here.			
7.	Overall, I am satisfied with my job.			
8.	My job is more satisfying than it was 2 years ago.			
9.	I'm given reasonable selection among projects to work on next.			
10.	Our employee benefits package compares well against those of other firms in the area, given our size and market.			
11.	I am satisfied with my career development opportunities here.			
12.	I provide others with the information they need.			
13.	I receive constructive, adequate, and appropriate input as needed.			
14.	Firm members generally get along well and readily help each other out.			
15.	Firm members effectively communicate positive reinforcement, praise, and recognition.			
16.	Strong egos very seldom create friction within the firm.			
17.	Comfortable and open communication among us, regardless of status, age, or job position is a major reason people work here.			
18.	Firm members trust each other and can frequently anticipate each other's responses and project decisions.			
19.	Old conflicts and hidden agendas very seldom get in the way of our holding effective meetings.			
20.	The fact that all of us share an agreed-upon vision for the practice and a clear set of annual goals, contributes to good firm performance.			
21.	Firm members treat each other with respect.			
22.	Everyone here is very accessible and approachable.			
23.	Firm members give criticism constructively.			
24.	We have a well-understood organizational structure and each member understands his or her role here.			
25.	Our capabilities and equipment for correspondence, financial info., project data, reproduction, filing, storage, and retrieval are effective.			
26.	Our voice, fax, data communication, and computer systems are appropriate for now.			
27.	We have an organized and useful approach to learning from mistakes and turning them into practice improvements.			
28.	We have a quality system to assure we prevent errors and that we meet or exceed client expectations of service, and for the project.			
29.	We encourage and recognize appropriately the attainment of improvement in written, verbal, leadership, and management skills.			

PROJECT DESIGN AND PRODUCTION

#	Statement	Current Conditions	Preferred Future	Gap
30.	We have, and monitor, comprehensive backup systems for all electronic files. Backup is safely stored off-site.			
31.	Recognizing that every member of the firm is a marketer, we meet regularly to develop and report leads, progress, and plans.			
32.	Our initial programming for each project calls for consideration of individual learning goals as well as for expansion of project services.			

GAP SURVEY

PROJECT DESIGN AND PRODUCTION (cont.)

#		Current Conditions	Preferred Future	Gap
33.	We effectively maintain, use, and upgrade our systems for project quality in terms of using current regulatory requirements, industry standards, product information, standard details, and standard specifications from which to work.			
34.	We develop, update as needed and comply with a work plan for each project which addresses the detailed needs for staffing, roles, assignments, schedule, and budget.			
35.	Each in-house project work plan includes scheduling adequate time for review (by someone other than those who worked on it) and we provide all deliverables prior to issuance.			
36.	We maintain organized files for every project of all communications (verbal, written, digitized, or graphic), relative to status, decisions, changes, or quality assessments of the project and our services.			
37.	For each project, we develop and reach a shared understanding with the client as to the scope of our services and who will provide other services required in order for the project to be successful.			
38.	We regularly track our "on-time/on-budget/on-target" project performance.			
39.	We have and use standard project forms, procedures, and documentation that are appropriate to the needs of our projects and clients.			
40.	Our CADD hardware and software, processes, and procedures optimize our productivity and quality appropriately for our current projects and needs.			
41.	In case of a project upset or dispute, we have a proactive early action plan or system in place which we all know and follow.			
42.	We regularly maintain and update information on current construction costs to use in developing anticipated project costs or checking contractors' submittals.			

CONSTRUCTION ADMINISTRATION

#		Current Conditions	Preferred Future	Gap
43.	Except for certain government projects, we secure and include in all contracts adequate scope of services during the construction phase.			
44.	We follow standard written procedures for bid document distribution, addenda, prebid conferences, questions during bidding, and bid opening.			
45.	We follow our office procedures on all projects regarding processing and documentation of shop drawings, field directives, requests for information, change orders, site visit reports, observations, etc.			
46.	We systematically use construction phase and post-occupancy feedback from clients, builders, and vendors to improve the quality of our client service as well as our processes for design, production, and construction administration.			
47.	At the end of our projects, the project team meets to recognize what went well, who made it happen, and to plan future improvements in project process.			

FINANCIAL

#		Current Conditions	Preferred Future	Gap
48.	We develop an annual profit plan, a marketing plan and an overhead expense budget. We manage and monitor performance. All members contribute in the process and are appropriately knowledgeable about the firm's financial goals and our progress.			
49.	We monitor our utilization (efficiency) ratio periodically on the basis of cost, and every member commits to an agreed-upon personal utilization ratio on the basis of time.			
50.	Standard time sheets are used and regularly submitted by all of us. Our system of coding hours provides adequate data for reliable pricing of fees and regular monitoring of project financial performance.			
51.	Cash flow and aged accounts receivable reports are regularly prepared, analyzed, and used as the basis for action.			
52.	We consistently use an invoicing and collection process which ensures smooth cash flow.			
53.	We only provide additional services upon proper modification of the contract, or after full discussion in-house to agree that the work will be done at our own expense.			

Every one of the people from whom you'd ask for peer review is virtually certain to be in a position to give you, or recommend you for, a project at some point in the future. Open discussions with them about strengths, weaknesses, and possible improvements does a lot to ensure they will do that. You might consider asking your favorite engineering consultants to fill out the gap survey as though they were members of the firm. They know things about your firm that you don't.

Final thoughts on using the gap survey: If you can find a way—or a third party—to make the input for form redesign and the resulting feedback anonymous, staff tend to be reassured there will be no reprisals and therefore will participate more honestly. A major objective of this gap survey process is for firm principals to do their own evaluations and then be able to compare their perceptions of themselves and the firm with the perceptions of other stakeholders. Works best when a copy of such a form is sent to each member of the firm along with a personal letter of assurance and a stamped return envelope, so they know the boss won't see their feedback. Having everyone in the firm take the gap survey can be a valuable way to get very quickly and explicitly down to what in the system needs attention. As might be expected, the most compelling message often is that of needing additional or better communication. Typically, principals are absolutely certain that they—and all staff—have been clearly and mutually understood, while staff are absolutely certain that neither side has. Best shot at keeping sides from being taken? Keep attribution out of it, except generically. One way is to have results reported in a summary report to all stakeholders, listing high, low, and mean ratings from staff, from principals, and from the firm as a whole.

2. **Mission statement.** Most of the literature lists this as a mandatory first step,* but it's often only after years of practice that the need for a statement of core values makes any sense at all to most design professionals in small and midsized firms. After all, don't we all have the same mission? To do good projects, serve our clients well, leave the world a better place than we found it, and find joy in what we do?

Lot of truth in that, but it's not the statement that matters so much as the interaction, participation, and reflective conversation needed to arrive at one. I've used the term *mission statement* here because that's what we're all used to hearing. Actually, what I'm suggesting you consider is closer to Collins and Porras's discussion of core values—a list of your essential and enduring tenets that won't change with time, market conditions, or technological breakthroughs.† The test of whether it's really *core*, rather than just part of today's strategic market response, is to ask yourself: *If conditions change and years from now we get penalized in the market for holding this value, will we still hang onto it?*

It's reported it took 10 years of reflective conversation, study, and circulation of written drafts before our nation's founders were prepared to declare *We hold these truths to be self-evident. . . .* The mission statement process can produce incredible bonding, appreciation of diversity, and true consensus building around core values—which is what holds firms together, over the long haul. The real key is to make the interaction an ongoing effort—a discipline—through which the shared vision is reflected on and retold, till it becomes the operative truth of every member of the organization, the myth that we live out.

---

*The exception: J. Collins and J. Porras, *Built to Last* (HarperBusiness, 1994), p. 7, the first *and last* of 12 "shattered myths."
† Ibid., p. 221.

3. **Pick a project—and make it one.** All the above has been leading—among other things—to your being able to identify what to do next. Each previous exercise can provide useful—perhaps vital—information for your analysis in the crucial process of defining the problems to be solved, in deciding which comes first. But even if, by now, you've documented and analyzed the causes of rework, have conducted both peer evaluations and self-evaluations, have identified your core values and purpose, I still advise that you rely on your gut to decide what systemic change to tackle first.

Decisions we can live with in life are those we make from the centers of our beings rather than with our left brain logic. Check your intuition; confer with your team; give it time. Or try this—list again all the options that have high priority—this time, each on a separate 3 by 5 card—and leave them spread out, "forgotten" on your desk overnight. Go home with breezy self-assurances that the decision will come easily for you tomorrow, no need to worry about it tonight—*so don't.* When you arrive next day, allow yourself only 2 seconds to select a card, pick one up, and that'll be the one to work on. This process forces a centered, intuitive, subjective decision, provided you've had the self-discipline to avoid compulsively obsessing in the interim.

The reason for these precautions is that design and implementation of systemic change requires investment of considerable commitment and resources. Transforming your practice is a major project, typically with no demonstrable return on investment for a very long time. I advise you test your level of commitment quite seriously before you accept such a project. If you do undertake it, then make it a real project. Assign a job number, set up a file, start a project record book—do whatever you normally do to initiate a big project.

4. **Programming.** Like the rest, this step is best done with all the stakeholders participating. As a group, agree on a reasonable date for project completion—a deadline by when the system will have been changed to eliminate the chosen problem. Then, as a group, imagine you've already won. Imaging success is important here, and *in the present tense.* Then describe the situation—how do you know you've won? What happens, and no longer happens, as a result of having won? Simply brainstorm—but do it the right way—simultaneously, on separate pieces of paper, and racing the clock (this is no laid-back B.S. session). The result: a composite, inclusive description by all the stakeholders of what project process is like, now that that problem no longer occurs—just never comes up anymore.

What you're doing here is developing a statement of project design aspirations, and I recommend you err on the side of superlatives. Using a flipchart, or bold markers on yellow Post-its stuck to the wall, display everyone's contributions to compile a composite description of what the improved system does. Not how it's done—just what gets accomplished—what it's like to work here now, in this best of all possible worlds.

Given adequate motivation—and a tolerance for reading about other disciplines and orientations, you may want to extend this phase, as advocated by Peter Schwartz, *The Art of the Long View;* by Collins and Porras in *Built to Last;* and by Senge and associates in *The Fifth Discipline Fieldbook.*

Of the three, Senge and associates provide the most comprehensive sourcebook, with the least focus on corporate and industry organizations. Schwartz provides tips for inventing alternative scenarios for the future and positioning yourself to be OK no matter which way the world goes. Collins and Porras advise setting "Big Hairy Audacious Goals" (BHAGs*) at the outer limits of possibility in order to challenge yourself to exceed the merely feasible. Passionately committing to scarcely feasible goals—and in the present tense—attains the power of affirmations, becomes a team's operative truth. That's what makes 10 out of a possible 10 scores the standard performance criteria for Olympic champions.

My own paltry (but nonetheless effective) version of this 20 years ago was to ask our team to select—as our competition—those architects at the pinnacle of what we considered admirable in the profession. We then set out to research, emulate, challenge them. Real trick was convincing the staff (never mind myself) that we were already undiscovered equals to our chosen competition and were expected to perform accordingly. Today we call that "benchmarking." However you go about it, remember that the admonition to "Dream no small dreams" applies to the design of organization systems as well as buildings.

5. **Design.** So now you have a project defined, the program statement, and a project schedule. Next step is a project work plan, and for this the process—as any good planner knows—is to work bass-ackwards.

Having projected when it's to be completed, and what it feels like to have achieved success, you now play all the "what-if" games to arrive at a plausible description and scenario of the events, changes, milestones that led to this stellar achievement. What was the last step in the process, and the contacts, resources, and procedures required? And what led to that, when, and how? Then the step before that, and the step before that, etc., etc.

As Schwartz recommends, you're spinning future myths, and though you're not bound by them, they provide a back trail of possible actions to the present. They lead to first steps for which you can set project budget and time line.

This method of present-tense future visioning and goal setting, followed by reverse engineering, is in strict accordance with classical planning technique. What's fascinating is that it's also consistent with Zen thought. Rather than the present constituting the causes for the future (western logic) it's a way of thinking of the past more like the wake of a boat spun out behind us, now that we've chosen to relocate ourselves into the future, For a good Taoist (or planner), apparently it's all in working from a present-tense mind-set. All I can tell you is that, without quite understanding it ontologically, I know from experience that it works.

6. **Design/build.** Obviously, the processes described up to this point are time- and labor-intensive, are most suitable for firms at least midsize and with a serious need for—or commitment to—systemic change.

---

* Ibid., p. 91.

If, instead, your firm is either sole proprietor, top-down (or big-daddy) in management style, it's probably more appropriate to have gone design/build long ago. Involvement of all the other stakeholders implies empowerment, and if you're not going to walk the talk, setting up all the implied mechanisms for stakeholder implementation can be detrimental. Besides, *empower* isn't the same as *enable*.

If, for whatever reason, the game plan is to make a top-down decision and go with it, simply go back to your survey and pick a gap. Works best to choose an easy win (with possible big returns on the investment) from among the problems identified. Then start with tentative yet focused trial and error. After all, doctors have always done this—they consider the options, make their tentative diagnosis, prescribe a treatment based on their best judgment, and tell you to call 'em if it's not working.

However you go about picking the problem and solving it, set it up as a design/build project—job codes, schedule, project file—all the rest. Redesign and reengineer how you do things—the system, the processes—so that the gap (problem) no longer exists. Learn by doing.

7. **Do it again.** Repeat any or all steps, setting up and doing quality projects, gap by gap. Then start all over again, always keeping adequate records so that you can:

- Know when you're winning and by how much.
- Celebrate it with stakeholders now.
- Prove it to prospective clients later.

PERFORMANCE EVALUATIONS

Dr. Edwards Deming, whose seminal work on quality management changed our work world, emphatically said *don't do personnel evaluations*. He held that the process is a huge drain on productivity, energy, and morale. That for 3 weeks prior to reviews, staff are angst-ridden, apprehensive, and relatively unproductive. That no one ever likes or agrees with the evaluations or how they've been administered, so they're angry or hurt and unproductive for 3 more weeks following the review.

Seems to me, the larger the organization, the more accurate that assessment becomes. The necessity and desire for equitable impartiality, the levels of review and approval required—all this adds quantum layerings of overhead with each increase in numbers or types of job descriptions. I cite Deming here just to underscore the need—even for so small a group as most architectural offices comprise—for a process that's fair, quick, and requires only minimum preparation and paperwork.

Should you provide performance reviews? *Absolutely*. First, two obvious reasons:

1. Employees won't let evaluations *not* be provided. 360-degree feedback systems, POE processes, team evaluations—you name it—staff still want to meet with, and get ratings from, the boss whose approval they've worked so hard to earn.

2. Done well, performance evaluation can become primarily a career planning session for the employee. It's an opportunity and a reminder for staff to evaluate how well their work fits with what's needed to advance themselves professionally through continuous improvement or diversified experience, to negotiate training or resources to facilitate that happening, and to propose how it can prosper the firm long term.

Use Performance evaluation as a process for staff self-motivation and choreographing their professional advancement

Try always to discipline in private.

And to brag on somebody at every public opportunity.

There's no way to get too hokey at this—provided you are absolutely sincere

The more immediate and understandable the feedback on performance -- the better.

Don't pressure-cook a grievance....
and don't let them

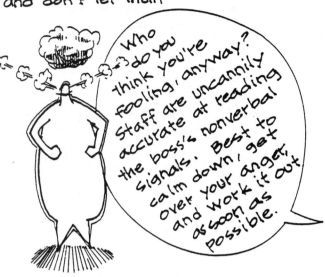

Who do you think you're fooling, anyway? Staff are uncannily accurate at reading the boss's nonverbal signals. Best to calm down, get over your anger, and work it out as soon as possible.

There's a third excellent reason to hold performance reviews. In all but the very large firms, it's the only opportunity for the leader—or boss—to get an evaluation. Like all of us, you too want and need to know how well you're performing.

How does that work? Simple. If there are any surprises—on either side of the table—during the evaluation interview, it means you as leader haven't done your job in a timely and effective manner. Consider the analogy of the basketball coach. When players aren't performing adequately they're jerked out of the game long enough for the coach to get in their faces, make sure they understand the best way to play it, and somehow motivate them to get back in there with high enthusiasm and all the right moves to help the team win. The pace is too fast and the teamwork too critical to allow disagreement or hurt feelings to generate repressed anger that impacts performance and gets vented months later at evaluation time. It's like that in architectural practice. If staff evaluation turns into a venue for staff—or you—to ventilate grievances, something's way wrong and has been for some time.

Evaluate your job performance as a leader by whether there are any surprises for either of you during the interview.

Money is almost always an issue, almost never the real problem. Look behind the symptoms for the true causes of job dissatisfaction.

The money? Sure, it's always an issue—which is one reason I push so hard for maximum disclosure. With a fully shared understanding of the way the firm is performing financially, salary is virtually *never* the problem, only one symptom. Because the nature of our work requires so much open communication, when job dissatisfaction has been seething undetected over time, it's serious. It often requires all the people skills you can muster to ferret out the real reasons, and provides yet another performance evaluation of you as leader. If you start getting hammered for salary increases at performance review time, it probably means you haven't been paying enough attention to the real problems. Money's usually way down the list.

Point is, it's your job to manage employees in whatever ways will help them succeed in the profession, and in the firm, and feel good about doing so. Managing well—leading—demands quality time, creative thought, and enormous flexibility on an ongoing basis, since what's needed by each staff member is always changing.

The accompanying four-box matrix from a training session years ago[*] illustrates a typical flow of management behaviors sequentially changing, depending on the degree of focus on relationship versus task.

The matrix is most easily understood by thinking of it as descriptive of management behaviors typically used relative to the length of time the employee has been with the firm.

First day on the job, we normally introduce new employees, show them around, where to find supplies, the coffeepot and restrooms, and explain only enough for them to succeed on the job the first week. All very directive. Fill out these forms today. This is your workstation. Do this by Friday.

Over time and as we get to know each other, the relationship builds into a coaching mode and, with growing trust, one of encouragement to excel with less direction needed. Somewhere along in here (3 months after hiring, 6?), they finally become worth the money they're being paid. Then gradually, like doubles partners in tennis, we learn to anticipate each other's moves and positions and play to the other's strengths with less personal time or even communication required. Eventually, delegation becomes assumed and intuited to a large degree.

What's actually important here is to realize that behaviors are appropriately predicated on capability, performance level, and mutual trust far more than on longevity. There are a variety of reasons—new assignments or project types, unfamiliar and risk-intensive services undertaken, or faltering performance due to personal problems, just to name a few—that justify or require adjusting management behaviors back to previous ratios of relationship versus task orientation.

---

[*] Robert S. Bailey, The Center for Creative Leadership, 1986.

ADJUST MANAGEMENT BEHAVIORS
TO FIT THE PERFORMANCE LEVEL
OF THE EMPLOYEE

Adaptable	Appreciative
Coaching	Considerate
Energetic	Encouraging
Interactive	Patient
Involving	Supportive
Resourceful	Understanding

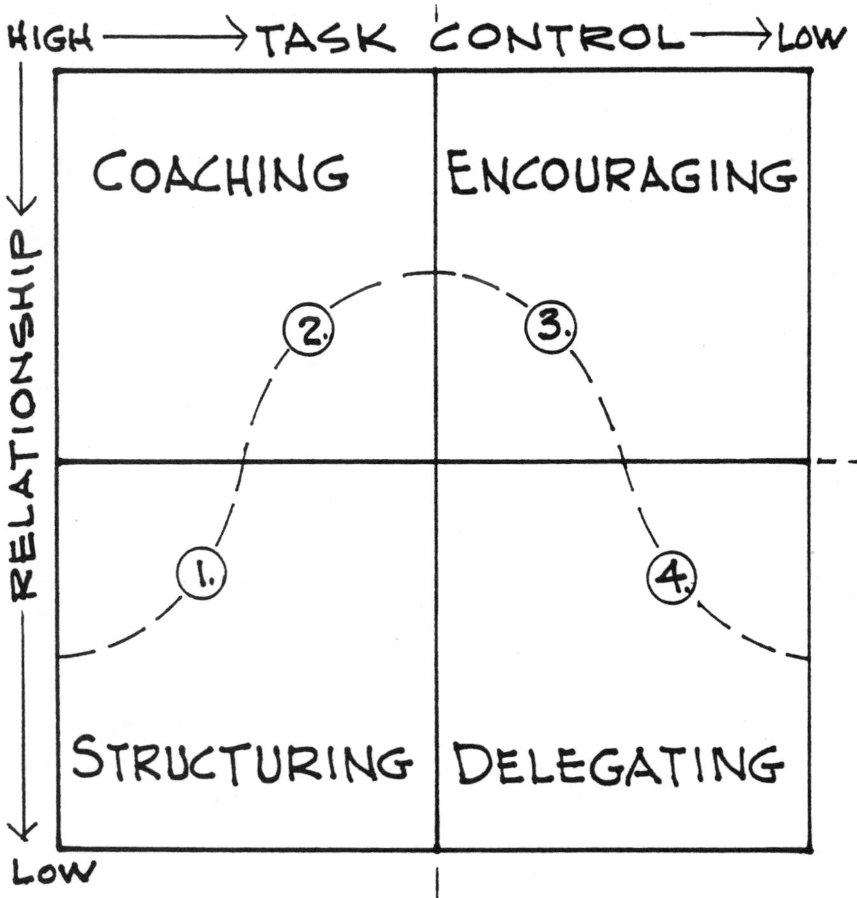

HIGH ——→ TASK CONTROL ——→ LOW

RELATIONSHIP

COACHING ②	ENCOURAGING ③
① STRUCTURING	DELEGATING ④

LOW

Decisive	Analytical
Directing	Delegating
Determined	Deliberate
Forceful	Methodical
Initiating	Organized
Structuring	Reflective

Obviously, such adjustments are made constantly, often intuitively, in the workplace without ever thinking of them as being a sequence. What's useful about doing so— and the point of including the matrix here— is that it's the basis for a neat performance evaluation system I learned years ago from Ron Battaglia at Canon Design—a large firm in upstate New York. I used it with equal success with firm sizes ranging from 15 to 85. It requires only a single-page form on which the employees summarize their work plans for the next performance period in five bulleted one-liners of their choice that describe roles and responsibilities.

Over time I found it beneficial to require a sixth item of each person—a proposed utilization ratio. Other than that, I allowed maximum freedom in what they chose to propose their job comprise for the next 6 months, provided we agreed that it was within their capability and would benefit us all. Seldom if ever was it necessary to push people to expand their aspirations—most were ambitious for personal professional growth and the whole process was one of self-motivation.

The only real negotiation came in what weight or value they assigned to each goal because, in this system, the total of the weights for the six one-liners has to equal 100 percent—the theoretical total of their contribution to the welfare of the firm. Doesn't have anything to do with the time allocated to each role or responsibility, of course—redlining sets of drawings for other teams' projects might require only brief periods of concentrated effort, yet provide incredible value. We'd talk about all that, since this form represents a performance contract between the individual and the firm.

The reason for the form occupying only about a half a page is to leave room for future amendments when their goals for the firm's needs change. In practice, however, it was most useful as a place to record in writing their personal goals that were not quantifiable, yet were important to acknowledge and work toward. Examples in my experience included their need to spend more quality time with children, or cultivate a more professional image in the community or the AIA. My self-evaluation of boss performance went up when staff would talk with me about such issues so important to their quality of life and self-esteem.

At the end of the performance period, the employee and I each rated the performance on each item and scored our respective copies of what we'd agreed to 6 months earlier. Took about 15 minutes for me, though I don't know how much they might have agonized over it. Then we met to compare details on the ratings and agree on a total score.

Great thing about this system is that it allowed me to be the good guy. Invariably they scored themselves lower than I had. I always had the benefit of experience, knew the client or contractors better than they, had stubbed my toe on that particular rock long ago. For whatever reason, I was aware of mitigating circumstances that warranted increasing their self-scoring more times than not.

PERFORMANCE PLANNING AND REVIEW

NAME: Stacy Project Architect   DATES: FROM: 6/1 TO: 12

MEASURABLE PERFORMANCE TARGETS	WEIGHT		x		RATING =		SCORE
	%	1/2	3/4	1	1-1/4	1-1/2	
1. Marketing: Make 4 cold calls each week. Write ____ Meet with Ext ____							
2. CADD Lea____ Form E Power ____				✓			10
	10					✓	15
3.							
4.	35				✓		35
	10	✓					5
5.	15			↗	✓		19
6. Target Utilizaton Ratio: 65%	30				✓		37
	100				TOTAL		121

(handwritten cloud note over top section): HOW TO USE THIS: The measurable performance goals and their weights (not hours) are drafted by the employee as a summary of all their roles and responsibilities for the period. They are negotiated and approved at the beginning of the period. Make sure each goal will produce quantifiable results -- what can be measured can be managed! 3 sections Time Specifications

QUALIFICATIONS AND AMENDMENTS

(handwritten cloud note): There are several good uses for the bottom half of the form:
1. To record clarifications or amendments made to the top part during the meet____
2. To list goals that can't be quantified, ie., "To achieve a more professional image in the community."
3. To document evaluation comments at the end of the evaluation period. Best to keep it all on one easily recognized 8½ x 11, so both parties can keep a working copy -- Use the back!

(handwritten cloud note): the weights must total 100%

(handwritten cloud note): At the end of the evaluation period, the employee & employer do independant ratings, then meet to compare and agree on the total score. They negotiate roles and responsibilities for the upcoming period

(handwritten cloud note): 150% is the max score

The next page is a clean form you can copy →

PERFORMANCE PLANNING AND REVIEW

NAME:		DATES: FROM: _____ TO: _____

MEASURABLE PERFORMANCE TARGETS	WEIGHT	x			RATING =		SCORE
	%	1/2	3/4	1	1-1/4	1-1/2	
1.							
2.							
3.							
4.							
5.							
6. Target Utilizaton Ratio:							
	100			TOTAL			

QUALIFICATIONS AND AMENDMENTS

Which takes us back to the four-box matrix. If you multiply the weight of each item times the rating on the form and add them up, it gives a total value to the firm within a range of scores from 50 to 150 percent. Setting aside the extraordinary situations staff might experience within a performance period (one may have gone through a divorce or, on the other hand, another been on an unprecedented 6-month roll with all the breaks), if you're dealing with a 50 percent performer for long, we need to talk reassignment or outplacement to a job where he or she can succeed better and be happier. If you're acknowledging a 150 percent performance record even twice in a row, you're either dealing with a future partner or your competition, take your choice.

Either way, and just as with design critiques, I was looking first for reasons to brag on them before getting down to what needed improvement or change. And of course the session ended for them with high hopes, affirmations, and a fresh set of goals for the next review period starting now. For me it ended later with quiet reflection, self-scoring on how well I'd handled it, and ways to improve my performance next time. I also usually resolved to meet with them and make interim amendments to the new agreement whenever their responsibilities changed substantively, or at least every quarter. In practice, this somehow never happened—we stayed too busy, which makes the case for holding evaluations and validates the usefulness of the form. Without it and the calendar, we'd never have gotten around to their long-term needs and career planning til one of us was angry enough to demand it. Which is never the right time to do it.

It can also be useful to look back at the four-box matrix of management behaviors in terms of rating the performance level of the employee. How much is required in terms of structured task control or intensive day-to-day relationship in order for them to perform at their best?

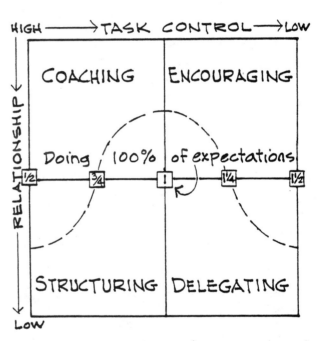

In the end, of course, it comes down to open discussion of judgment calls. Much of it has to do with the endless problem of quantifying quality. To the extent we can put numbers to it, we feel better about the system, more justified in our decisions.

CHAPTER 12 — TIPS FOR BETTER PROJECTS

The previous were tips for keeping the firm project-centered. The following are gatherings about practices used for getting better projects designed and built. Again, they're primarily from national design award winners, even two AIA Gold Medallists, but a lot also came from a bunch of other good architects. As always, there's no formula—if these tips resonate well with you, pick and cull, tinker and try, mash to fit. They're listed and numbered here to correlate with the sequence of project phases and processes, but that's only for reference. If they work, use them wherever they fit your needs. Preparing for negotiation, writing a proposal, setting up a meeting—each is a design project.

1. **Invest in the programming.** This is a sort of pay-now-or-pay-later proposition. Programming and design have a reciprocal relationship—each necessarily informs the other. I've yet to find an architect who recalls any project for which they did absolutely no programming. One of the biggest advancements made by the 1997 edition of the AIA B141 is that it both blurs accountability for, and attenuates the process of, programming. It was unfortunate—and patently not feasible—that previous standard forms of agreement set aside programming as a unilateral activity for the owner to perform. Attempts to comply with that edict can have negative consequences at least three ways:

   • Unilateral client programming denies the client of value-added opinions, questions, and options the architect can offer. We're not aware of the world's spinning because we're spinning too. In the same way, it often takes an outsider to our organizational system to innocently comment, question, and thereby provide new insights into our assumptions about what we do and how; what we need and why. The architect can play that role.

   • None of us enjoys rework. We don't like having to redo what someone else should have done better to begin with. Most of all, we don't appreciate people gratuitously redoing work we're proud of.

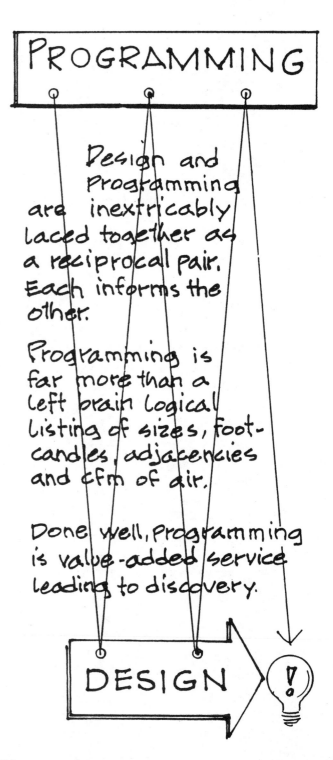

PROGRAMMING

Design and Programming are inextricably laced together as a reciprocal pair. Each informs the other.

Programming is far more than a left brain logical listing of sizes, foot-candles, adjacencies and cfm of air.

Done well, Programming is value-added service leading to discovery.

DESIGN

CLIENT PROGRAMMING

☐ The client misses out on value-added right brain ideas, questions, etc.

☐ Frustrates the designer, whose subsequent decoding & reconstruction probably will frustrate the client.

☐ Get's worse the "better" its done through systematic left brain work.

☐ Denies the client, the designer -- and the project -- the benefits of the trust-and-team building that could have happened through joint work.

Architects typically are frustrated by having to decode, deconstruct, often reinvent, the client's program statement simply in order to understand it. Their attempts typically frustrate the client, who has already invested heavily in developing a statement of assumed givens for the project, and considers it obviously self-explanatory. Far better to do programming up front and with them, rather than later and despite them.

• The "better" (more voluminous, detailed, and quantitative) the client program, the more it tempts the architect to accept it without question and settle for merely meeting expectations. We know from the mid-1980s TARP[*] study that customer *dissatisfaction* is measured in terms of unmet *quantifiable* expectations. *Satisfaction*, on the other hand, is *qualitative* and comes from getting more, or better-designed, results than one knew enough to require or expect in advance.

In negotiation parlance, it's the difference in dealing with positions, rather than interests. Delivering projects to meet measurable expectations is only the price of admission, the star performance is having the project achieve immeasurable aspirations.

Sorry, Phil Crosby[†]—quality is not free. You have to work for it, but it can provide incredible bargains in both quantifiable and ineffable returns that meets true interests throughout the entire life-cycle of the project. So, on every project—but especially those for which you're handed a handsomely prepared program—I propose that you:

---

[*] The study, performed by the TARP organization, was authorized by President George in 1985 to determine what U.S. industry could do to improve its global market share through increased customer satisfaction.

[†] Phil Crosby is a noted author on TQM. This is in specific reference to his book *Quality Is Free.*

2. **Conduct a predesign phase of services.**
People who specialize in programming like
to lump this one in with it. I differentiate
them because every star designer does, and
for good reason.

Suffice it to say here that unilaterally
generated client programming also denies
both owner and designer opportunities to
interactively develop relationship, trust, and
a consensus statement of aspirations for the
project. Our hopes and aspirations for the
project are the major deliverables for the
predesign phase. They can act in the same
way as a goals/mission statement for a firm
or organization; can serve as the scorecard
for assessing all future qualitative design
decisions. That's very different from the
program as we've come to think of it—the
alphanumeric heavy yardstick against
which all quantitative design decisions are
evaluated for compliance with expectations.

It's not a question of quantity versus quality.
Obviously both need be included. The
predesign phase of services (for which top
designers customarily get paid) must
therefore involve working intensely with the
client to program or reprogram, but also
includes any or all of the following:

- Exploration of client and user interests
  (versus positions).
- Scenario-building to envision users' ideal
  experiences of the project.
- Explorations of all forms permitted by
  the restraints—site, context, regulations,
  etc.
- Developing consensus about and a
  shared understanding of project
  aspirations and hopes.

The front-end phase of services -- reported by -- and about-- top design architects

PREDESIGN:

☐ To develop respect, trust, and good communication among all design team members.

☐ To discover and investigate--prior to design-- all possible building forms the site would allow.

☐ To reach consensus -- especially with the client-- on highest aspirations for scope, function, and quality-- what the project will do.

☐ To summarize those aspirations in 5 or 6 memorable goal statements, the standard against which all subsequent design decisions will be judged.

Sounds almost like partnering-- both seeking to build communication and trust -- but they're fundamentally different. Predesign works to set very high aspirations-- a challenge goal for design. Partnering tends to accept design as a commodity and deal with process and accountability to meet expectations.

PARTNERING CHARTER:

☐ To understand and agree on roles and responsibilities of all project stakeholders about:
  - Time
  - Budget
  - Quality
  - Risks
  - Rewards

☐ To jointly design a process to avoid project errors and delays.

☐ To agree on process and protocol for avoiding project disputes and, when they arise, for settling them quickly at the lowest possible level.

☐ To mutually commit to:
  - Effective ongoing communication
  - Dealing for equity and efficacy
  - Being personally accountable
  - Striving for error-free process
  - Maximum speed and profit

The key to good design is to start with a concept so strong it can withstand the erosion... inevitable in every project.

The detail of all this is covered in Chapter 14 which proposes you add a predesign set of services to your normal project processes—they're that important. The next five tips are actually part of this one, or at least could begin concurrently with predesign. They're listed separately here because each seems significant enough to warrant its own paragraph. The megamessage: What you do up front—and how—counts enormously.

a. **Ask the site**. The design process begins with listening to and understanding the site and its context, past and present. Context is far more than perceptions of surroundings and includes considerations from metrics to poetics, from physical to metaphysical. The mere fact that *letting the site speak to you* is a process that eludes both physiological and procedural rules in no way obviates the necessity for listening.

As an aside, Paul Laseau* ratchets up the pressure a notch with his observation that you can categorize all the parameters of any design problem as being need, context, or form. His concern is that most of us mistakenly think *need* and *context* are fixed givens, that the architect's only domain of action lies in designing and manipulating *form*.

Not so, Paul says—all three interrelate and the forms we create can change the other two.

I put it more strongly—changes in any one cannot *not* change the other two. They're all interdependent variables.

Function · Schedule · Image · NEED · Life Cycle Cost · Sustainability · Budget · Technology · Program · Circulation · Systems

FORM

Access · Microclimate · Topo · Site uses, past, present, and future · soils · CONTEXT · Sun & wind · Vistas to & from the site · Socio-economic · Local & regional · Vegetation · Seismic

You can never change just one thing.....

Too many of us assume the only thing we work with is the form. Our designs modify context and needs as well. Start with the site and seek the disclosed, rather than imposed order first.

* Paul A. Laseau, professor of architecture, Ball State University. Along with Norman Crowe, Paul is the author of *Visual Notes for Architects and Designers* (Van Nostrand Reinhold, 1984).

PREDESIGN

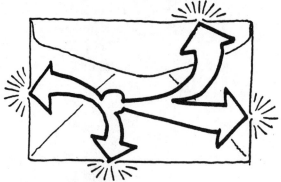

TEST THE
EDGES OF THE
ENVELOPE

SAY <u>WHAT</u> YOU
WILL ACHIEVE

NOT

DISTILL IT DOWN
TO SIX
MEMORABLE
GOALS

THAT'S
YOUR
SCORECARD

PREDESIGN

START WITH THE SITE AND THE CONTEXT

Cultural and Socioeconomic as well as physical

What other excellent projects do you know with similar site and context parameters?

What are the principals behind their solutions?

Any generative ideas there?

TRY TO IMAGE THE EXPERIENCE (rather than the) form

WHAT SPECIAL EXPERIENCES WILL THE PROJECT PROVIDE THAT WILL SET IT APART -- MAKE IT TRULY EXCELLENT?

b. **Defer judgment.** The one thing specifically excluded in predesign is *design*. This is Arthur Erickson* saying that, for him, *The secret of doing excellent design is to not design at all until it's almost too late.* It's Charles Gwathmey calling predesign *the discovery phase*. It's Charlie Dagget's firm insisting on providing a final presentation model *after* the schematics are approved as a way to test, tinker with, adjust the design—and obtain a 3D contract to which all stakeholders agree to adhere in subsequent project decisions.

c. **Agree on team learning objectives.** As the firm's aspirations for the project evolve during the predesign phase, so can the professional-growth aspirations of in-house project team members. It's at this time, in a true learning firm, that staff might volunteer—or be asked—to undertake some special research or unique role for the project. Staff might propose—and negotiate—that the firm provide resources, tuition, software, or other assistance in return for their focusing on some new or neglected expertise that will be of long-term benefit to the project, the firm, and the staff member. Setting explicit learning goals leads to individual mastery.

d. **Design the process to fit the project.** Design professionals commonly share the idiosyncratic tendency to approach most anything—from organizing and managing the firm, to quality management, to writing an invoice—as a design project. Should come as no surprise, then, that designing the very process by which to design the project is among the tips here.

---

* There's a lot of name dropping all through this. If I don't signal an endnote by a name, it means I assume you know—or should know—their names through their published architectural projects.

I admit, however, that it surprised me some-what to find the top designers I've interviewed volunteering that project-specific process is also one of their precepts. Guess I had hoped they'd have some universally applicable secret to share.

Instead, I found they simply anticipate opportunities and needs up front, rig an ad hoc process to suit, then remain thoughtfully flexible enough to let the design process itself change or evolve along with the project design. It's Joe Esherick saying, *The secret of doing good projects is paying attention.*

e. **Anthropomorphize the project.** Probably no need to bring this one up, since it's so ubiqui-tous a habit among us. I include it here for the more left-brained among us, remembering the *aha* experience one of my favorite lawyers[*] had, following an afternoon of lis-tening to architects discuss design, *Why, they talked like those buildings were people!* she said in amazement. We do. It works.

It is this ability to evoke for the project its own identity with personality, needs, and wants that is a major secret in the art of designing. It's an artist's and inventor's strate-gy, reported widely by authors, physicists, and painters, as well as by preeminent designers of the built environment.

Ira Progoff,[†] noted psychologist and author, once told me he always kept one personal daily journal for himself and another for the book he was currently authoring. In morning meditations, the work in progress told him where it wanted to go each day.

Try giving your project a persona -- an identity and personality all its own -- through doodling, journaling and sketching, find out what it wants to be.

---

[*] Ava Abromawitz, Esq., former Deputy General Counsel, the AIA, then Vice-President at Victor O. Schinnerer, and now a consultant to architects and engineers.
[†] Ira Progoff, author of such books as *Jung and the Theory of Synchronicity* and *At a Journal Workshop.*

3. **Once you start, design all the time, out loud, and with lots of alternatives considered.** The act of designing comes in lots of forms. It can involve the roomfuls of rough Styrofoam models a Pelli or Gehry are known for talking their clients through. Or an Esherick saying his best design approach is to sit down with the client, some blank paper, and start sketching—*We talk our clients to death. . . it's the secret of our success,* Joe said.

There's George Hartman: *The only reason I'm any better at design than anybody else is, that's all I do.* And Hugh Newell Jacobssen: *I'm always designing—in the shower, driving to work. . .* It's Graham Gunn reporting he gives some 19 design crits on a typical day in the office.*

On the one hand, it's such luminaries as these reporting they actively design through the daily crit process. On the other, it's also all those lesser-known firms out there constantly evolving their own latter-day versions of Bill Caudill's squatters' sessions, holding design charrettes on the clients' turf.

As an aside, for the last 15 years of my active practice, we designed virtually every project in 4-day charrettes with the clients present, and actively involving as many of the users as possible. I instigated the process selfishly when the firm grew so large I was about to lose my chance to design—too much management to be done.

One of the best things about it was that it forced us to take the predesign phase very seriously indeed, because the one cardinal rule for successful on-site design charrettes is that you *do not* go into one with *any* preconception of how the design will turn out or what it will look like.

---

* Quotes from the AIA 1989 Signature Firms Roundtable, or follow-up phone interviews. Most of these previously reported by me in *In Search of Design Excellence* (AIA Press, 1990).

Given a good predesign phase, everybody on the team can sing from the same sheet music.

So delegation is no problem

With consensus on, and full communication of, design goals, everybody is capable of offering meaningful design alternatives and crits.

Trying out and talking over lots of design alternatives improves the odds of ending up with the best one.

TO MAKE AN ON-SITE DESIGN CHARRETTE WORK

- Involve clients in a comprehensive predesign phase and strongly resist anybody's designing—one key to success is going into the charrette with no preconceived ideas of what the project will look like.

- Monday morning, set up an ad hoc studio on their premises—I've used boardrooms, classrooms, conference rooms, and nearby motel rooms. Schedule them (in sequential sessions of subgroups if there are lots of stakeholders) starting Monday afternoon.

- Have all the site, context, and program information posted on flipchart paper on the walls, along with the five or six project goals that came from the predesign work—that's the problem statement to confirm or amend with each subgroup at the start.

- Involve representatives from all the stakeholders including user groups, administrative support, and maintenance people. Encourage them to make suggestions while you conceptualize freehand and in big felt-tip. Sketch or diagram the 3D implications of all suggestions from the stakeholders. They can all recognize quality (and the lack of it) when they see it—they just can't draw.

- Have all consultants on call and bring them in early and often to surface options, restraints, concerns, recommendations (and why) with the stakeholders.

- Stay up late bringing each day's work to scale, sketching perspective studies, making rough study models, finding out what works, what can be improved and how.

Keep repeating the last three steps and, even on big complicated projects, by Friday evening you can leave with a user-group and team consensus on a conceptual design. Full ownership by the client means no redesigns!

Instead, you post the statements of predesign aspirations on the wall as a beginning. Then you start the clients talking function while simultaneously sketching on a flipchart the 3D implications of options discussed. At each step the group can judge the work in progress against the goals statement and discuss which should be changed, if either, and how.

You stay up nights (typically in the clients' boardroom or classroom) bringing the day's hot ideas to scale. By the time the client arrives for work the next day, you're equipped with all the reasons why the previous day's concept will and won't work, and what you think needs improvement. At some point the client invariably takes the felt-tip from you and starts sketching too— that's when you know you're winning. And if all this sounds hokey and dangerous, I can only report that over a 15-year period we won more than that number of design awards.

But to return to the reports from the star designers, whatever the process they use, it virtually always involves the client's active participation at a very early stage, and lends additional importance to having a previously committed predesign consensus firmly in place about project aspirations.

4. **In-house, talk design, *with the client, talk everything else.*** This one surfaced when top designers spoke of retaining full control of the project design. That brought up the obvious question: Sounds easy if you're paying the salaries of all the project members, but how can you not talk design to the client when they're included as participative members of the design team?

Turns out that when clients bring up questions about design, the stars eagerly discuss it endlessly. Except they talk about it in terms of technology, life cycle costs, microclimate, function, schedule, or construction materials, systems, and methods—everything except aesthetics! Nor is this necessarily manipulative. For these designers, everything in that list is clearly a design issue.

Charles Gwathmey: *If the client feels the commitment and excitement of the architect. . . it's making a believer and a participant out of the owner because you're passionate. . . it's all about how it* works. *How it* looks *is your thing—the reason you're here. . . it's more than trust.*

Star designers simply expect clients to expect them to control the aesthetics, so with no fanfare, they do. They couple that seemingly natural self-assurance with:

- A relentless demand for quality solutions to the technics of project systems and details.
- And an ability to:

5. **Keep a holistic approach—it's *all* design.** Interviewing top designers revealed that for each of them, every project activity is an act of design—and they treat it that way.

That's an interesting tip, in light of the sequential mentality from which most of us feel we have to operate, with design clearly set aside as a discrete phase—only some 20 percent of the total. Then there are all the experts and managers among us railing that we too often overrun budgets because we don't know when to stop designing.

At every opportunity -- in-house, talk design.

With clients, talk everything else.

Top designers report they simply expect the client to expect them to control aesthetics, so they do.

Clients are to expect full involvement in:

Financing the project
Project scope
Technology
Cost control
Schedule
Marketability
Life-cycle cost
Project uses
Function
Aesthetics

All this stuff in the middle gets endless discussion

Top architects expect total involvement in providing solutions concerning:

For them, everything on that list -- except the financing -- is a design issue.

DESIGN IS CONSEQUENTIAL --NOT SEQUENTIAL--

Try frequently changing media, scale, venue, viewpoint, mind-set.

Sections

Orthographics

Macrosketches

Quick study models

Diagramming

Journal keeping

Doodles

Axonometrics

Perspective studies

Styrofoam mass models

Write... Wom if.... Wnal if.... what if.... what if.... What If... WHAT IF.. WHAT IF..

Write
Research
Talk about it

Anything to keep that right brain momentum going.

Give yourself left brain permission to play creatively, to experiment, to challenge, to approach the problem as though for the first time -- again and again.

Lots of star designers must have put up with that stuff, too—wonder how? Early on, were they adamant? Subversive? The ones I've interviewed were probably cheerfully self-possessed and somehow immune, but I don't really know. Not many around these days who knew the young Joe Esherick or Fay Jones.

Probably the answer lies in their fascination with how things really go together and actually work, an ability to constantly access both left and right mental lobes for *both/and* design solutions.

After years of helping write the design portion of the Architectural Registration Exam, the University of New Mexico's Don Schlegel, FAIA, researched who passed it and who didn't. His finding: Those who approach a design problem sequentially and with a checklist to follow have far less chance of success than those who maintain a holistic approach.* Design—even the pragmatic version focused only on public health, safety, and welfare—is consequential, not sequential.

6. **Respond to obstacles with lateral moves.**
When the roadblocks to conceptual design are external, this one invokes the "lots of alternatives" precept listed earlier. When the obstacles are internal, don't just doggedly persevere, contending against "artist's block" or colleagues' contrary opinion.

My best advice: Try radical changes in process—jump scales, change media, build study models, gather options—do *anything* productive that prompts a fresh viewpoint and keeps right brain momentum rolling.

---

* Several AIA conventions in the late 1980s featured Don presenting these findings to interns preparing for the A.R.E. and coaching them on how to pass the exam.

Progoff's apt analogy is to paddle where the current flows, rather than banging stubbornly into the rocks in the river. More prosaically put, when the going gets tough, switch to working on the part where the going gets easy.

Your subconscious will continue processing the hard stuff—and have an easier time of it—without your left brain compulsiveness getting in the way. "Sleep on it" while you're doing something productive.

7. **Use precedent as a launch platform.** The ideal of the modernist school of design—that each project should be a venue for the reinvention of architecture—was an interesting concept. One that, in terms of feasibility, ranks right up there with the prediction of worldwide sociopolitical reform through design. Or there's today's special strain of hubris—that a design must always be only self-referent.

Don't worry about copying. Every client, site, and context will present its own set of specific, real problems; and by continually focusing on solving these you'll easily achieve plenty of aesthetic innovation.

Charles Eames said, *Innovation is the last resort,* and it is Eames whom Herman Miller's Max DePree* credits with teaching him the usefulness of repetition:

I often repeat myself, by design, to establish something and then connect it with something else. A new situation requires another connection because things appear in a new way and need new relationships to what I already know.

---

* Max DePree, *Leadership Is an Art* (Dell, 1989), p. 3.

Use PRECEDENT as a launch-pad--a departure point. Venturi said, "You cannot not know history." All that stuff you learned in school Plus the richly varied, often mutually exclusive theory getting published these days....

Better yet, travel around and do comparative shopping with your sketchbook. Find a sidewalk with five-foot spacing of expansion joints where you can periodically recalibrate yours to a 30" pace. Heights I can easily guess, based on 7' doors -- horizontal dimensions, I can casually pace off, silently counting by fives on every other step-- without looking like Groucho!

Helps a lot in learning how others dealt with scale and proportions.

Equipment-- MY sketchbook and a 30" natural pace

PHOTOCOPY PRODUCTION TIPS FOR THE "*CAD*INGLY" CHALLENGED

For those of us beyond the generation gap from CAD addiction, a good photocopier, sheets of clear Mylar, and a roll of transparent tape can work wonders. Examples:

The Kentucky architect who *starts* drawing—just as he did in school—on 30 x 40 illustration board. He works fast with pencil, felt-tip, whatever—making quick corrections on yellow-trash overlays, and layering a photocopied collage of increasingly better ideas onto the board. After he stands back from the resultant mess of paste-ups and declares it finished, he copies it on Mylar with his prized 36-inch-bed Xerox to produce his "original."

There are many architects who produce everything at 11 x 17, happily cannibalizing and pasting up bits and pieces from previous projects. Again, the finals are Mylar prints from collages. Small-project practitioners across the country routinely limit their specs to about 11 to 15 pages, of 8½ x 11, on Mylar taped to the drawings where the builders can't help but see them.

Or there's the Maryland architect who uses what she calls a "pennybar" system. She has one pin bar on her drafting table, another on the photocopier. Every overlay she draws can be precisely registered, as can the Mylars she runs from them. Up to three Mylars then can be registered for layered photocopies—i.e., base plan, reflected ceiling, electrical, etc. The Mylar closest the glass prints like new money with each succeeding layer increasingly half-toned. I've seen her work—beautifully crafted, succinct 11 x 17 sets of drawings.

And there still are those who freehand drawings for small projects, then reduce to half-size for improved visual quality. All the illustrations in this book were done that way.

Use what works for you, rather than what the CAD salespeople say you can't live without.

Design strategies involving the use of precedent might include research on how famous design solutions addressed similar site conditions or functional issues—followed by speculation on breakthrough advantages of diametrically opposed approaches.

Fay Jones* recounts considering how the Chateau de Loire and Fallingwater had each responded to a site with a stream, then explored an exact opposite approach for Sam Walton's house. Whatever your methods, for the sake of aesthetics, profitability, risk management, and efficacy—design your projects based on (which is different from cribbing) precedent—as a guide, but more importantly as a springboard for bold departure.

We all rely on our own precedent. Sustainable design (in all its varied definitions) requires we document performance, analyze it, and try it again adaptively. Obvious production strategies include libraries of so-called standard details stored in CAD files for adaptation to project-specific needs.

In terms of managing your projects (and your clients), the key to benefiting from precedent lies in documenting how, why, and by whom decisions get made and remade.

---

* In a talk to students at Cal Poly, San Luis Obispo, CA, Winter 1996.

Learning from precedent is the key to continuous improvement. Charles Nelson,* FRAIA—guru of ISO in Australia—predicts the time is coming when there'll only be two kinds of firms—those with time card codes for rework and those without. His implication is that those without will get left out—that you can't improve the system without identifying where within it problems tend to occur.

8. **Honor your quality assurance promises.** We all make promises—to clients, bosses, consultants, and ourselves—that we'll check our work. And we all know the rules—put a two-week review window into the schedule, pick people who haven't worked on the project, and ask them if they could get the project built from the documents.

It's like landscaping in the construction budget—the first to get skimped when the crunch comes. Don't know the answer, but there have to be better ways than plans-check charrettes. At least get the building system layouts all drawn to the same scale and acquire a light-table so you can see the conflicts when overlaid.

Or there's the group of six Carolina sole practitioners who—though competitors—provide plan checks for each other. They get together for a Dutch treat lunch each Christmastime to set a common rate, exchange bills, and write each other checks. The rest of the year they never see each other—they messenger their 95 percent complete documents across town to a competitor for redlining and critique at the agreed-to hourly rate. They barter quality-assurance services, adjusting for slight inequities with a year-end check.

---

* Charles E. Nelson, *TQM and ISO 9000 for Architects and Designers* (McGraw-Hill, 1996), to workshop attendees, AIA Convention, Minneapolis, the same year.

TIPS FOR REDLINING

First, role-play the scenario that you've never seen or heard of the project before—you've inherited it along with the obligation of faithfully carrying it to completion with no changes to the original concept and no additional input from your predecessor. Is there enough information here to do that? Organized to clearly communicate intentions and depicted accurately? Any graphic nonsequiturs or oxymorons? Can you locate it on the site and build it from what's on paper?

Next, check for life safety—ingress, egress, ADA compliance, etc.

Then, on a light table (sliding glass doors will do in a pinch), overlay all plans and sections and elevations of the same scale—especially those from different disciplines. You're looking for at least three things:

- Physical elements (doors, windows, columns, beams, walls) that have gotten unintentionally relocated or misaligned in the reiterations of drawing.
- Incorrect relationships, i.e., light switches behind doors.
- Adequate clearance for and conflicts in location of physical elements by different trades all shown occupying the same critical space, i.e., ducts, pipes, and beams.

The point of all this is not to solve problems but merely to identify them. Question everything with notes and diagrams—bleed all over it with red pencil or marker—the cures come only after full diagnosis.

9. **Call for and participate in frequent construction-site meetings involving all specialty contractors.** Used to call them subcontractors until, at a workshop recently, several reminded all of us that they're the ones who actually build the project—and provide detailed design services for significant parts of it.

A San Antonio architect tells me they've been actively coordinating the work of specialty contractors since they found it's cheaper to help get it done right the first time than to be dragged into fixing things after they've gone wrong. Again, some timecard coding and analysis might be in order, if you want to check it out. Roughly put, it's the cost of a weekly site meeting and some follow-up versus the cost of a large part of the RFI stuff you're currently living with.

10. **Schedule—and hold—project reviews and postmortems.** Few firms do much of a job of scheduling and budgeting—much less carrying out—this obvious tip. The number of big firms hiring consultants to do performance evaluations through formal surveys of previous clients is increasing, but is still amazingly low. The majority of us unfortunately continue to emulate Frank Lloyd Wright, who when asked which was the greatest project of his career, reportedly quipped, *The next one.*

Too many of us never look back after final inspection. Exceptions: The occasional midsize firm I've found, whose sole marketing efforts are to volunteer post-occupancy inspections for past clients. Meanwhile, there are a few learning firms out there that routinely meet at project's end for in-house (and informal) evaluation of the process—not just the results. How could we have done better or differently so those problems never happen again?

Sure, many of these practices add overhead, but so does rework, answering RFIs, and dealing with change orders. Not sure how you'd figure your long-term cost/benefits ratio, but you'd be doing better projects and resting easier at night. That's worth a lot.

CHAPTER 13.   PROJECT MANAGEMENT AS LATERAL LEADERSHIP

Whether you're honing your skills, deciding whether you're ready to take a project on, or evaluating your staff's potential, here's a quick summary of the exemplary project manager's personal attributes.*

In my view that's a lot more useful than attempting any checklist of all one has to do to run a project, or a tiresome rehashing of job descriptions. Here's why. Though the industry is full of books, consultants, and schools dealing with project management, all the systems I've reviewed seemed limited to quantitative processes aimed at eliminating surprises. They're top-down control mechanisms to anticipate all that should or shouldn't happen and then assign responsibility and accountability to make it come out right. But since every project is unique, there's no one-size-fits-all quantification process, so most of the generic systems get cumbersome in attempting to be comprehensive. The danger, then, is needlessly loading your overhead and quota of frustration til the system becomes a burdensome tool of last resort, a mechanism for fixing blame.

My advice—use minimum checklist or quantification procedures you believe will assure that all bases are covered, that people are clear about what's to be done and how, and that adequate records can be kept of who did what when. But remember what really makes an architecture project go well—people enthusiastically bringing very different sets of skills and expertise to bear on amazingly complex problems, all in a smoothly coordinated way. Rather than any generic set of control mechanisms, at essence project management is a project-specific and ongoing design problem having a lot more to do with a holistic vision, lateral leadership, and the ability to deal with paradox. You could say project management is mostly about mastering paradox.

Leader/Manager.
Architectural project managers, more than traditional business managers, are only as good as the commitment, ability, and energy of others whom they don't directly boss. That is, they must be lateral leaders— visionaries, coaches, masters at transferring passion to others. On the other hand, the grind of being on top of all the boring details naturally comes with the turf of being manager. In fact, to run a project effectively, architects need *matching* passions in three very different areas:

- A passion for inspiring others to achieve true design quality (leading)
- A passion for the complicated and interdependent technologies of architecture (coordinating)
- A passion for the details of process, scheduling, accounting, and documentation that gets the job produced, bid, and built (managing)

---

*If you think this is written only for architects, take a look at very similar advice from business management guru Tom Peters (to whom I am greatly indebted) in *Liberation Management: Necessary Disorganization for the Nanosecond Nineties* (Knopf, 1992), p. 212.

PROJECT MANAGEMENT IS MOSTLY ABOUT MASTERING PARADOX

The sign of a true intellect is to be able to keep two mutually exclusive ideas in mind at the same time and still function.

F. Scott Fitzgerald

I like complexity and Contradiction in Architecture.... I prefer "both-and" to "either-or," black and white and sometimes gray, to black or white.

Robert Venturi, 1966

Yeah, but that's all design side talk--the art of architecture. Project management is also-- and mainly--about the craft-- getting the design produced and built. It's a meta-paradox of multiple dialectic pulls between standing firm for the either/or decision versus using lateral leadership to accomplish both/and. And the approach you choose on this issue can affect choices available on other issues later.

PM

Ambiguity/Perfection.

Ubiquitous to any architecture project is ambiguity. Things are always unfolding and evolving, sometimes with near whiplash impact and the only thing certain is the unexpected. The accomplished project manager handles ambiguity and uncertainty with élan—and a sense of humor. But he or she must couple that with an equal zeal for perfection. Taking a last look—then another *really* last look—to make sure the mistake we caught in specs got changed on all sheets of the drawings. *Oh, and what about the finish schedule? Did the mechanical engineer catch it?*

Oral/Written/Graphic.

Peter Drucker characterizes two kinds of people—readers and listeners.* I'd add a third category—those (especially architects) who can't talk (much less think) without sketching and diagramming. Good project managers are not only fluently multilingual these three ways, they know when to use which means of communication to best effect. On the one hand, they're off base (not to mention schedule) to insist upon an audit trail to document every last thing. On the other, they're subject to being hung out to dry if that *crucial* something-or-other can't be verified later in writing, drawings, at least dated sketches and notes. Dealing orally and on the run comes easily to effective project managers, but they must also be masters of the detailed work plan, the daily checklist, the memo to owner, the sketch to file.

---

*Peter F. Drucker, *Management Challenges for the 21st Century* (HarperCollins, 1999), p. 169.

Generalist/Specialist.

Project managers must appreciate forests and trees equally—or as Orstein[*] would put it—deal simultaneously (and always) with both text and context. It's the project manager's role to keep so holistic a perspective as to be able to anticipate the opportunities and problems inherent in the whole system.

- Project designers can't be expected to do so while they intensely focus on form, systems, and finishes.
- Builders and owners can miss the big picture—even the life-cycle value part of it—if focused too exclusively on immediate schedule and cost.
- Technical experts can have their exclusive tunnel vision.

So along with the big picture, project managers must also talk the talk of specialists, attend the detail, and coach the very people for whom they work.

Action-driven/Schmoozer.

On the one hand, project managers must be action fanatics: "Get on with it; try it; forget about yesterday's foul-ups; move on to tomorrow." But at the same time they're "running" a network and often dealing with several dozen fragile (by definition) egos, cultures, and relationships at once. In fact, they're not "running" the network at all. Leadership comes only by consent of the followers, and, at best, project managers are leaders among equals.

Complexity/K.I.S.S.

Nothing short of a moon shot seems more complex than dealing with a sizable architectural project. Kansas State research[†] some years back found over two million yes/no decisions to be typical.

The effective project manager must juggle—literally for years on a large project—hundreds of balls of differing (and ever-changing) shapes, sizes and colors. In my view, the best help for systematically organizing to deal with all this complexity comes from the AIA in the 12th Edition of the *Architect's Handbook*[‡] and in the D and G series of AIA documents.

But in selecting—much less trying to consistently use—forms from among that stack of detailed tools, the project manager needs to remember this paradox: He or she must also be a fanatic about the keep-it-simple-stupid dogma, making sure that a few simple rules and values dominate the project.

- For top design, it may be a scorecard of short, memorable aspirations for building performance, against which all later decisions are judged.
- For in-house process, it may be *Nobody misses the 8:00 A.M. Monday meeting!*
- For client management it may be the scheduled twice-a-week phone call, the ubiquitous fax to confirm.
- For project-wide coordination it may be the daily care and feeling of a project intranet system.

In every case it relies on personal contact, since the project manager in architecture is totally dependent upon each team member's unique skill and passion for improvement. Smart, interdependent leaders spend lots—and lots—and *lots*—of time on relationship building and networking. It's exactly as important as perpetually pushing for action.

---

[*]Robert Orstein, *The Right Mind: Making Sense of the Hemispheres* (Harcourt Brace, 1997), p. 176.
[†]Reported to me verbally by Frank Zilm of the graduate school in approximately 1992.

[‡]David Haviland, ed., *Architect's Handbook of Professional Practice*, 12th Edition (AIA Press, 1994), pp. 544–602. Fifty-eight pages of useful, densely packed, how-to information. Adding in the 116 pages of D and G documents and instruction sheets makes it 174 pages available to you.

Ego-driven/Ego-free.
Successful project managers know you can accomplish almost anything so long as you don't need to take credit for it. That doesn't mean they have no ego involvement—the norm is a tremendous and highly personal identification with "their" projects.* Project managers assume full accountability for a daunting array of factors for however many months, even years, the project may take. They tend (if only privately) to hold themselves fully responsible for its daily success or failure; they're "consumed" by it; it "becomes" their project.

But project managers must also perform as though totally free of ego, since success depends on the performance of lots of insiders and outsiders whom they hardly "command." They live in the fishbowl critique culture of architecture where anybody can and frequently does have a say. There's a preponderance of subjective decision making required that relies on the expertise of clients, user groups, and especially the array of engineering consultant-specialists to whom most outsource. Not only that, those over whom the project manager *does* have formal authority must also have high ego involvement. The project manager must be expert at letting them take full credit for what they've done *and* an inordinate amount of credit for overall project success, regardless of how small their contribution actually may have been.

Autocrat/Participative Manager.
When the chips are down, it's the project manager who has to make the call, sometimes on the spot, and with no clear rules to go by:

- *Postpone the bids till we get this right* (and take our lumps for the delay).
- *Reject that change order proposal* (when the cure is worse than the curse).
- *Tell the owner he's wrong* (when what he demands is not in his own best interest).

There are a lot more verses, but it's the same song: *My project—my decision.*

On the other hand, the participative project manager, through lateral leadership, will have vested ownership of quality assurance in the team members long ago—mainly through a process of self-delegation involving ad hoc systems theory. As individuals, as a learning organization, such a team will have anticipated problems, taken steps to see they never come up, developed collective abilities to respond immediately when the worst does happen in spite of best efforts. In such a project team, members hold themselves mutually accountable, making "Who's in charge?" a wrong-headed question. It goes without saying that the project manager really has final say.

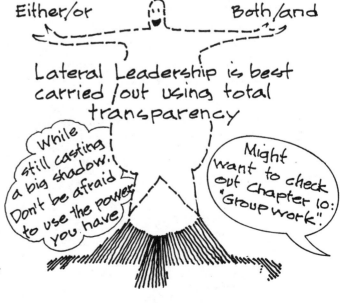

Either/or   Both/and

Lateral Leadership is best carried /out using total transparency

While still casting a big shadow. Don't be afraid to use the power you have

Might want to check out Chapter 10: "Group work"

---

*In the late eighties, working with groups of architects who had been laid off, I was struck by the extent to which those architects had identified with their projects, how very difficult for them it was to reaffirm their sense of identity and self-esteem based on who they were, rather than what they did.

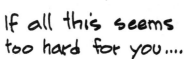

If all this seems too hard for you....

It's not rocket science. Perhaps you've read the foregoing shaking your head over the complex technical knowledge required for managing architectural projects. If so, consider the following:

Q. Give an example of something involving an understanding of aesthetic design, geometry, algebra, manual dexterity, strategic planning, color theory, ergonomics, and allotment of resources.

A. *Making a Halloween costume.*

Q. Give an example of something involving chemical processes, arithmetic, timing, weights and measures, aeration, biology, and behavior of materials.

A. *Doubling a cake recipe.*

Q. Give an example of something involving politics, economics, kinesiology, systems theory, psychology, negotiation, and sociology.

A. *Little League baseball.*

Sure, the technology is complicated—that's why we outsource to experts. Yes, the coordination is demanding—that's why the AIA publishes 174 pages* of detailed how-to information from which to fashion your project- or firm-specific system. And yes, it's time consuming—the project has a life-cycle of what? Fifty years? And how many people will it serve?

On the other hand you may have read the foregoing shaking your head over the *nontechnical* and coordination demands. Perhaps you're one of those who was hired for your technical knowledge, CAD skills, design ability, attention to detail—whatever—and now here's all this warm-fuzzy people-skills lateral-leadership *stuff* in those eight paradoxes. They didn't teach that in school and you've been fixated on a computer most of the time since. Truth is, you've probably already had plenty of training opportunity *off* the job. Managing your day-to-day affairs already exposes you to most project management challenges. Families, pairs of significant others—even close-knit groups of best friends—frequently find themselves operating as self-managed teams faced with complex trade-offs, budgets, networking and yes—projects with outside vendors, no job descriptions, and long-term goals.

First time I ever thought about my old backpacking buddies that way, but it fits. Check your own analogy against the preceding and if you happen to have made it past your mid-twenties—especially if you've started a family—you're probably well along in the advanced course on project management readiness.

---

*Haviland, op. cit.

CHAPTER 14

POST-OCCUPANCY & PREDESIGN

We'll get into all the reasons later, but, up front, I'm proposing that for *significant work* you add two brief phases of activity to your typical project process:

- **A post-occupancy evaluation survey** after a project is complete.
- **A discovery phase** prior to the design of the next project.

Why couple them together? I can just hear it now. *Why on earth try to make a package out of two sets of services at opposite ends of—and both clearly outside what's* actually required for—*the doing of projects?* The short answers:

1. **To get better projects designed.**
2. **To get projects built faster, cheaper, better.**

And besides,

3. **Both processes involve the same people dealing with the same issues.** Predesign (or the discovery phase) and post-occupancy evaluation (POE) are similar in three ways.

- Both include and invite input from all appropriate stakeholders in the project.
- Both services—one prospectively, the other retrospectively— deal with the same issues that are key for every project—*quality, scope, time,* and *money.* Though they bookend the project timewise, providing either of these two services informs the doing of the other as sequential loops in a learning system for continuous improvement.
- Both are value-added services which can improve not only design, project delivery, and performance, but—over time—market share.

Doing either predesign or POE will make doing the other easier. If, by providing both services, you can improve the next cycle, future projects, yours and the client's systems of project design and delivery, you will have added great value to your package of professional services. The provision of predesign and POE services can furnish you a value-added competitive edge, since (as of this writing) virtually no one else is doing them, certainly not in a collaborative, interactive, inclusive way.

Both sets of activities have as their immediate and overt goals:

- To clarify and manage communications.
- To improve performance and accountability.

Guessing you may have choked a bit on my mention of accountability, let me quickly add that we're talking *everybody's* accountability here, not just yours. If you didn't take the quiz on p. 2.50, now might be a good time to find out how much money you're spending these days on value-free project activity. That's the WIIFM—the what's-in-it-for-me factor. The average is about $27,000 worth of billable time a year—perhaps most of that spent in trying to figure out who should have communicated what, how, and when. Who's to blame and why it isn't you.

I said *significant work* above and that's a relative term. So before we get into all the reasons to provide these services—in addition to the immediate what's-in-it-for-me factor—here are some ideas as to the range of activities, from minimum to maximum, from which you might choose—or begin your own design—of what's applicable in a given situation.

POST-OCCUPANCY EVALUATION.....

THE MINIMUM OPTION

• Hold an in-house plus consultants project post-mortem. The Army calls it "ground truth." What happened in the field differently from how it was planned and what can we learn? No finger-pointing allowed. Keep it to how the team—as a team—can get better at the communication/response cycle, how the system can be made simpler.

• Get back in touch with the clients. Pay whatever attention to news media you always do, but now with past clients' interests in mind. Make yourself a tickler file in your calendar pages to remind you to contact them and, when you do, pass on whatever you've noted would be of interest to them. Having signaled you've still got their interests at heart, ask about project performance— a debriefing on how they felt the project had gone, what could have been improved.

And yes, this is also good marketing— changing your practice from a series of one-time projects into a wealth of career-long client accounts. But in the process you can be getting better at what you do.

THE FULL-TILT MAX OPTION

When post-occupancy evaluation (POE) is used in business and industry for decision making about whether and what to build, it can become a lengthy and complex multidisciplinary process. Some architects have developed it into a specialization, a market niche often linked with a practice in building forensics.

MY PROPOSED OPTION

What's proposed here limits the process to quick 360-degree feedback from users and immediate project members—the project stakeholders—but getting immediately useful information.

Never look back. Something might be gaining on you.

(satchel Paige)

Somewhere between the two extremes, we need to find efficient, cost-effective, reasonably reliable ways to not only learn from our projects (we all do that individually), but respond with systemic change.

The outlook for definitive statistical proof is steadil...

One approach is to circulate a survey form at project's end. The one offered here seeks stakeholders' evaluation of the five major categories of driving forces that shape every project and must be juggled continuously throughout:

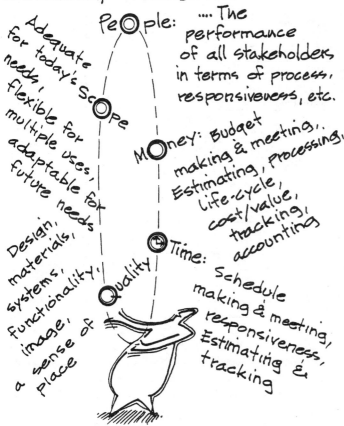

People: .... The performance of all stakeholders in terms of process, responsiveness, etc.

Adequate for today's Scope needs, flexible for multiple uses, adaptable for future needs

MOney: Budget making & meeting, Estimating, Processing, Life-cycle, cost/value, tracking, accounting

Design, materials, systems, functionality, image, a sense of place

Quality

Time: Schedule making & meeting, responsiveness, Estimating & tracking

Often, a major usefulness to get from such a process is to identify those you should follow up with -- or not work with again. Those who decline to give meaningful feedback are doing so by default.

The obvious purpose is to evaluate the performance of the project and of the participants in getting it designed and constructed.

Take a look at the generic form that comes next. The front of the double-sided form seeks evaluation of the building in the four categories summarizing the major forces—the imperatives—that drive decision making on virtually any project—*quality, scope, time,* and *money.* The flip side seeks ratings of participants' performance in the course of getting the project designed, approved, and built. To this point, then, respondents are being asked to evaluate project process and results.

Then the form asks them to rank the four driving forces dominating decision making for this particular project. Since all respondents may not agree on which imperative had (or should have had) priority, their individual rankings could shed light on, lend context to, their performance evaluation ratings in the previous sections of the form. If you're so inclined, the rank order of imperatives can help you categorize buildings in a database over time. The objective would be to better forecast for your clients which project delivery systems coupled with which project imperatives can be expected to produce—or mitigate—what types of problems.

The focus then, of this proposed POE survey, is that it be used as much for system development and improvement as for evaluation and score keeping. A long-term goal could be identifying what team lineups, what processes, what systems of project acquisition might be most useful—or most usefully modified—in order to get better projects faster for the money available.

PROJECT EVALUATION FOR:

From: (Your Name)   Date:

The purpose of this questionaire is to improve future projects and their delivery.
It will help a great deal if you will please rate each of the statements listed below in the column to the right, scoring each from 5 to 1 (or N/A) according to the following legend:

5. **Strongly Agree**   4. **Agree**   3. **Neither Agree nor Disagree**
2. **Disagree**   1. **Strongly Disagree**   N/A   **Not Applicable to this Project**
                                                              or Don't Know

		RATING
	A. QUALITY	
1.	Overall, the quality of the construction is excellent.	
2.	The public image created by the project is entirely appropriate.	
3.	Given the building purpose, the experience of entering and using it is excellent.	
4.	The finishes selected (both interior and exterior) are highly appropriate to the uses of the building.	
5.	The details of how finish materials fit together shows good design thought.	
6.	Given the site and what's around it, the building's design statement is excellent.	
7.	The sizes, shapes, and locations of the building's openings make an interesting and inviting design.	
8.	Changes necessary during construction were generally unforeseeable during design. The contract documents were appropriately comprehensive and complete.	
	B. SCOPE	
1.	Overall, the sizes and shapes of the built spaces properly accommodate their functions.	
2	The layout of and proximities among the various rooms works very well, given their uses.	
3.	The circulation spaces and systems work well. People easily get where they need to be.	
4.	Window sizes, shapes, and locations take good advantage of views of and from the site.	
5.	Ceiling heights are very appropriate to the sizes of the rooms and the numbers of users.	
6.	Overall, the building is very user-friendly in terms of:	
	a. Security and signage systems	
	b. Lighting controls and availability of electrical connections	
	c. Ventilation and air quality, delivery, and controls	
	d. Restroom facilities and other plumbing fixture provisions	
	e. Communication systems	
	C. COST	
1.	Overall, the building was a good buy for the money at the time.	
2.	Life-cycle costs were appropriately considered in the design.	
3.	Ease of operations and maintenance was clearly thought through in the design.	
4.	Environmental concerns were appropriately considered in orientation and design as well as in the selection of materials and building systems.	
5.	This project demonstrates highly cost-effective selection of:	
	a. Communication systems	
	b. Mechanical and plumbing systems	
	c. Structural systems	
	d. Exterior finishes and window systems	
	e. Lighting systems	
	D. TIME	
1.	Project delivery was highly efficient given restraints of design, regulatory process, and site conditions.	
2.	Project processes were consistently appropriate, timely, and effective on the part of the:	
	a. Owner	
	b. Construction Manager	
	c. Architect	
	d. Engineers	
	e. General Contractor	
	f. Subcontractors	
3.	The project acquisition and delivery system selected responded in a timely fashion to meet owner needs.	
4.	Project documentation and communication systems were timely and effective.	
5.	Project decisions were made in a reasonable amount of time.	

	E. TEAM PERFORMANCE:	RATING
1.	The architect consistently and effectively represented the owner's best interests.	
2.	Team meetings were appropriately scheduled throughout the project, well led and documented.	
3.	The project process was clearly set up, well coordinated, and implemented.	
4.	Participation in project meetings was very consistent and collaborative with timely, cooperative, and reasonable follow-through from the:	
	a. Owner	
	b. Construction Manager	
	c. Architect	
	d. Engineers	
	e. General Contractor	
	f. Subcontractors	
5.	Proposed design and construction changes were appropriately considered and equitably dealt with by the:	
	a. Owner.	
	b. Construction Manager	
	c. Architect	
	d. Engineers	
	e. General Contractor	
	f. Subcontractors	
6.	Cost estimating was appropriately reliable and comprehensive on the part of the:	
	a. Owner	
	b. Construction Manager	
	c. Architect	
	d. Engineers	
	e. General Contractor	
	f. Subcontractors	
7.	The request and payment process was appropriately detailed and expedited by the:	
	a. Owner	
	b. Construction Manager	
	c. Architect	
	d. Engineers	
	e. General Contractor	
	f. Subcontractors	

PRIORITIZATION OF FORCES DRIVING PROJECT DECISIONS Do not score the following as you did the ones above. Instead, please rank these in their order of relative importance (from 1 to 4, with 1 being least crucial) to indicate their influence as forces driving decisions for the project. Thank you.	RANKING 1 – 4
a. **QUALITY:** Of materials, systems, finishes, design.	
b. **SCOPE:** Was the built project consistent with the program?	
c. **COST:** Both construction and life-cycle costs.	
d. **TIME:** Meeting deadlines and the overall schedule.	

What was the worst part about being involved?

What was the best part about being involved?

We invite any additional comments you wish to make. Please feel free to attach a separate sheet. THANK YOU.

If you don't mind a follow-up phone interview, please provide your name, phone number, and the best time to call:

NAME: PHONE NUMBER:

BEST TIME TO CALL:

PREDESIGN: THE HOW-TO PART

At minimum:

- Fill out Article 1.1, Initial Information, of the B141 or jot down (I like to use bubble diagrams) the equivalent in discussions with your client.
- Ask how they're going to know, after it's built, that you've done a wonderful project together. If that's a bunch of quantifiable expectations or requirements, jot those down and hang onto the list—it's your POE scorecard to review with them at the end of the project.
- Keep them talking till they reveal their hopes and aspirations. Ask questions like, *In the best of all possible worlds, what would change in your life as a result of this project?*
- Later and over time, jot down your own aspirations for the project. Work in the present tense as though it's already built, winning awards and not just for its design—for how it functions better than any other building of that type.
- Force yourself to at least doodle every possible alternative massing diagram *before* you jump into design (check back on the learning's from the top designers—discipline yourself to not lunge at project design).

At maximum, say for big institutional clients, predesign can rightfully become an entire phase of services, a series of work sessions with the client, or sub-groups of clients, sketching options, reviewing rough study models of the site and all possible massing options, stacking plan diagrams, circulation patterns, etc., etc.

For some major medical or corporate clients, full-scale room or workstation mockups can be appropriate.

If there are complex user groups to be served, this work might lead to a well-facilitated *discovery phase* workshop including appropriate representatives of all stakeholders in the project.

Obviously, predesign does not readily lend itself to the use of generic forms or by-rote process for major projects, each being so complex and unique. But here's a to-do list you can start from to design what's appropriate.

PREDESIGN CHECKLIST

- Introduce and begin to build relationship among project stakeholders—especially those expected to function together to design, approve, and build the project.
- Clarify and confirm quantitative expectations synopsized in the project program and budget.
- Surface, identify, and share qualitative aspirations and hopes from all project stakeholders for project performance, functions, impact, and image.
- Set out the appropriate communication channels, procedures, and requirements.
- Explain and agree upon required paperwork—from whom and by when, and in what format.
- Establish the timeline for deliverables and frequency of project meetings.
- Identify decision makers and clarify project design review processes and responsibilities.
- Discuss and clarify early conflict resolution processes.
- Prioritize the basis—the imperatives—for decision making for the project to come.
- Clarify billing and payment procedures.
- Develop in advance the scorecard by which future performance of the project and of the project members will be evaluated. (The POE survey included here can be a starter kit.)

What follows is an unabashed homily, so skip it if the preceding has already sold you on the need for predesign and POE to the extent you're ready to rush out and do them.

Actually I've already said about all I'd want to say on the subject. That's provided I thought you were convinced enough about the need and usefulness of these services to start doing some version of them. Trouble is, I don't. In my experience, everybody talks about them and nobody does anything. That experience—with some 20,000 architects over 12 years—prompts me to go into detail here as justification of predesign and post-occupancy evaluation.

Besides—assuming you're a convert, you may need this later to convince a client (your partner? your staff?) that such services are value-added and worth the time and trouble. Think about it: (A) You already know how to do, manage, and document projects. (B) Every other project stakeholder knows how they do, manage, and document projects. (C) Probably no two of you agree on the specifics of all that. Where you do, there may be unnecessary redundancy in effort, in documentation. Where you don't, there's clear basis for conflict.*

I like to ask participants in my continuing education workshops to set their own agenda. Not once in 12 years have the topics of predesign or POE even been suggested. Neither ever seems to get mentioned unless I bring them up,† at which point they're services to which everyone assembled gives perfunctory lip service and which virtually no one admits to providing.

Part case study tips -- a lot of it sales pitch....

If this convinces you -- or even if I'm singing to the choir-- this may be very useful.

It can provide credibility when you're proposing POE and predesign services to partners or clients -- might help you justify equitable fees for these value-added phases of work.

---

* J. Stuart Eckblad, Associate Director of Design & Construction Services, Kaiser Permanente, in a presentation to the Executive Management Program of the Cal Poly Department of Architecture, Winter Quarter, 1998, pointed out that traditionally redundant project documentation is kept by owner, architect, and builder—that, in case of disputes, none of the three agree.
† In the eight workshops in 1998, I specifically asked about POE services; for a decade and a half I've asked about predesign.

What becomes immediately obvious in seminar discussions about predesign is initial confusion as to whether I really mean programming. Worse, there then emerges the *if-it's-in-the-contract-I'll-do-it* attitude so ubiquitous in the workplace. The vast majority of architects seemingly never think to convene even so obvious an effort as the minimum list as the previous pages suggest.

Too many of us take the contract at face value, accepting the owner and the architect, *hereinafter the parties*, each as a single entity, forever separate and necessarily defendable from the other. That's until the abrasions of cost estimating and design review begin. By then, the putting together of faces with names, of beginning to form teamwork relationships with the actual people, can be uphill work—particularly if either you or the project are already in deep yogurt.

I'm saying predesign is a prudent investment. It can make the difference between having a transformative collaborative relationship with clients, consultants, and builders instead of another of those potentially adversarial situations permeated with cover-yourself overhead and delays.

You can do this by starting the project with consensus agreement on—at least acknowledgment of the differences in— priorities about intentions, aspirations, and project processes. Predesign is the place to set up the processes, the interpersonal chemistries needed to carry the project team through the hard times of contention sure to come at some later point.

At best, by end of the predesign phase every stakeholder should be motivated to contribute whatever's necessary to this project's being best-of-class in terms of meeting certain agreed-to functional aspirations.

At the least, the process should yield a scorecard of expectations that project stakeholders jointly develop and have consensual agreement on in advance of ever beginning the project.

In *any* event, the process should equip any stakeholder to feel entirely comfortable in dealing with any other on a personal basis, should a project situation make it appropriate.

Back to my continuing ed workshops: When the topic of discussion is POE, maybe 3 percent of the attendees say they have provided these services "occasionally" and at the owner's request. Only a few of those say they've gotten paid for it, though the AIA B141, 1997 Edition, now includes opportunities and reminders for you to negotiate providing and getting paid for *both* predesign and post-occupancy services.

So the money's a symptom, not the cause. And what becomes evident from the comments that ensue is a shared perception about post-occupancy evaluation: *POE would be just another final inspection, and who needs to hear all over again the grievances about what didn't get built right?*

I agree. Were it the sole purpose of POE to merely quantify things you'd hope would have been corrected under warranty—who needs it? And while any post-mortem necessarily will include a list of what doesn't work and what might be required to get it fixed, that's only the first level of inquiry.

Predesign
for
Stakeholder
Alchemy

The second level of inquiry in the POE process lies in getting seasoned consideration of the performance of all the stakeholders in the enterprise of design and construction. Chances are that future opportunities—or necessities—will arise for you to work again with the same people. Monday-morning quarterbacking now can optimize relationships and performances later.

The tertiary level of opportunity in the POE process is in the lessons learned about—reconsideration of—the process, the system.

In addition to these considerations, the *what's-in-it-for-me* factor, and the tired truism of *faster, cheaper, better* with which all this starts out, there are some even broader challenges.

Litigation. Costly litigation continues to plague project acquisition. You don't need any and we know that ineffective project communication and lack of clarity on project expectations and accountability accounts for most of it. A goal of what's proposed here is that joint communication management will provide process, a level of personal comfort, and a forum for early resolution of conflicts before they get serious enough for lawsuits.

Fragmentation of the design and construction industry. The design and construction industry has traditionally been rigidly divided into different trades and professions. In recent years these divisions have become even stronger and more finely delineated with increased specialization.

New technologies have further fueled the trend. Every project faces problems, the solutions of which could best come through collaborative, coordinated efforts of you, your builders, clients, and consultants.

The relationships and goal setting begun at predesign can lay the groundwork for such interactive collaboration. Joint development of the POE scorecard can heighten the awareness of the need for communication. *What gets measured gets managed.* Even when the measurement is subjective.

The complexity of doing business with committees and many organizations. In their efforts to trim costs and improve productivity, many client organizations have undergone—or are in the throes of—far-reaching cutbacks and changes.

Problematic—or even merely complicated—characteristics of the client organization can beget problematic behaviors in consultants and builders, and typically you'll catch the job of being go-between, whipping boy, or both.

Understanding the bureaucracy and putting names, faces, and communication channels together with a project organization chart could be a real discovery phase breakthrough for consultants and ease your project management load considerably.

When the POE form tells the client where their system needs to be tinkered with to make responses timely and to expedite project processes, it's not just you complaining. POE might even be pivotal in the client learning how to become better at what they do. When this cuts their in-house project costs, and there's a good chance they'll be your repeat client in the future, you'll have provided true value-added service to them as well as to yourself.

POE for converting project ground truth into strategies and alliances that can improve future performance.

Project participant turnover. Typically any project of considerable size will lose original members of the project team through normal attrition, downsizing, reassignment, promotion, etc. Their replacements—people who come to the project late and with new mental baggage—often have a different agenda than that developed by the team with their predecessors.

Such a newcomer, if presented with a previously agree-upon documentation of project aspirations and expectations, should feel clearly obligated to either accept the team's terms for measuring success, or to initiate due process to have them modified by the team.

Given those larger issues to confront, here are more immediate reasons to get into—or sell others on collaborating in—these services.

The elusiveness of design excellence. There's an obvious similarity between the preceding and the current TQM partnering admonitions that we must start each project *right* through a chartering session. This final challenge is very different, dealing as it does with starting projects off *well*.

To architects it's a matter of uppercase RIGHT, rather than lowercase rights. Slight semantic difference there, but a critical shift from adverb *well* (implying effective process that empowers the RIGHT solution to evolve) to adjective *right* (meaning correctness and entitlement or rights). RIGHT and rights. . . .

Philosopher Don Schön got interested in doing his seminal studies on architects' design process through the observation that we use language *decoratively*, rather than precisely.

If you're as sloppy with semantics as most architects, the adjectives and adverbs sort of interchange, mingle, and mix—and I say let's not change—that's probably the most efficacious way to deal with architectural design. But for a moment, lets examine and analyze.

The *rights* part of preproject work isn't easy sometimes, but that's often the result of so many project participants being involved—each with roles, entitlements, and proscriptive definitions of *yours* versus *mine*. Every one of them has a specific certainty in the demands to which he or she feels entitled.

So partnering starts off a project with openly acknowledging the rights of the parties and their project goals in terms of self-interest, then making common cause for the good of the project. In practice—and, I'd like to think, largely because of the presence of architects on the team—the focus moves back and forth from *rights* to *well* throughout the project.

The processes reported about top design architects are similar, except that they have more to do with aspirations that transcend immediate self-interest. Project goals have more to do with long-term good than immediate gratification and ego—how well the project will function for clients and users, how much it will stir them, heighten their awareness, expand their experience, arouse their emotions, startle, tickle, challenge, or relax them. Pretty hard to make any of that quantifiable. Accountability?—tough. We all acknowledge the value added by good design, but its very hard to measure. Especially in its absence.

WHY POST-OCCUPANCY EVALUATION

1. **To rate performance—and the experiences provided.** Post-occupancy evaluation ought to tell us how well we did. In *Paradigms*, Joel Barker* says excellence—quality—is no longer merely a firm goal—that it's become the price of admission in today's market. Reminds me of Dana Cuff's working definition of design excellence as being the *quality of experiences* the project brings to all the categories of stakeholders involved—design team, builders, clients and users, the public, the profession. Acknowledgment by the public (enthusiastic use) and the profession (design awards) is readily apparent over time. The others we need to ask, so we can improve our performance—or our selection of team members for future projects.

2. **To help in establishing strategic alliances and selection of team members for future projects.** An obvious bonus of using some POE system such as the form suggested would be to learn to "see meself as others see me," as Burns said. The megabonus can come from seeing how others regard the various team members with whom you've collaborated—or contested—to get the job built.

A lot of how you might use the POE survey results depends on the size of your firm and your normal project types. For midsize to large firms, such project evaluation can help you in prequalifying consultants and builders for future projects. It can be used in proposing to clients or CMs the selection of complementary teams. In-house it might suggest project-specific staff assignments to compensate for, or take full advantage of—anticipated strengths and weaknesses of given teams.

---

* Joel Barker, *Paradigms* (HarperCollins, 1992).

The 1985 federal TARP study found customer satisfaction is not measured on the same scale as dissatisfaction! Dissatisfaction comes from quantifiable expectations (rights)

In architecture:
- Roofs leak
- Slabs crack
- Footings settle

DISSATISFACTION

SATISFACTION

WOW WOW

The point: Quality resists quantification

is measured by the extent to which people get more than they knew enough to expect.

It's <u>experiental</u>, especially in both service and design.

The major focus of POE, then, is to expediently <u>quantify the quality</u> of the experiences of all the project stakeholders in order to:
- Identify what processes worked best and tinker with--or redesign--the rest.
- Identify top performers and build alliances.
- Look for systemic change where possible.
- Demonstrate to all stakeholders we're working for continuous improvement.

3. **To provide benchmarks for systemic change.** Survey results can also assist the client in determining which of its communication, administrative, and oversight processes might best be improved to avoid costly project conflict or delay.

It would be possible over time, of course, to derive a Demingesque assemblage of Pareto charts and analyses of statistical means and variances.[*] Unless your practice comprises site adaptations of identical building designs, however, the principal value of such tedium, seems to me, would be to finally find a place to use that course in calculus you took all those years ago.

Far better to trust intuitive judgments of those involved and team up to redesign—at least tinker with—the systems, or those parts of them, that are amenable to change.

Though the potential for project teamwork is great, as Katzenbach[†] argues, calling ourselves a team doesn't make us one, and there are real limitations to what is best done by teams. The challenge is to discipline ourselves to relinquish what we can to single-leader action, work as a true team when it's appropriate, and minimize current norms of positional behavior that lead to additional overhead costs, project delays, and contentions among stakeholders.

For example, Jeffery Gee,[‡] AIA, Campus Architect at Berkeley, envisions an extranet for his projects where all stakeholders will simultaneously see and track RFIs, change orders, pay requests, the entire project record as it evolves.

Lots of project decisions and actions are best handled by single-leader work-groups. Some require true teams. Trick is deciding which is which with seamless lateral leadership hand-offs and full disclosure to keep the project moving & accountability clearly acknowledged.

Such initiatives toward paperless project process can work to avoid duplication of paperwork and lots of meeting time. By providing full disclosure, single-leader actions can be empowered, yet monitored by the entire team of stakeholders.

Stuart Eckblad,[§] describing the same sort of systemic change on Kaiser Permanente projects nationwide, contrasted it with the present system requiring three sets of project documentation being kept (by owner, architect, and builder) and no two versions being in agreement when claims occur. He's pushing for individual parties to the contracts splitting up the project administration.

4. **For marketing.** Circulating a post-occupancy evaluation form and following up where appropriate can tell those other stakeholders—the builders, clients and users—that you, as an architect, care about the quality of others' experiences with the firm and with the project. Just being asked to complete the survey can reinforce the message to clients and users of the buildings that you care about their opinions and seek to improve their working, living or learning environment—in today's jargon, that you're customer driven. Given the percentage of architects' projects coming from repeat clients and direct referrals, in the long term, this one may be one of the most beneficial reasons to provide POE services.

---

[*] E. M. Baker, "Springing Ourselves from the Measurement Trap," in Peter Senge et al., *The Fifth Discipline Fieldbook* (Doubleday, 1994), p. 455.
[†] Jon R. Katzenbach, *Teams at the Top* (Harvard Business School Press, 1998), p. 11.
[‡] Discussed with the Cal Poly Executive Management Program attendees, July 18, 1998.

[§] J. Stuart Eckblad, Associate Director of Design & Construction Services, Kaiser Permanente, in a presentation to the Executive Management Program of the Cal Poly Department of Architecture, Winter Quarter, 1998.

WHY PREDESIGN -- CASE STUDIES

When Collins and Porras*—who wrote the book on visionary companies—talk of the importance of the BHAG (big hairy audacious goal) in companies that have led the world in their fields, that one's easy for me to extrapolate from for project-specific examples. Sets me thinking how every project I've ever done presented—for me, at least—its own BHAG to be attained.

With hindsight the question arises—how compellingly did I succinctly state and share the excitement of that vision? How much better would those projects have been and how much easier to manage if the entire project team had fully shared that vision?

Or consider Senge's work on systems thinking. In their field book for learning organizations, Senge and colleagues[†]spend 50 pages on how to inculcate the "shared vision" among the members of a learning firm.

A learning organization can be thought of as a team of people, working collectively for common purpose through complementary skills and abilities, who jointly respond immediately to problems as opportunities to eliminate problem causes. They seek to win by solving not only the immediate problem, but by having that problem simply never come up again.[‡]

Senge's groups' analogy[§] is, *While striking it rich by winning the lottery certainly is an extraordinary achievement, it in no way improves your capacity to win future lotteries.*

What makes that so apt a metaphor is that predesign can feel a bit like setting out to win the lottery. Too many variables—the people, site, building systems, and market conditions prevailing for each project have never been brought all together at one time

and place before. Developing a shared vision—understanding the joint aspirations for the enterprise—can be a first essential step. The second lies in how the team members will interact in order to respond to the inevitable setbacks later.

Makes quite a case for the need for shared vision and team building before the project starts. Nor is it necessary to go outside our profession to make a compelling case for predesign. What follows are several different versions of how the good guys do it—most of it large-firm stuff, but useful case studies for all of us.

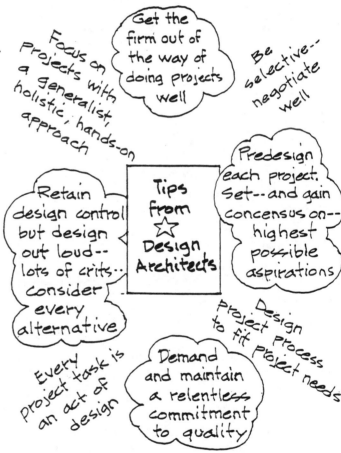

Tips from ☆ Design Architects

- Focus on projects with a generalist, holistic, hands-on approach
- Get the firm out of the way of doing projects well
- Be selective-- negotiate well
- Retain design control but design out loud-- lots of crits.. consider every alternative
- Predesign each project. Set--and gain concensus on-- highest possible aspirations
- Every project task is an act of design
- Demand and maintain a relentless commitment to quality
- Design project process to fit project needs

THE STAR DESIGNER APPROACH
Providing predesign services is one of the project processes that I find sets exemplary design architects (those who consistently win design award "lotteries") apart from the wanna-bees.

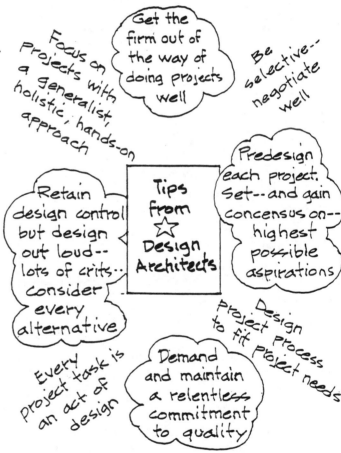

---

* J. Collins and J. Porras, *Built to Last* (HarperBusiness, 1994), p. 91.
[†] Senge et al., *The Fifth Discipline Fieldbook*, p. 297.
[‡] Ibid., p. 23.
[§] Ibid., p. 48.

In 1989 I organized two national research roundtables and led a nationwide investigation of what we mean by *design excellence.** We found ready consensus on an inclusive list of characteristics of design excellence, but no agreement on how that list might be prioritized.† It was as Bill Caudill had said—we all know great design when we experience it, yet we can't describe, much less *prescribe*, exactly what makes it great.

So the study evolved away from the *what* of design to become a compilation of the *how*—useful methodology tips collected from design architects whose projects were studied and emulated—the indirect leaders‡ of the profession at that time.

Among the behaviors of these exemplary designers, perhaps the most remarkable was that, as a routine phase of services, they all had some version of predesign, or, as Charles Gwathemey§ called it—the discovery phase.

They were all adamant about predesign not being confused with design. Arthur Erickson put it this way: *For me, the secret of good design is the self-discipline to not design at all until it is almost too late.¶* They were equally emphatic in their clear differentiation between predesign and programming as we have been taught it.

Programming, as it is typically practiced in the world beyond the profession—by our client base—is grounded in the *tyranny of the or*— the *no/but* theory of scarcity. Resources are limited, therefore only functions and amenities with compelling and quantifiable rationales get funded and required.

The star designers regarded programming as largely the setting forth of expectations—a sort of performance specification of room sizes, adjacencies, lighting levels, air changes, flame-spread ratings, etc.—all quantifiable. Instead, what they were after in their predesign activities was qualitative— shared aspirations, intense motivation, and joint commitment to work together to make each project the best of its kind *functionally.***

Predesign seeks to add the *genius of the yes/and* quotient of hopes and aspirations—to operate on a theory of abundance through good design, to the extent that's possible.

Interestingly, virtually none of the two dozen or so "signature designers" I've interviewed admits to even thinking of design awards, certainly not at predesign stage—their whole concern is with function. Joe Esherick told me that, for him, awards are fringe benefits—spinoffs—that just seem to happen if he really focuses on solving the client's problems well.

Star designers report using the discovery phase to accomplish the following:

- To clearly and succinctly define the client's problem to be solved.
- To establish and agree upon the scorecard of only 5 or 6 memorable goals against which all subsequent design decisions can be judged qualitatively and openly.
- To establish interactive, creative relationships and good chemistry among the design team members (all these people seem to work out loud).
- To discover the limits of what's possible by testing and thoroughly discussing (with the client and all the team) the widest polarity of formal extremes feasible, given the site, the program, and the budget.

---

* Reported in two publications by the AIA in 1990: *Keys to Design Excellence* (this author) and *In Search of Design Excellence* (an anthology edited by Tom Vonier, contributed to by D. Cuff, R. Shibley, and me).
† See the three-track What Best Describes Design Excellence exercise on p. 1.23 of this manual.
‡ For the difference between direct and indirect leadership, see H. Gardner, *Leading Minds* (BasicBooks, 1995), p. 6.
§ Frankly, I like Gwathemey's term better than predesign, which is used here only for clarity, because it clearly says when in the project it occurs, and which serves as an admonition to the vast majority of architects who lunge at design as their immediate response to every project opportunity.

¶ At a state convention of AIA Michigan in front of some 300 assembled architects in 1993.
** It's interesting to note that the signature designers reported they do not talk aesthetics—either in predesign or in project presentations later—they focus instead on function—how the building or its systems should work to solve the clients' problems.

For these practitioners, clearly the processes of a predesign phase, the working relationships forged during it, are as important as the documented results. They report the phase takes anywhere from 3 to 6 weeks of highly interactive work—first among in-house teams, but involving the client early on in the process.

THE COMPARABLES APPROACH

A very different but equally inclusive predesign approach was reported separately in 1994 by staff architects from Dow Chemical and by practitioners from CRSS.[*] Both groups stressed how essential some version of predesign is to achieving better projects faster, cheaper, with less hassle. Both these firms recommended a bracketing method using comparables as a way to work toward consensus among project user/owner groups as to the quality of the building to be designed.

In their view, everything can be quantified—even quality. For each system of the built environment to which users could personally and directly relate—the building's skin, lighting, automation, interior finishes, landscaping, air treatment and delivery controls, etc.—these architects developed a project-specific, five-layer continuum from simplest (cheapest) to most sophisticated (expensive).

Each layer of each system's continuum was illustrated by comparables from well-known projects or project types with which the user groups were familiar through the media or by personal experience.

With the program and budget already set, and using gross estimates of comparative system costs available by computer, these architect/CMs were able to engage the user groups in prioritizing their options using easily understood language and examples.

Obviously, there's a lot of quid pro quo involved—"If we can't afford best-of-class in every category of building system, which ones are most important, and what do we downgrade to get our top priorities funded?"

THE STORY-BOARD APPROACH

A third very different example of exemplary predesign is that of Disney's Imagineers.[†] On every project team, they include a "rides-operator member"—someone who manages customer sales and service—as well as a member whose role is in the film-making side of the Disney operation. The other four or so members are design professionals, though each from a different discipline.

For their work there is set aside a major conference room with one entire wall of tack space. Over a period of weeks they cover that wall with a collage of sketches, diagrams, clippings, Post-it notes, torn-out cartoons—whatever contributes to their *what-if* and *let's suppose* interactions. Their goal—to create a story line or "plot," a script for the *experiences* of the users of the project.

They move from highly tentative collage, to very precise storyboarding, sketching the visitor's views in all directions from each point of progression through the facility—not just where the designer wants you to look, but what you'd be able to peek or crane your neck to see. Last, they move into model building of the "set." Since it's all in-house, the shift from predesign to project design is relatively seamless, though carefully sequenced through explicit deliverables.

Diverse as all these processes are, perhaps the most telling thing they have in common is that they each—in very different ways—image the user's experience of the building. That comes first.

Only later—during the design phase—does the form of the design take shape and then, more than anything, it's as a three-dimensional form that evolves holistically—in its entirety—rather than as a plan being extruded vertically.

[*] AIA Corporate Architects Committee symposium on quality management, Indianapolis, October 1993.
[†] This one comes from my visit with their head architect in 1993.

HOW ARCHITECTS DESIGN *

The Design Solution is actually known to the designer only when the quality of the experience in the virtual world of the sketch matches that of the experiential image prior to design.

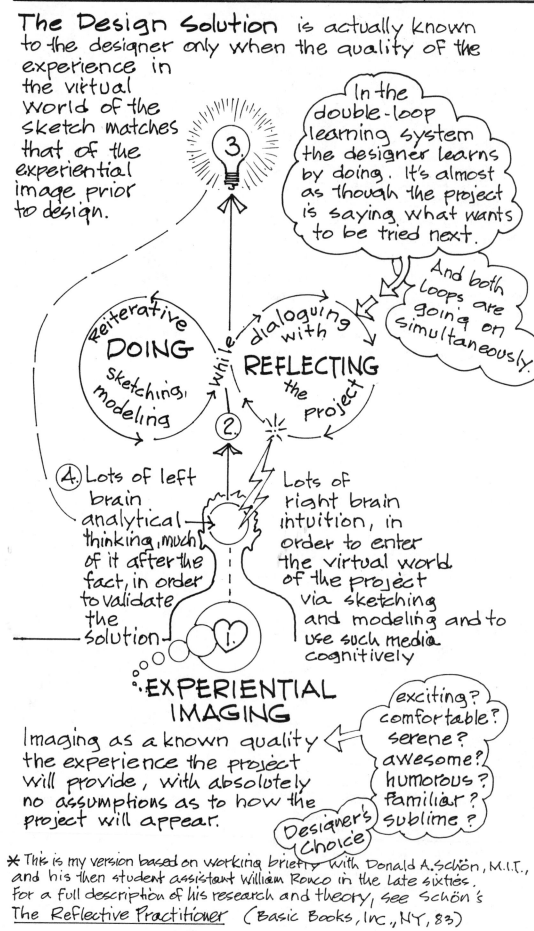

3.
In the double-loop learning system the designer learns by doing. It's almost as though the project is saying what wants to be tried next.

And both loops are going on simultaneously.

Reiterative **DOING** sketching, modeling

while dialoguing with **REFLECTING** the project

2.

④ Lots of left brain analytical thinking, much of it after the fact, in order to validate the solution.

Lots of right brain intuition, in order to enter the virtual world of the project via sketching and modeling and to use such media cognitively

1.

EXPERIENTIAL IMAGING

Imaging as a known quality the experience the project will provide, with absolutely no assumptions as to how the project will appear.

exciting? comfortable? serene? awesome? humorous? familiar? sublime?

Designer's Choice

✱ This is my version based on working briefly with Donald A. Schön, M.I.T., and his then student assistant William Ronco in the late sixties. For a full description of his research and theory, see Schön's _The Reflective Practitioner_ (Basic Books, Inc., NY, 83)

AFTERWORD

It's at this point that I'm supposed to succinctly and brilliantly summarize the major themes and findings contained in the book, warmly affirm your ability to successfully implement what's proposed, and express complete confidence about the future as a result of your doing so. Truth be told, I thought I'd been doing all that as I went along. Besides, succinctness and brilliance are not among my strong suits or—in my experience—even prerequisites for being a good architect.

What is required—at least in my ideal architect—is paying attention and caring. It's not what we do that sets us apart so much as how—as much a matter of mind-set as it is talent, skill, or technical capability. As Maister[*] says, *The opposite of the word* professional *is not* unprofessional, *but rather* technician. . . . *A real professional is a technician who cares.*

Or as Peter Senge says in his Foreword to *The Living Company*—Arie de Geus's excellent book[†]:

> *As we enter the twenty-first century, it is timely, perhaps even critical, that we recall what human beings have understood for a very long time—that working together can indeed be a deep source of life meaning. Anything less is just a job.*

Which is why I have resisted calling them "jobs" here. They're projects, subsets of the ultimate practice of working together collaboratively to give life meaning. Here's how such a practice—as a true professional's path of life-long learning—is summed up by best-selling author and blackbelt Aikido master George Leonard[‡]:

> *Ultimately, practice is the path of mastery. If you stay on it long enough, you'll find it to be a vivid place, with its ups and downs, its challenges and comforts, its surprises, disappointments and unconditional joys. . . but it might well turn out to be the most reliable thing in your life.*

Leonard goes on to say that coming to love the practice for the sheer joy doing of it . . . *might eventually make you a winner in your chosen field, if that's what you're looking for, and then people will refer to you as a master. . . . But that's not the point. What is mastery? At the heart of it, mastery is practice. Mastery is staying on the path.*

To help me stay on the path, I'd appreciate hearing from you. Hence the form that follows so you can tell me how the next one might better meet your needs. Thank you.

---

[*] David H. Maister, *True Professionalism: The Courage to Care about Your People, Your Clients, and Your Career* (Free Press, 1997), p. 16.
[†] Arie de Geus, *The Living Company* (Harvard Business School Press, 1997), p. xi.
[‡] George Leonard, *Mastery: The Keys to Success and Long-Term Fulfillment* (1991), p. 79. Used by permission of Dutton, a division of Penguin Putnam, Inc.

James R. Franklin, FAIA, ASLA

Resident Fellow

College of Architecture and Environmental Design

California Polytechnic University

San Luis Obispo, CA 93407

Tel: (805) 781-8420   Fax: 781-8421

Your name and address

_____

_____

_____

_____

Telephone, fax, e-mail _____

What is most useful about the book?

_____

_____

_____

_____

What got left out you wish had been covered?

_____

_____

_____

_____

What is wrong-headed in the book and could be harmful if architects actually tried to do it?

_____

_____

_____

_____

What is your best hot tip for practice that others ought to know about?

_____

_____

_____

_____

_____

_____

POSTSCRIPT: ON THE DHARMA OF INEFFABLE DRAWINGS

I came to this too late to get it in the body of the book, but since it's rich and helpful information, it's appended here. To me it's that important, and actually I'm glad this is set apart from the rest. This is a case study on design processes that may be old hat to some of you, but to most architects they suggest powerful new ways of evolving the design of architectural forms that are also separate and set apart from the main body of what's being built today. Even if you're not envious of the leading-edge, architecture-as-spectacle design solutions being published at the moment, the rigor and comprehensiveness of the processes reported here are compelling. So is the ongoing active participation of the client in the design in collaborative ways that *don't involve drawing.*

Designing without drawing is a startling concept to an old guy known for sketching fast and well enough to have made my living at it for a long time. I grew up drawing, doodling my way through classes, sketching when I should have been studying. In a sense, I've profited all my life from the habits of a misspent youth, and have long argued the efficacy of the sketching process as a cognitive tool.

As communication, I hold that one freehand sketch is worth a gigabyte of word processing, even AutoCAD. I admonish that computers can say only *yes* or *no*—never *what-if.* I tell students that CAD capability is only the price of admission to today's profession—that quick communicative sketching is their competitive edge for upward mobility.

Students come to me these days because they want to draw better, or at least overcome their fear of drawing. So in undergraduate design studio, I stress drawing as a design tool—as communication rather than art. I coach learning with and from your hands, Donald Schön* style, through a simultaneous double-loop learning system. That calls for reiterative sketching combined with an almost Zen-like awareness of what's happening in the virtual reality of the sketch at hand *while it's happening.* To me, that's designing, but I must admit it's far from collaborative.

I urge architects to draw fast rather than well -- to use graphics as a tool for learning and communication.

Orthogonal Projections

ME

Just never occurred to me to abandon Euclidean geometry for even the quickest sketches of our design thoughts.

---

*Donald Schön, *The Reflective Practitioner* (Basic Books, 1983).

Yes, I know that top designers "design out loud" through endless crits. But I'd assumed that meant lots of overlay sketches ....

Which, like mine, were all derived from Platonic shapes and forms:

, etc.

I was taught, like most my age, to organize a project in plan to be extruded vertically. It was a bold departure when I discovered the benefits of starting the design by sketching in section.

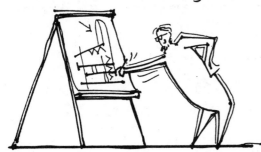

Even then I never imagined repealing the law of gravity or creating collisions of sensuous bulging or crumpled forms ....

Recently that whole premise—that the better you draw, the better you can learn, design, and communicate—has been called into question. For me that's a seismic shock to the very ground on which I stand professionally. The first slight tremor—not even registering on my Richter scale at the time—came some 10 years ago in 1989. Then a staff vice president at AIA, I'd worked with Weld Coxe to put together the Signature Roundtable and heard a number of the top design architects of that day reach immediate consensus. As I reported in *Keys to Design Excellence* (AIA Press, 1990) they all held that good design process is inevitably a highly verbal interaction with staff and clients. They reported talking a lot, along with sketching, as they gave indefatigable dialectic crits to explore design possibilities—designing out loud, they said. That part I guess I glossed over—knowing as we all do that talk is cheap. The sketching part I took to mean that like me, they drew quick explicit depictions of geometric forms Plato would have recognized. After all, their clients were able to follow what they sketched, and up until that point we'd all agreed on Euclidean as the common geometric language.

But times change, and since 1989 we've incrementally ventured with design into the realm of the sublime and ineffable—or at least well past what Pythagoras could have condoned. For me the big quake didn't hit until 10 years later—in the spring of 1999—when I saw a slide presentation by Randall Stout, AIA, billed as an emerging talent by CCAIA at their Monterey Design Conference. Along with—or as part of—his presentation of some stunning and truly admirable architecture, Randall showed parti sketches that are incomprehensible. Literally. You can't tell what they refer to until you see them side by side with the final formal statement.

It's not possible that Randall, a graduate of the University of Tennessee, then Rice, SOM, and finally Frank Gehry, doesn't know how to draw intelligibly, so what's the answer? Nor will I accept the statement of Thom Maynes (Morphosis) at that same conference, "Most of what I'm thinking about these days I'm not able to draw." It may be hubris—more likely limited thinking—but I *know* that anything I can think, I can draw.

Puzzled, I then recalled the parti sketches of le Corbusier, Kahn, and Gehry. Until now I've somehow assumed those were curios chosen for publication only to show that the gods have clay feet, are sometimes sloppy and lazy with their graphics, or are abstract expressionist artsy types. But for whatever reason—to a man, and at least occasionally—they've drawn sketches fully as illegible as those Randall Stout happily presented at Monterey.

Now comes the aftershock. *What if top architects don't* want *to draw understandably, because doing so will impede the design of good architecture?* What if the essence of producing a wonderful piece of architecture lies more in the dialectic verbal process evoked by a scribble, rather than in working from a readable sketch? What if the social art that *is* architecture is best accomplished by a team struggling to extrapolate all the things an ineffable sketch *might have intended*, within a work environment where any artful attempt is openly and critically considered, and all are open to any possibilities? Have I stumbled upon the Dharma* of Ineffable Drawing?

With these questions in mind, I ventured to L.A. to talk with Randall Stout, along with staff member Ann Yu and former staffer Chip Mennick. Confessing my conviction that the means *should* justify the end, I asked, what do they do to move a project forward *before* design starts? What processes work for them? When does actual design start, what happens, and in what sequence? Here's their process as described to me:

_____

*Dharma: A Buddhist "word with multiple meanings. Its primary meaning is 'phenomenon.' Since phenomena are impermanent, according to the law of causation, its second meaning is 'law.' Since impermanence is a fact, the third meaning is 'truth,' and since Buddhist teaching is based on truth, the fourth meaning is 'teaching.'" L. Shainberg, *Ambivalent Zen: One Man's Adventures on the Dharma Path* (Vintage Books, 1997), p. 314.

Came as a shock to find that when star design architects sketch an illegible, squiggly parti, it's not just the start of the idea -- it's the whole idea.

Here's my graphite stick drawing of Corbu's charcoal sketch for Ronchamp.* Let's see .... Is it Plan? Section? Elevation? All three?

* Actually, it's said to be part of a site-plan study from the *Le Corbusier Archive*, Vol. 20 (Garland Publishers, NY, 1982). Courtesy Fondation Le Corbusier, Paris.

WHAT IF--in order to design better projects "out loud"-- it helps when the team is challenged by a dialectic process? Suppose they creatively work to discover all that might be implied in a holistic representation that is

☐ Ineffable?
☐ Illegible?
☐ Emotively Scrawled?

Me at the thought of it....

So I checked it out for this case study with Randall Stout in L.A. Turns out those non-orthogonal forms aren't just dreamed up. ←---

They evolve after rigorous research and analysis --from lots of model building. It's a series of down-to-earth processes, starting with stuff we all know and have done. What's different? That it's so systematically thorough and that the whole time Randall focuses on capturing those "free associations" that involuntarily come to mind.

Though I'm told Bruce Goff worked to implement forms from his dreams' images -- those being his most "emotive ideas."

Was at?

Must take a lot of awareness to not brush aside those emotive images in the midst of the hard data gathering and processing.

1. **Context, program, and client research— stating the problem.** These are closely interwoven, often happening simultaneously, and as parts of a holistic jumble of input to be sorted, but always kept all together as interactive data:

- *Programming* starts with the usual list of owner expectations in terms of functions, rooms, sizes, adjacencies, etc. It's then enlarged over time and through discussion to get at precedents, aspirations, and future hopes.

- *Researching context* includes considering all the things we always think of in terms of site, soils, topography, traffic, access, natural forces, flora and fauna, microclimate, neighboring buildings' scale, style, uses, materials, etc. It's then expanded to include site history as well as users' socioeconomic and cultural history, needs and conditions. Randall casts a wide net.

- *Site model.* A small-scale model is made of the site and relevant surroundings. This is a model of woodblock building forms—roof slopes and all—on a wooden topo base with streets and cars. It's all handsomely crafted, painted, and landscaped with the site left vacant so that a series of massing studies (plugs) of the project can be tried later and discussed.

- *Free associations.* Throughout this extended process, Randall—and as the design principal, he's hands-on in all this— is carefully holding himself alert to and aware of his free associations that come unbidden. *What did that remind me of? What have I seen that came to mind just as they said that, and why now?* In one case it was a 10-year-old photo he'd snapped of sunlight filtering through the underside of the Santa Monica Pier. In another, it was an Arizona desert canyon of sensuous rock that had provoked momentary aesthetic arrest. In both cases, these had been remembrances of the fleeting epiphany of wordless wonder that James Joyce wrote of in his definition of true art.* Interestingly, neither of these free associations related to art objects,

---

* James Joyce, *Portrait of the Artist as a Young Man*, as quoted by Joseph Campbell in *A Joseph Campbell Companion*, Diane Osborn, ed. (Harper Perennial, 1991), p. 246.

much less other buildings—they were merely about natural phenomena with strong configurative impact.

2. **Functional organization studies** are begun—perhaps continued from programming—but now with quantitative measures and design components being fully defined; again, all of this with close cooperative input from the client. It's interesting that neither Randall nor his staff were comfortable with setting a point in the project process when design actually begins. The requisite discipline for them is not refraining from starting the design too early, but rather in keeping every option open so all potentialities can evolve concurrently for as long as possible—it's all design, and that includes:

- *Functional research, i.e., How large will that machine be and how much operational and maintenance clearance will be needed? What size space is required to seat 12 comfortably and what supporting equipment will they need in order to function well? How many and what kind of toilet fixtures should there be for each sex? How are supplies to be delivered, stored, and accessed?* Etc., etc.—endless specifics to list and later deal with, but the immediate goal is to set the optimum footprint and nominal height of each room or space in the program.

- *Volumetric organizational studies.* Simple three-dimensional rectilinear large wooden blocks are now quickly cut to scale of all the design components described in the research, and each is labeled with name and size. The real organizational study comes from shoving, stacking, and arranging these blocks endlessly to try every possible combination, until the team—and especially the client—agree *That's it!* Randall reports this process comprises a verbal and visual contract among himself, the client and all staff. It safeguards against clients' second thoughts based on misremembered

discussions, hazily understood plan sketches, or late realizations of what that compelling PowerPoint presentation actually depicted. We all know, no matter how wisely they nod, many clients really can't read plans. It's the client's full participation in the three-dimensionality of the process that fully communicates in memorable ways, that evokes commitments to be honored throughout all the process yet to come. Photography is used to maintain a record of the studies as they evolve. Massing "plugs" of the overall forms derived through various arrangements of the large blocks can be tried on the site model.

It's useful to note that these volumetric organizational studies are carried out with blocks large enough to be easily manipulated—say at a scale of ¼"=1'0" —and that while those design elements to be largely glazed might be cut from Lucite, most are wood with a light stain finish. In some cases for definite reasons, particular blocks may be shaped a bit, but by and large, they are kept to the simple forms Plato called "pure"—orthogonal blocks reminiscent of child's play. Perhaps there's a subliminal message here to the client who says he always wanted to be an architect but never could draw a straight line?

Instead of plans being drawn to organize the project, large to-scale wooden blocks are stacked and shoved around by the team -- including the client -- until they all agree they've got it right, that it works.

3. **The parti.** Here's where the process description necessarily gets hazy. Somewhere at about this stage or during the next one, Randall evokes the parti. He says it's best not to force it, but that the pressure to derive one does begin to build. If he's hitting artist's block he may resort to having the entire team sit around a table, sketching and discussing. But in the best of all possible worlds, it's as though there's a force pulling the parti out of him alone and into instant representation.* It can happen on an airplane, in the midst of things at home, and although Randall reports it's yet to happen for him on the back of a napkin, it may get captured on any kind of paper anywhere. It's a gesture drawing, a right-brain alogical and nonorthogonal expression of the project in its totality. It's the essence of the project, and when he's hit on it Randall knows that (and so does his staff) from his own resonance and excitement.

I ask what he's thinking or feeling when he draws the parti. Randall replies: "Someone said that seven is about the maximum number of different things a person can focus on at one time and deal with simultaneously. I try to reduce the project problem statement to about that many key factors.[†] Certainly they have to cover what is important in terms of how the building must respond to:

- Context
- Client and function
- The free associations—the art

If any one of those three gets left out, someone's going to be unhappy with the project."

It's interesting to note that in several hours of discussion this was the only time I heard Randall use the word "art." He *is* an artist, committed to his calling, and expects you to know that. What he talks about are materials, costs, finishes, and detailing—a perfect example of the truism: *When art critics get together they talk art. When artists get together they talk about the cost of paints and canvas.*

Somewhere about now the parti gets drawn. It's best when it just happens, but to evoke it, Randall culls through all he's learned so far

data codes stuff stats

He gets it down to the 6 or 7 vital issues that must be satisfied by the design.

These he mentally juggles til the parti....

erupts on paper!

Working models like those get built from little more than parti sketches like these (which are actual copies)

---

* Frank Gehry is quoted in an interview as saying, "You have to hold the image in your mind while you're doing it, and I can't hold the image for longer than 3—I think I made 3.4—minutes. I clocked it." *Architectural Record*, May 1999, p. 189.
† There's direct correlation between Randall's report of the "seven things" and the predesign process reported at the AIA 1989 Signature Firm Roundtable and reported by me in *Keys to Design Excellence* (AIA Press, 1990), p. 36. The only difference being that the star designers of that era reported limiting themselves to five or six seminal forces or issues on which to base the design.

As for the gestural character of his parti sketches, he says that allows room for more subsequent interaction between him and project systems or materials, between him and other people. It's as though he's capturing the essence in a way that won't prescribe implementation, thus allowing room for, as he put it, "Discovery, which is what you're after." He then shared with me a sketchbook in which, traveling through Europe, he had worked at the reverse—looking at the final architecture and sketching quickly to capture the essence—the bold impact—with none of the detail. He says he came to this approach after finding that he was asking his drawings to do more than they were capable of representing—that his careful renderings could no longer convey all he needed them to express. Finding the essence, he says, means editing out all but the minimum without which it would lose reality. It shows that to which nothing less than *everything else* would have to be added in order to keep from changing the meaning. Randall says the parti is the gestalt—it's about reality.

His staff, meanwhile, affirms that a great deal of information—much of it specific—is contained in even his quirkiest gestural parti. For them, white space may refer to unbroken expanses of either glass or solid, scribbles of overlap or redoubled lines have great significance, and curved versus straight lines are key volumetric distinctions rather than a slip of the pen. Chip said that having worked his way through one project with Randall, he now feels comfortable with intuiting the intent embodied in the parti.

Is the parti shared with the client, who until now has had a hands-on role every step of the way? Yes, sometimes, but it depends on the client. Most often Randall talks about and explains the parti to both staff and client in terms of how it works—how the building will function and serve, or what materials and systems will be used. Randall says, "I don't have much patience with 'talkatecture,' and in the end, the seven things (embodied in the parti) mean absolutely nothing if the building doesn't work."

Steinhuder Sea Recreation Island Facilities,
Niedersachen, Germany
Randall Stout Architects, Inc., Los Angeles

GIVEN THE PARTI
the team now starts the "paper-bending" phase of design-- building models big enough to visually experience all major interior spaces. Every model has to-scale human figures.

Which the staff say they readily intuit, having worked through this process so long.

✳ *First comes a quick study model to discover, test, and define the building form contained in the 2-3-minute parti and fit it to the organizational block study.*

✳ *Next, an entire series of progressively more detailed working models lead to final decisions on systems, materials, finishes, placement, location, connections, interfaces.... all the details*

4. **Working models.** At this point in project process the scale jumps again, as forms—often non-Euclidean compound curves—begin to evolve through building a large working model—perhaps at ½" or ¾"=1'0"—quickly searching for form in what Randall refers to as the *bending paper* stage of design. Foam Core, illustration board and chipboard, balsa sticks and Mylar sheets, photocopy paper—whatever can be worked with fast and experimentally to aid the search for discovery and resolution of all that the parti implies. It's here the relationships among design elements get resolved and materials get selected. Yet another model or series of models is now built to focus on framing and structure, to continue the refinement and decision process.

These decisions later get translated to data on CAD, but the real design is all hands-on in the model building.

Randall warns, "This process (to work successfully) consumes an exorbitant amount of fee, so a real commitment must be made from the standpoint of business as well as creativity and talent. Like other design processes, I have seen it work with a wide range of aesthetic success and failure, so it's not a design panacea.

"To work well with it requires years of practice. Like any powerful tool, this one takes a while to hone your skills. It is not the actual making of the model parts that is tricky. It is learning how to 'read the model' each step along the way and have a vision of what design moves to make next."

5. **CAD depiction and modeling.** Asked about the use of CAD Randall says, "It's hard for me to design at the terminal," and sees both the potential and the danger of CAD as a design tool.* Yes, given a project and fee of adequate size he would add computer walk-throughs as yet another way to experience the virtual reality of what he's designing. On the other hand, every model he currently builds—and there are lots of them for even the smallest project—invariably has human figures to scale. All are incessantly studied and photographed from eye level with the human figure prominently featured. Moreover, all working models are of a size and level of craft to clearly depict the design intent necessary for proper detailing. Randall has found that computer modeling glosses the issue of project-specific detailing and can lure the architect into doing so as well.

---

* Gehry, op. cit.: "My problem with it is that the imagery on the computer takes all the juice out of the idea; I can't stand it. You have a great idea and you're dreaming of this thing, then somebody builds a model or a drawing, and it looks like hell. Oh shit, you think, my idea is in that. You get that icky feeling."

So for now, although the only drafting board in the office is piled high with books and papers in Randall's own office, design is done through freehand sketching and model building. The CAD is primarily a production tool. Chip Mennick: "For us the computer is used to report the work done in the model and the decisions made there—to represent the phenomenon that *is* the model. Our models are used as design tools and to communicate to the client and the builders. It's only *blob* architects who use computers for design—all the permutations that the computer can do might intrigue you intellectually, but they leave out the response to the context and the client."

Randall adds, "Models are 3D placeholders for complex thoughts. Interacting with models allows you to explore and experience more geometric possibilities and formal relationships than the mind can preconceive. In computer terminology, they serve as a visual 'extra hard drive' to hold data while you react to the results and continue to juggle seven thoughts. This allows you to engage the work more dynamically, and for me results in as more creative process."

So what does all this mean for you?

Maybe nothing, if you (and your market) feel good about your processes, services, and design.

Unless you already have a model shop, even trying this out can get expensive... Time, space, equipment, materials

On the other hand, if it's your long-term aspiration to:

☐ Venture into the hot market for leading-edge design
☐ Recruit and retain the best and brightest
☐ Involve clients so much in design decisions they never second-guess you
☐ Escape consignment to the "production firm" category
☐ Perhaps realize a dream you've always had....?

Then you may want to try some of the tips from this case study-- after all, none of it is rocket science.

Conclusions. To return to the question as to whether I've discovered the Dharma of Ineffable Drawing, it's clearly a phenomenon, a fact, and a teaching as Shainberg requires in his definition of Dharma.* As for a law about how to do projects, it's clearly not. Architects are all different in many ways, but nowhere so radically as in their design intents, which in turn governs their process.

If you are among the vast but dwindling majority of the orthogonally bound, and committed to staying there, then cluttering your practice with models—from volumetric organizational studies to framing and structure models—is probably overkill. Takes time, space, money, and equipment. Even in the previous tiny start-up office in his apartment, Randall had a full model shop. But it seems to me that even a

devout modernist (if any still exist) could evoke better design from so rigorous a process as described here. And if the out-of-town big-name designers are picking you off, there's even more reason to consider a change. Probably your market will prompt the answer, or your ability to recruit and retain the brightest and best with whom to grow the firm. But more than anything else, the answer about whether to try such a process lies in your design intent—that's at the heart of it.

I'm not talking here about project-specific design intent—that's a given for all of us, or should be. Rather, I'm aiming at your understanding your own intent for the body of work for which you will become known and remembered, long term.

---

* Shainberg, op. cit.

One way to start at this is to truthfully consider just who it is for whom you're actually, consciously, day after day, doing all this work:

- The client who pays the fee
- The users of the project
- Yourself
- All who might be influenced by its presence in the context of their lives
- The profession (as denoted by publications and design awards)

You might rank that list in the order of your priorities, even strike from the list any you don't consciously consider, or have commitment to and awareness of, in daily work. Clearly, in the case study just given, the terms "context" and "client" embrace the larger society, and probably all five of the categories of people served figure largely on Randall Stout's list, perhaps even in the order I've suggested.

That's one place to start evaluating how well your current design process can meet your long-term aspirations. The shorter the list, the less I'd consider change—or if I were to consider it, I'd work on the list before the process. It's a matter of mind-set and values.

There's yet another way to address the issue, suggested by something Isaiah Berlin wrote long ago, proposing there exists a fundamental polarity between those he differentiated as being either hedgehogs or foxes.

The hedgehogs, he said:

- Relate everything to a single central vision, one system somewhat (sometimes highly) coherent and articulate.
- In terms of that vision they understand, think, and act on a single, universal, organizing principle.
- Everything that they say and do has significance in terms of, and spins from that big idea—it's all centripetal.

On the other side, he posited the foxes about whom he said:

- They pursue many ends, often unrelated, even contradictory.
- Their actions and goals are connected, if at all, only in some de facto way, for some psychological or physiological reason, unrelated by any moral or aesthetic principle.
- Their thought is scattered and diffuse, moving on many levels, seizing on the essence of a vast varity of experiences and objects for what those are in themselves.
- They work without seeking to fit these diffuse ideas into—or to exclude them from—any one unchanging, much less fanatical, unitary inner vision (as a hedgehog might).
- They lead lives, perform acts, and entertain ideas which are centrifugal rather than centripetal.*

In our profession, it's easier and more accurate to fit projects rather than architects into those categories. Le Corbusier's concepts for multifamily housing seem to spring from a hedgehog conviction, while his single-family residences and Ronchamp get decidedly foxy. Frank Lloyd Wright's prairie houses stand in clear opposition to the Guggenheim.

So think of your projects and, suppressing for the moment any negative connotations you may attach to actual hedgehogs or foxes, run the matrix on the next page for clues as to which appellation might apply to the body of work you're doing now and what you hope to do.

---

* Isaiah Berlin, *The Hedgehog and the Fox* (Simon & Shuster, 1953) as attributed by Colin Rowe and Fred Koetter in *Collage City* (MIT Press, 1978).

CURRENT APPROACHES TO ARCHITECTURAL DESIGN

Hedgehog	Fox
Seeks a universal, abstract language for design with which to provide site-specific, original objects faithful to (and correct within) the given syntax. Only one big idea can be read.	Seeks to experiment with a project-specific syntax, juxtaposing and relating elements—even fragments—of any (or several) design language(s). Multiple readings possible.
The method of design is often sequential: adjacency diagram, to plan, to vertical extrusion. Even when begun with section studies, the result is almost invariably expected to be susceptible to orthogonal representation.	The plan is often developed—or modified—to accommodate previously or simultaneously intuited formal approach(es). If not orthogonal, the form is assumed possible to represent—or perhaps discover—through use of computers.
Emphasis is often on structure—a preference for expressing it as the (or a) predominant and explicit design statement.	Structure is regarded as only one of many possibilities for expression and by no means necessarily dominant or even to be revealed.
Focuses using materials in accordance with their innate qualities and characteristics. Glass is typically considered either a void or a mirror, most often in (or comprising) the plane of a wall.	Focuses on combinations of materials exploited to take advantage of their characteristics and contrasts—often to their technological limits. Glass is available to layer and selectively reveal other claddings, elements, or visuals.
Preferred colors: whites and grays, with accents in primaries.	Preferred colors are project-specific choices from a full palette.
Highly Platonic—strong concern for Euclidean geometry's "pure" shapes—squares, triangles, and circles. Within those constraints, the objective is to be original.	Accepting of non-Euclidean geometry or, alternatively, juxtaposing and combining familiar shapes and forms in hybrid and unexpected ways.
Distinct articulation of abstract volumes corresponding to functions housed, and their hierarchical status—form follows function.	Overlays or interpenetrating forms, layers, and elements with multiple interpretations possible. Less is not more, complexity is.
Ornament typically comprises abstract design elements, usually of tectonic significance, and denoted at most by contrasting color, finish, or shape. Mimesis is equated with plagiarism.	Permissive of applied ornament, even decoration, to support the narrative of the design—what it's saying or is about. Therefore other objects or times are sometimes recalled—or predicted.

Obviously, considering projects from such luminaries as Meier, Botta, Gehry, and Silvetti, great design can be done through using either approach summarized above, and many others besides. This is a period of such fragmentation and multiplicity that for once practice is leading the academy in design theory—an exciting time with the current market in enthusiastic contention over design approaches. *Postmodern* only says what it's not. The whole world seems waiting for what the next style will be. All I can say is that wherever you recognize yourself in the matrix above, or the list that preceded it, your process should support your vision. Yes, I'm still convinced the means should justify the end, but only if the overarching goals—the visions, hopes, and aspirations of both you and your clients long term—are all supported by those means at every step of current project process.

My advice:

If you're a confirmed hedgehog, go ahead with:

- Programming (but expand the clarification of intent—both yours and the client's).

- Schematic sketches (but now include the client more, and more often at least jointly consider options, rather than selling *the* solution).

- Evoke a parti (and try to do it early enough to invite critical thinking by the team before the design is fixed).

If you aspire to foxhood, consider some of the alternative processes presented in this case study, such as:

- "Child's play" with blocks to elicit your team's creativity and the clients' full understanding of what they're buying into.

- Build study models of a size to make apparent the details needed beyond those currently stored as "standard" in your computer.

- Stay alert to and record the configurative impacts of whatever you experience anywhere— then be aware enough to capture the fleeting images and remembrances that pop into your mind as you work on each project—honor the emotive free associations that can become central driving forces of the design.

- Look for the literal and present aesthetics lurking in every aspect of what's happening on the project as it's happening.

- And sure—sketch ineffably when the parti comes upon you and grab it fast—draw for speed, not quality, not even communication.

You may want to consider trying some or all these as a launch platform toward evolving your own space-age design process. But then—how do you feel about free associations and drawing ineffably?